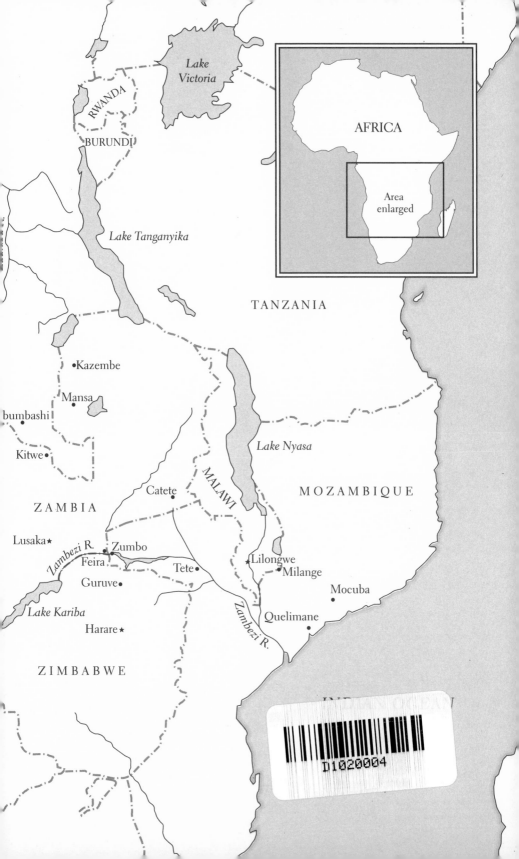

BAY OF TIGERS

PEDRO ROSA MENDES

BAY OF TIGERS

AN AFRICAN ODYSSEY

Translated from the Portuguese
by Clifford Landers

HARCOURT, INC.

Orlando   Austin   New York   San Diego   Toronto   London

www.Harcourt.com

This is a translation of *Baia dos Tigres*.

Library of Congress Cataloging-in-Publication Data
Mendes, Pedro Rosa, 1968–
[Baia dos tigres. English]
Bay of tigers: an African odyssey/Pedro Rosa Mendes;
translated by Clifford E. Landers.—1st U.S. ed.
p.   cm.
Translation of: Baia dos tigres. 1. ed. 1999.
ISBN 0-15-100655-5
1. Angola—History—Civil War, 1975—Social aspects. 2. War victims—Angola.
3. Angola—Description and travel. I. Landers, Clifford E. II. Title.
DT1428.M465 2003
916.7304'42—dc21   2003002501

Text set in Electra
Designed by Linda Lockowitz
Endpaper map by Patti Isaacs, Parrot Graphics

Printed in the United States of America

First U. S. edition
A C E G I K J H F D B

For Dulce

We have come to the end.
We have eaten our horses,
our birds, rats and women.
And we are still hungry.

—VICTOR SEGALEN, *Stéles*
   "Written in blood"

CONTENTS

AUTHOR'S NOTE   xi

TERMINUS   1
AFRICA HOTEL   123
VILLA MISÉRIA   249

ACKNOWLEDGMENTS   309
GLOSSARY   311

AUTHOR'S NOTE

This is a book about simple things: the calmness of fear, the vitality of death. In June 1997, I landed in Luanda with the intention of journeying to Quelimane by land. My purpose was the most noble of all—that is, I had no purpose in particular. These pages are the atlas with which to read my trek: the emotional map of a route whose locales bear people's faces and where space and time are the coordinates that lie the most.

Everyone warned me: The war is still going on there. Some of my travel companions died. There was no guarantee I would return.

TERMINUS

"The dead stay behind!"

In every inch of this ground is the last moment of my life. I can contemplate my last moment as far as the eye can see. It's the reason they transport me only at night. They're preserving me. I don't mind. Right now it is night, and there is much of it. It is always at night that I find myself restless. I have stopped feeling fear, because fear has deserted me, becoming an external territory. An enormous lack of stability: I have nothing to cling to, and that can be fatal. The ground, the road, the savanna, the country: fear is a map and the obligation it imposes. I don't know how many days' wide it is. We are crossing it at night. Crossing fear through the night is the only thing I have.

I can also tell you that I'm sleepy, cold, and possessed of absolute calm. Later I'll speak of a small crate of wine waiting to be drunk, tea leaves, and salt. There is also a precious cassette of Marilyn Monroe, with Billie Holiday waiting her turn before the end of the show.

In Menongue, the head of the CARE mine-clearing project in the Cuando Cubango Province showed me a map in very small scale that occupied an entire wall. A mosaic of military charts glued side by side, it was infested with red pins. There were also hand-drawn rectangles of red. And small blue flags, almost all of them around Menongue and along one bank of the Cuebe River, some inches to the southeast.

"The red ones are minefields. Not all of them are here, there's lots more. These are the ones we've identified. The rectangles are strategic locations that were surrounded by mines, such as barracks, powder magazines, and the airport. The blue ones are the areas that have been cleared of mines. Since June we've removed 24,000 from that zone. We store them in an old barracks that belonged to the Cuban logistical team, behind the Catholic mission. Then we destroy them, the way we're doing now: 3,000 on Friday, 860 on Saturday. And then there's the insanity of explosives in private homes. A few days back, a person came to see us because he was remodeling his house, and when the masons started digging in the yard, they discovered eighty-two mortars. You never know when they'll be needed . . ."

A single blue line leads to Menongue, starting at Bié. There are two more small lines with no outlet, toward the south as far as Caiundo, as far east as Cuíto Cuanavale. That is the extent of land communications, in a territory larger than Portugal.

"What about this blue rectangle along the riverbank?"

"It's the beach on the right side of the dam. The UNAVEM soldiers swim there.* The other side is still mined. They swim only halfway across."

"Where's the road south of Caiundo, on the way to Jamba?"

"There isn't one."

"In Luanda they told me there might be one."

"There's no road, and what there is is completely mined. We've managed to clear the road as far as Caiundo, nothing else. You still can't walk on the shoulder. Some time back, there was an accident with a truck that tried to back up. People died in the back of the truck, which is the way they travel here. South of Caiundo the minefields haven't even been located. UNITA and the government haven't given us the maps. No one takes that road, not even UNAVEM armored transports."

---

*For clarification of abbreviations and unfamiliar terms, see the notes on pp. 311 ff.

"How do the NGOs there get around?"

"There are no NGOs down there. There is nobody! Most of the province was never recognized by the Mission. Do I make myself clear?"

"But my plan is to get to Zambia through there. By way of Jamba. There's no other road."

"I'm telling you there isn't any road! No one is authorized to leave from Caiundo. Go back and catch a plane to Luanda and from there to Zambia, if it's so important to you."

At the office entrance, the CARE personnel had bamboo shelves with a display of some of the types of mines and explosives found in the city. There are Russian mines, Cuban, South African, and Chinese mines. Some carry instructions engraved by the manufacturer to ensure proper placement: "This side toward the enemy." The most dangerous are the Chinese plastic mines.

"I'm going to Caiundo. To try to get through."

"In three days you'll be back here telling me I was right. And if you're not, believe me, it'll be because you're dead. In three days you'll be back on the plane to Luanda. Retrace your steps and don't cause problems for us."

I didn't see him again. At the top of the street is the train station that no longer has any trains; they used to arrive from Namibe and Lubango, in the war years, loaded with ammunition and massacres. At the bottom is the river, and before that, the End of the World, a discotheque. It's closed, either because of its redundant name or because it's bankrupt. I left, heading down.

The last instant, therefore. Through the night. There is no scenery, no villages, no people around fires, or elephants silhouetted against the sky. I could speak of such things, I was hoping to, but it would be a lie. There is no horizon, nothing that stands out in relief, no time, no direction. Everything is compressed into the two frames of the windshield. We advance upon a tribe of ghosts illuminated by the headlights. They return to darkness when we run them over, to the deafening sound of the engine. Bushes, rabbits, faces, bats, lullabies, a zoo full of memories.

Our conveyance is a Kamaz. Soviet manufacture.

They used to make some colossal vehicles: a keel with four-wheel drive (each tire the height of a man) to cut through the stubborn sand, the currents of savannas, Cuando Cubango's unbridged rivers.

The right door has no glass. It needs it. The Kamaz charges forth into the cold and the vegetation like a blinded buffalo, with sudden lunges and jolts of fury. We struggle for hours in a network of giant thistles. The trees are of medium size but solid. They block our way, lashing against the truck with brutal power, the rhythm of waves in a storm. The thorns are tough, unbreakable. When the bumpers fracture their spine to the root and we leave them behind, they rain blows on us from every side, scratching against the metal of the chassis like fingernails. In the cab, my feet are burning from them. Little by little, the thorns tear at the arm of my coat before they fall to the ground (I see them in a sliver of the mirror). They have already pierced my skin and caught an ear in the process: my neck bristles with that knifelike flora. I don't dare remove my hood.

The lieutenant colonel is in the middle seat, sleeping the sleep of his rank. I envy him and elbow him aside because he is pushing me toward the thorns. I defend myself by reflex, no longer able to feel my body.

Three days ago, or two, maybe four, it doesn't matter, we had to take apart the jeep's engine. We were in the middle of a mined stretch between Caiundo and Cuangar. The jeep in the middle of the sand, the parts in the middle of the sand, two guerrilla fighters lying down with oil on their arms and sand in the oil. An entire day to clean the engine. The colonel, smoking, told me about the day he stepped on a mine. He felt the click on the sole of his foot and instantly froze. He cried at the top of his lungs. Get me out of here. It was an old Portuguese mine. With them, one second separates the click from the explosion. The click activates the mine. The explosion occurs when the pressure from above is released. Desperation and survival have only that one second to act. The colonel asked for a stick, which they tossed to him. Weeping and sweating, he inserted it beneath the toe of his boot and applied pressure so he could remove his foot without setting off the mine. Then he leaped forward onto the ground. The mine went off behind him. He was in a state of shock for several days. Nothing else. The two of us looked at his feet: intact. Hungry, we gathered twigs, carefully treading on the parallel tracks of the jeep, and boiled a pot of tea. I passed around the small white bag they'd given me in Menongue, and we sweetened it. The colonel took a sip and spat. The bag was table salt.

Every twenty minutes someone is killed or maimed in this world by an antipersonnel mine. There are more than one hundred million mines buried in seventy countries, close to a tenth of them in Angola. In Cuando Cubango, where it is believed 45 percent of Angola's mines are located, mines outnumber people. There were not a lot of people to begin with, and in recent years many have died.

Above our ears and above the dolorous noise, a guerrilla with his Bedouin head wrapped in a rag acts as copilot, shouting through the rear window of the Kamaz, which has no glass.

"To the left at that tree...At that one, to the left. Then to the right...To the right at the bramble bush...To the right, through the sand...To the right, the right! Back, go back! Now that way, straight ahead."

We hope that the copilot knows the terrain well. That his mask of youth conceals the face of a seasoned veteran of war. That he knows the minefields because he helped plant them.

"Right!"

We hope that this is not the first time he has crossed this field in the only way possible, by slashing through the undergrowth.

"Left!"

And we hope that he has done this at night.

"Right!"

And we especially hope that he has no desire to commit suicide. Not a speck of such desire, in this night that never ends.

"We're there! Wake up."

I have no words. My eyelids are heavy with sleep, and the northern lights are exploding in my brain.

"I couldn't sleep. Did you notice that we were being watched?"

Everywhere, a roaring that doesn't seem to come from the engine. "This side toward the enemy."

Dirico is the name the map gives this place, but where have we arrived at? The coordinates are ephemeral. My birthday was yesterday, therefore today must still be yesterday. I get out of the Kamaz with bruised hands and bump into two mirages: a house in ruins and a river in the depths of the savanna. It is the sight of water that I dream about now, there on the cold cement, grabbing the dream in my hands: my two feet like stone but intact.

"Marilyn." Those fearful, fantastic aerial bombs that a Portuguese captain showed me; they are waiting to be destroyed. Six-foot cylinders that have not exploded, rusting in the grasses of Menongue, with graffiti in French: JE T'AIME, BRIGITTE!

It was when the mine smashed into the road that Zeca realized he was dead. This comfort lasted only for the duration of a thought. A needle of sound pierced his ears, and a cyclone swept away the ground, launching his feet into the air and laying bare his spine from neck to chest. The lash of pain took away all sensation from his body. He saw the sky whirl, tumbling without color, and plummet flat onto the ground. The world disappeared in the same instant. There wasn't time even for panic.

Zeca Cambuta — "Shorty" — was born in Bengo, a northern province unpopulated along its shoreline. But on the land side it extends into the interior for a considerable distance. On the map, Bengo is on the Angolan coast; Zeca, however, didn't see the ocean until he was fourteen. This, like everything else, came from the dictates of war. For safety he was sent to the home of those charged with his upbringing (an Aunt Olga who later found a house in Portugal and changed countries as well as quarters). Zeca wasn't acquainted with Luanda. In his mind it was like what they say nowadays about Portugal.

In the forest, things are known that cannot be seen. But the ocean is not known, because when one lives in the forest, there is always ignorance. On his first day at the seashore, Zeca took a bar of soap, a towel, and toothpaste, convinced he was going to the river to wash. His sister Carmita was surprised. When he got to the beach, near the Slavery Museum, Zeca wanted to see whether or not the water was salty. He looked at the expanse of water and stood motionless as he watched the children dive. It was low tide. He was afraid that the current would sweep him away.

Zeca still hadn't tried the water. He finally ran and plunged into the blue novelty with his mouth open. Yes, it was salty, but he kept the secret and told no one. He did not return to the sea.

Ten days after Independence, Zeca moved from an old wattle-and-daub shack to a masonry colonial house in Ferreira do Amaral Square, a small corner redolent of the exhilarating smell of whites in flight. In the square, a self-selected division emerged between "indigenous" and "assimilated," where, years earlier, agents of the International Police for Defense of the State — PIDE — had gone to arrest a doctor named Agostinho Neto. Those Angolans engendered sovereign sons in metropolitan beds as wide as a crucifix made of Cabinda wood. But the houses themselves were merely an act of occupation. The greater conquest was to inhabit the memories of their former owners.

In the gaudiest house, painted in shades that coruscated under the Luanda sun, lived Sr. Leal, owner of Fotofilme and a Mustang that arrested the eye. His son, Eduardo Nunes, filmed Agostinho Neto's arrival in Angola; they also made animated cartoons. His wife, Adelaide, died from a stray bullet. She was sitting in a chair on the veranda when they fired from the terrace of a nearby building that was once a hotel. It was during the confrontations in 1974 and 1975 among the MPLA, the FNLA, and UNITA.

Zeca did not know them or the other whites in the square. His aunt told him they had left for their own country. They built huge wooden boxes without room for the dogs, which to them were obviously thoroughbreds. They sold cars hastily and broke down when they saw the ring of the bay embrace, in them, the longing that they would soon feel. They elbowed their way past one another at the dock and slept on the landing strip. The planes came from Lisbon, and the whites left like the tribal chieftains of Luanda: leaving life, taking with them the utensils for colonizing death. Luanda danced the comba for them, the ritual commemorating death, treading—at last!—upon the absence of their bodies on this red soil.

Of the whites from Ferreira do Amaral Square, only the family of Fernando Alvim, or Nando Pula—meaning "white"—remained. He and Zeca were midfielders on the local soccer team, the Brilhantes Football Club (a reference to the glittering house). They formed a team with Zeca Mulato, son of the family that inherited the rich man's residence. Nando, José, and Zeca: a trio of geniuses in the square, in outlying districts like Cazenga, or in the soccer field along the railway.

A white, a black, and a mulatto ("from the slums, if you please").

Those were the best days, the only ones in which Zeca was always happy. A brief eternity. At eighteen, a mixed police-FAPLA patrol knocked at the door of his sister in Praia do Bispo. It was 5 A.M., and he was there. They asked him for identification, but no draft dodger carries his identity card in his pocket. Carmita was pregnant, so the soldiers tried to let Zeca off the hook. To one of them, however, there was nothing to be discussed: if Zeca stayed, another would have to take his place. Carmita sobbed and went to the kitchen, where she prepared some Musseque flour and a can of powdered milk. She wrapped her good-bye in a plastic bag.

When day broke, Zeca was already in the Autodrome, south of the city, in the midst of other "recruits." He gripped his provisions tightly, for now nothing else was his. That morning they bound his future into a uniform.

He went first to the Sergeants School in Lobito, then returned to Luanda and the Gomes Spencer Commanding Officers School in Huambo. Inevitably he ended up in Cuando Cubango as cannon fodder for the governmental troops. A living hell. He had no choice, but he went there with no illusions: he knew no one was expected to return.

Zeca died in installments. The first was being recruited when he had finally got a verbal contract with a sports scout to be transferred to the Electro team in Huambo. He was going to play soccer and train to be an electrician. The second happened on October 19, 1986, on the Menongue-Longa road, when he fell on the mine. Zeca, in the 36th Brigade, was defending the Longa perimeter. The mine exploded eleven miles from the position. The last voice to speak without shouting said on the radio: "We interrupt this broadcast of Angolan National Radio to announce the death of our beloved comrade the president of Mozambique, Moisés Samora Machel, killed in a plane crash in Zambia."

In Zeca's vehicle, an IFA truck manufactured in East Germany, were three other soldiers. Two in front, two behind, making four on a journey to nowhere.

The news spread in the camp, and Justino knew that his sentence would continue. The president was dead. His plane had crashed.

Justino is a free man. When he was a prisoner—half his life—it was not power that confined him. No one can.

"It wasn't FRELIMO that punished me. And it wasn't the Portuguese government that punished me. It wasn't PIDE that captured me. It wasn't FRELIMO that arrested me. No. Yah... I have a destiny that lights my way. My destiny doesn't fit in with politics."

One accepts one's destiny—that's what destiny is. Justino knows and accepts this. Otherwise he would be able to fight it. The Portuguese agents who arrested him for the first time in December 1964 for subversive activities learned about his destiny. Three white men came and put him in a car to take him to the administration building. The car wouldn't move. They all got out. The car started. The agents and their prisoner got back in. The car wouldn't move.

The Mozambican driver realized what was happening. "The car won't start because of that man."

Justin said no, it was the driver.

They tried again. They got out once more. The car started. They got in.

"Hold tight to that man. He knows how to keep the car from starting."

Justino told them he didn't know how. He wasn't at the wheel.

They finally got under way. At administration headquarters, as Justino was being interrogated, the handcuffs—clang!—fell to the floor.

"Why are you trying to run away?"

"If I wanted to run away, I would, and you couldn't catch me."

The chief of the brigade ordered Justino slapped a couple of times; soon the officer's arms swelled so much that he couldn't get them out of his uniform sleeves. They didn't beat Justin again after that. The prisoner was taken from Inhambane to Lourenço Marques.

Justino knows and accepts his destiny. But first he had to learn it.

Justino's corps was Portuguese. Three years. Then he fled the colony by clandestinely crossing the border to Tanganyika. Dar es Salaam. Then Algiers. In Algeria, he learned the use of various weapons as part of the first group of FRELIMO guerrillas: he was among the founders with Samora Machel, Alberto Hispano, Osvaldo Casama, Francisco Maianga, Samuel Cancomba. There were other revolutionaries in Algiers. Justino, without ever seeing them, heard talk of the Portuguese, including a famous man named Galvão who had hijacked a boat...

Justino's first FRELIMO mission was to escort Admiral Américo Tomás to Mozambique, in June 1964. He recalls it, in Beira: Tomás assured the Portuguese that Mozambique would never become a terrorist camp and that no one would change the age-old ideas of Portuguese dominion.

"Where is he now?"

"Dead."

"I can't feel ill will toward those who fought with dignity at that time. They were trying to make a livelihood."

In Lourenço Marques, the PIDE inspector explained the situation pragmatically, something that Justino very early began to accept.

"You see this map? The naval minister left it for us after his visit.

These sections of Mozambique, all these provinces, they're Mozambique because they're Portugal. This northern part belongs to Madagascar. This other part of the north belongs to Tanganyika. This here is Swaziland. This other one belongs to South Africa. Mozambique is Mozambique because of us, the Portuguese, who defend it from its neighbors."

"South Africa, maybe. Malawi, maybe. But the others have no interest in occupying Mozambique."

"You don't believe me?"

"No, because I know the situation. I built the country of Mozambique."

"You have a different ideology, I know, but don't forget you're in the claws of the PIDE."

"I don't know the PIDE. I only know what FRELIMO brought out in Spanish and Portuguese. PIDE catches a FRELIMO leader and puts him in a cage with lions, out there in the garden, or else they put him in a sack, tie it up, take him in an airplane, and dump him over the ocean. That's what we know."

"That never happened!"

"I left here when I was little. Now I'm seeing certain things in concrete form. You say I'm in the claws of the PIDE. It's the lion that has claws..."

"Why are they creating all this confusion? Going around indoctrinating the population? Just what is FRELIMO?"

"It's an organization made up of all Mozambicans holding political opinions that the Portuguese government doesn't accept. FRELIMO tried to negotiate, but Lisbon didn't answer the letters. It did reply indirectly to the second one: Salazar will never agree to sitting at a table with his shoemakers."

"I'm going to tell you the truth. We know very well that you people have a right to your land. Our coming here led to bloodshed. Our leaving will also be costly; closure means bloodshed. Did you people think all you had to do was pick up a broom, and we were gone? That can't be. We have to end the story the same way we began it: by killing."

"Yes sir, thank you for that. We too want a page of history that shows our strength and our ability to win back our country."

They gave him enough paper for three months on which to tell his story. The judge read the pages at a hearing, and the lawyer Almeida Santos, who was present, asked to know where Justino had written that he was trained in Kenya by the Mau Maus to attack whites. Perhaps that had been added by PIDE.

In the end, the maximum sentence: six years in Machava, with an additional year courtesy of the PIDE-DGS. When he was paroled, Justino was sent to Nampula, to the Psychological Action Group of the Portuguese political police. He was ordered to do counterpropaganda "among the population and rebut everything about FRELIMO, to say that FRELIMO is the Chinese and the Chinese eat people. Or it's the Russians. Things that didn't make the least bit of sense."

Later transferred to Inhambane, he handed over to PIDE reports saying "the population isn't with FRELIMO. There are few active bases. The district isn't sensitive. Terrorism has little penetration, and Mozambicans are in good spirits." Until the revolution in Portugal, when all that came to nothing.

After the revolution of April 25, Justino was an active FRELIMO militant in Inhambane and continued in politics after Independence, in Morrumbene. One day he had the unfortunate idea of asking if his wife could have lunch with him at party headquarters. They didn't know what to tell him: the district commissariat sent him to the provincial commissariat, which sent him to Maputo, to the national commissariat. In the Liaison Office they checked on who he was.

"You worked for the puppet organization!"

He was arrested by order of the vice minister of the interior on October 14, 1977.

His argument, that his time at Psychological Action was forced upon him by court order to exert better control over an individual they considered dangerous, fell on deaf ears. Justino remained at general headquarters before being sent to the penitentiary, from there to Machava, finally to be dumped for good into the Ruarué reeducation camp in Mueda, in the Cabo Delgado province.

"Life was nothing but farming. Uprooting large trees was the punishment. Digging, cutting roots until the tree fell. If you don't finish today, you sleep right there and continue tomorrow. They bring you your food. If it's going to take two or three days, you don't go to the barracks. It was a very hard life."

Every day there were political lessons and literacy classes, "A-b-c-d-e-f-g. Everyone had to participate, and it didn't matter if you were a college graduate. And the ones chosen to be leaders were people with no formal knowledge. They chose real idiots, to tell the truth."

Samora Machel discovered Justino on a visit to Ruarué in 1981 and couldn't understand why his old friend from Algiers had been arrested. Not even the president had jurisdiction over the camp. Machel ordered Justino, along with a group of deserters, sent to a camp in the province of Niassa, from which he could have Justino brought to him. Justino was subsequently transferred to the camp at Mussauize, in the Mavago District.

There, he waited for the president. One day Justino was told Machel was going to visit Niassa with a foreign delegation and come through Mussauize. The prisoners began cleaning up but were later told that the president was first going to Zambia.

"That was when Machel lost his life. I was totally forgotten here. I went on clearing my field. I decided I'd take the first opening at the district level in Mavago in a field growing bananas, papaya, and other fruits. I was there until 1989 and didn't leave until all the confusion got close to us."

Justino, one of the founders of FRELIMO, owes his freedom to RENAMO, which on August 11 attacked the area where he and the deserters were being held prisoner, in the old reeducation center.

Justino fled to Lichinga, where I first met him in 1995, as night watchman for a nongovernmental organization. His time in the labor camps had estranged him from his family.

"I started this family here. My first family was forcibly separated. They stayed in Maputo. I had two little girls. I don't know anything about them or about my wife. I found another one here, and we live well. But one day I'll go to Maputo. I'll keep looking for my daughters and find out about my first wife's situation: whether or not there's the possibility of getting back together. If not, so be it, it's fate."

I still have a photo of Justino, untaken because it was midnight and the small Olympus had no flash. Justino's face in his shack, looking out into the darkness toward the cold of the Upper Niassa, his hands on the glassless window.

If the photo had sound, it would be Justino's measured voice speaking of his life with wise deliberateness, gazing at the unreal landscape of Lichinga. I didn't go inside, the time wasn't right—I would leave for Lichinga before dawn. I didn't go inside, and Justino didn't come out; the time wasn't right.

Photo of an interview: a small recorder pointed at Justino's mouth, gathering in words scattered across the windowsill, and my flashlight pointed at his face. The man reduced to theatrical horror lighting, lit from below. Me reduced to the small red dot that indicated the moment: REC.

Lichinga, in the cold that coursed in and out of Justino's glassless window, reduced to its landscape: the brilliant sheet of light of Lake Niassa hovering in the distance, distinctly, above the mountain range, touching stars more fragile than ourselves. Justino asked for a cigarette. I don't smoke. I left him a pack.

"Thank you."

An ember very like REC lit up at the contact with the first match, then faded. The sound of an owl could be heard during Justino's pauses and, from inside, the breathing of a baby.

And the smell of pines.

"Yahhhh—"

Justino was born April 5, 1941, in Morrumbene, in the province of Inhambane. He was a cellmate of the writer Luís Bernardo Honwana. He learned to write sonnets. His first described the landscape of the Mavago plateau. He learned to read and translate English, solely through books. He learned on his own always. He learned everything. After fleeing, he went from prisoner to nonperson. When I met him, he did not legally exist, because he had no documents recognized by the nation that he had helped found.

"Really, from everything I've seen, government is government. I can't say different. I came to the conclusion that there's no such thing as government of the people, no such thing as democratic government, no such thing as socialist government... It's all—government. Yah... Because, to rule, anyone in power depends on what's in his heart. So I come to respect as the government whoever's in the government. A force of the nation. Not because he does well. It's not easy to do everything well. The People's Republic of Mozambique got worse, yes, but the country can't put itself right all at once. But, more or less, we know how to wear shoes, because they used to be tires— ha!—if you were lucky enough to find them. I wouldn't want to get involved in politics again. I've had enough."

The sky came back into existence a few hours later. Or just after the explosion. It is impossible to say. One eye was blind, burned to a lump. The other hovered high in the blue, the most expansive and immobile of colors. When he lowered his good eye, the green line of vegetation came into view. Lowering it further, the sand, strewn with twisted metal. What about the others, had anyone else survived? As he turned his body, the pain shot up into his clavicle. If the "little brothers" were nearby, they'd have heard his shouts, and it would be the end. But he had managed to turn over. Now he was lying on his belly. His body had rolled. Below his right knee, his leg was at an impossible angle, the kneecap exposed. Only then did panic come, tardy and irremediable: the others were dead, and he wasn't.

"The other three were killed by the mine. But not Zeca. With mines you only die when it happens. Fate wasn't ready for him."

"Where did you find him?"

"In Luanda. In a café in Baixa." A small man at a small table, staring hypnotically at his beer, his eyes clouded and red, his tongue perpetually dry, sighing for the foaming malt.

The voice of old Artur, without the slightest tremor, pierced the serpent of smoke, stiff from cold, that rose from his pipe.

"Does he have his health?"

"He doesn't have a job."

"Heroes don't work while they live. Zeca died many times, and people like that never survive."

Artur's words continue to speak about Zeca's silence in our midst, while a woman, a bit younger than he, ceremoniously places fire into a hubcap from a truck, outside the hut. At the end of the afternoon, fog from the Cuíto and Cuanavale Rivers creeps into the small sandy ravine where the village stands. The people dissolve into the sleep of the bonfires. A dense phantasmagoria, inhabited only by sounds, settles into the spaces among the huts. Artur takes a twig from the flames to scratch in the sand at our feet. He makes sixteen dots, in a four-by-four grid, then joins them with lines. Children arrive, and the woman leaves.

My sister-in-law,
I have been ill.
I thought of you in Caiundo.
How pretty you are.
I'm happy to see you.
I was sad, but now I'm fine.
Take this salt I brought for you.
I hope to see you tomorrow.

The dots were connected by eight lines.

"Nhari. Sister-in-law. It's the name of the drawing. We Ganguelas used to communicate by drawings. Only the elders knew it."

"Is there a book of such drawings?"

"No. They're done in the sand. No one does them any longer."

"Are there others?"

"More than you could know. But I can tell you some of them."

"Do any speak of war?"

Artur motioned behind his head with his arm, with a gesture that included both himself and the devastation of the village. Then, with a sweeping curve, pulling an imaginary hood, he brought the hand forward to the ground. We were seeing another drawing.

"Gunpowder. It's this."

Artur drew.

The road that formerly linked Menongue to Mavinga and Jamba ends at Cuíto Cuanavale. The bridge that crosses the savanna was dynamited early on, when the war had still not hit the area, and beyond this point the road has yet to be cleared of mines. There is no traffic. There are no cars, no engines, no machines. There is no fuel, and all these shortages buttress one another in a vicious circle. From the canoe borrowed by António, for whom the enormous bushes make way, bowing as we pass, can be glimpsed a world cursed with primordial peace. António, on his knees, rowing the hollowed-out tree trunk, rides the water's crystalline muteness, conveying me into the quacking of ducks and the memory of the worst battle of the civil war, which took place here.

In the battle of Cuíto Cuanavale, in the eighties, Angolans from FAPLA, SWAPO guerrillas, Cuban troops, and Soviet planes fought against Angolans from UNITA, South African commandos, and French planes. Thousands of men died from bombs, mortars, rockets, mines, tanks, machine guns, hunger, swamps, crocodiles. Alongside the madness: an incalculable number of others, who left and returned to Moscow, Havana, or Johannesburg smuggling nightmare-filled baggage. Cuíto Cuanavale is the center of nothing but possesses the only paved road in the district, invaluable for transport of troops and matériel. Gaining control of it could determine the war, as came to happen. The final combat occurred long after horror grew commonplace, on March 23, 1988—the day there was no dawn.

Colonel Q., who arrived in Cuíto Cuanavale in 1985 and rose in the ranks because they didn't want to remove him from there, agreed to share some unpleasant memories. That probably means a referral preceded me, sent by radio from FAA headquarters in Menongue by the friendly master of Mobutu, a black dog born the day Laurent-Désiré Kabila's Angolan troops took Kisangani, capital of Haut-Zaïre.

"I was in the Thirteenth Landing and Assault Brigade, assigned to counterattack the enemy flank. The South Africans were across the river. On UNITA's side, for example, was Ben-Ben. The head of the FAPLA general staff was General Ngueto. Cinta Fría was in command of the Cubans. Did you see his bunker in Menongue?"

Cinta Frías, of the Revolutionary Armed Forces, landed in 1978 and left in the withdrawal of the Cuban contingent in 1989. He rose to commander of the military mission that Fidel maintained in Angola. He is a member of the Central Committee. The bunker is a massive structure of earth and cement shored up by beams made from cross ties of the Moçâmedes railroad. Discreet, for a hole that withstands half-ton bombs. It is located on the street near the station, behind an innocently civilian colonial residence; but two minutes after you enter, someone in sneakers knocks at the door "to see how the chief's Sunday is going. Is there any beer?"

"What most left its mark on me in the first and second wars was March 23, 1988. That day you almost couldn't see the sun from the smoke of the explosives. You couldn't hear the infantry, only the artillery. The South Africans were ready to take it. The most intense attack began at two in the morning and didn't stop till twelve hours later. G-5s, 106s, the Kentrons (a South African cannon), and the tanks were all over us. From this side we shot BM21s, which are vehicle-mounted artillery, 130-type cannons, D30s, 76 mm fire, and the artillery from the tanks. The most dangerous is the G-5, which has a greater range and more destructive power. In the retreat, the South Africans launched gas with their cannons to injure the population. On a normal day we would suffer ten casualties, but in the final assault we couldn't even see the bodies. The Cubans were removed at the end of the war..."

A few miles before Cuíto Cuanavale, behind government lines, Fidel's boys were completing their interventionist mission in deep graves of fine sand—a posthumous discharge enjoyed in the caress of Cubans' beaches. The cemetery is still there, abandoned in a clearing of mines and weeds, with three logs similar to the gates of the Boer farmers the Cubans fought until the eve of their sacrifice. Crowning the entrance is a sign: THE STRUGGLE CONTINUES. The rest has rotted away, but the colonel recalls what the dead men read: VICTORY IS CERTAIN.

This is the obsessive slogan chosen for the banknotes of the National Bank of Angola, under the likenesses of António Agostinho Neto and José Eduardo dos Santos. The two are in profile, the arrogant lower lip of the former and the melancholy gaze of the latter. Two leaders who achieved, beyond the millions of devalued kwanzas, the abbreviated limits of their farthest horizons, after which nothing more is conceivable. Victory is certain. Within reach of the two presidents, but hidden invisibly in the watermark, is the traditional figure of the Thinker, sitting, silent, anonymous, his head in his hands and his elbows on his knees. The watermark authenticates the whole.

António, who speaks an incomprehensible Portuguese, takes me downriver without a word, gathering with his oar the heartbeat of the water. The sun, ever lower, spills honey from his hair to his shoulders. In a traveling shot virtually motionless but filled with gestures, a riverbank of seminude women bathing in a group passes by us. People still die on the shores of this river after every rainy season. Here, the mines are even more treacherous; left by the thousands in the unstable soil of the Cuíto Cuanavale, they shift with the sands and drift toward the place where everything flows: the river. The men, with neither modesty nor fear, bathe farther downstream, robed in soap and the gleaming cellophane of wet skin.

António waves to them. His middle finger is missing, severed by a bullet that went through his left hand. He fought five years for that village and can still hear in the sky the instantaneous hiss of MIGs and Mirages. They came from far away, from Lubango or Southwest Africa, their wings skimming the savannas' treetops. Suddenly they would emerge from behind a corral (stakes driven vertically into the ground at short intervals, forming a circle higher than a goat can jump). You ran for your shelter, if you had dug one. If there was time.

"Bad thing about planes is we didn't see them till they were leaving. War planes are like that: you hear them only after they bomb you," explains António.

"Je t'aime, Brigitte."

Artur shows me the third drawing, in the same sand where gunpowder dissolved.

"*Kalunda*. Cemetery."

Artur's hut is in the lower part of the village. Cuíto Cuanavale has little to distinguish it from other *municípios* that the settlers erected in Cuando Cubango before 1975: a handful of single-story houses of somewhat eccentric lines, along a road in the middle of nowhere. One house was for administration, others for the police, the post office, and what was evidently a small school (with its whitewashed open-air classroom and its paved walkway). And a few other walled structures for small businessmen. Today not a building remains intact—as is the case in virtually the whole of the Angolan interior.

The population lives in the surrounding "neighborhoods" of huts, constructed of wooden poles, sandy clay, and fused metal remnants from the war. The local leaders, in the UNITA zones (in Cuando Cubango the UNITA movement controls the entire province except Menongue and Cuíto Cuanavale) or in the government's, are distinguished from the general population only by their title and by the right to arbitrate. They rule from masonry ruins, their low-slung castles, but are subject like the rest to the absence of electricity, running or potable water, plaster, sanitation, windows, glass, communications, sometimes even roofs and doors. Almost always the absence of furniture, and always of a complete bathroom. In such a setting, the settlers' houses provide no shelter: they serve only to obey a statute and purchase loyalty.

Someone important lives in this house, in the middle of the street, as poverty-stricken as all the others, though it rises above the ground and the rest because the owner can enter his fortress without crossing the moat of sand: there is a helicopter blade, forty feet long, over which you can make your way to the pavement. Someone important, for sure:

a nouveau riche in the circus of destruction, high up, doing a balancing act to enter his house, with no dust on his feet, his unequaled power, his pride and joy a house with no lock.

António has no house. He found work as a janitor at the United Nations team site. The night I arrived at his village, he was the first to press his nose against the window of the UNAVEM all-terrain vehicle that gave me a ride into Menongue: two restless, staring eyes, as if terror had removed his eyelids. He shares the work—washing, cleaning, hauling, listening, watching, recounting—with an even stranger individual, Domingos, another Cuíto Cuanavale survivor. A bullet shattered his right leg, which is still twisted. Seen from behind, when Domingos walks from place to place with his faltering step, his right knee turns inward: his legs form a K in a lopsided rhythm. A K for Cuando Cubango and Cuíto Cuanavale—the terrible KK of wartime Angolan slang.

Domingos takes great pride in a lady's comb, made of red plastic, that he wears, horizontally, in the hair at the back of his neck. A large comb, it sticks out past his ears. At times of boredom, I watch António and Domingos dance away their idleness from the kitchen to the jango, from the tent to the living room. Two phantoms flying through the mosquito netting of the doors.

At the end of the street, in a house missing one corner because a howitzer opened a hole the size of a double display window, a young man is playing a Total banjo (the sound box was once an oil can). Three ragged children dance to off-key scales of wire. The day has ended, and there is nothing to eat in the tents of the small "market" off to the side.

The house, uninhabited, still displays the sign on its facade, ORGANIZATIONS BAKERY WE SHALL RETURN.

Zeca was rescued and taken to Menongue. He spent three months convalescing in a hospital. His third death occurred by telephone. A fellow veteran, having heard the communication that Zeca's IFA had run over a mine on the Longa road, phoned Luanda and informed

Zeca's aunt that he had died. The family tried to organize the comba, but Uncle Manuel was opposed: no need make the death official until the body was found.

When Zeca phoned from Menongue, the call smelled of Lazarus. His aunt couldn't believe it. It was necessary to send for his wife, Belita, to confirm that the voice was that of the dead man and that the dead man was there, though not in person, reinstating himself. That was in 1987. Belita went down to Menongue with a death certificate for her mother-in-law (who is still alive today and in good health). The commanding office gave Zeca eight days' liberty, and Zeca was already in Luanda on the morning that Operation Mavinga took place.

After his leave, he was supposed to present himself to a unit in the capital. They wanted to send him to Moxico, in the east. The soldier didn't comply, covering his tracks with the quickness of the clandestine and camouflaging his desertion in the labyrinths of Prenda, a Luanda slum. He stayed at home, taking care of his three children. He would sometimes go out, but warily.

In 1992, enjoying the minipeace of 1991, he presented himself at the headquarters in Funda to be demobilized. He went from deserter to unemployed. He met Nando Pula again in 1993. He recalls with emotion the man's having offered him fifty dollars. His eyes become a bit damp, then quickly regain the cloudy look of one on autopilot, an alcoholic rosy tinge trembling on his eyelids. Zeca grasps the sandwich with the concentration due a chaplet. He shrinks away upon the arrival of an employee in a uniform that has lost its color at the elbows and in the folds — there is always a uniform to intimidate him. Zeca is uneasy there. It's the first time he's been in that café in Baixa, the only one without bars on its windows. The addicts press against the outside of the glass, like tentacles brandishing packs of American cigarettes.

"I did a course in general logistics in the army. I worked as a stock clerk in a store. But at the moment I'm not working, been a year... I live off friends and family. If not for the army, today I'd have a career in electronics. I'd play for the Primeiro de Agosto team. Cuíto Cuanavale was constant torture. I did the military for eleven years, till I deserted. What they promised wasn't honored. Soccer would have been possible. It's a lost dream. I get perspective help from my friends."

Zeca, losing his words, concludes by bitterly flailing his arms.

"It was territorial integrity... But instead of defending, I was offended. Yesterday all I had to eat was a piece of bread..."

It accompanied me against my will, like a moon and a shadow. When I was forced to stop, it went on running, but as days passed, it began to notice me and turn. I was calm, it was not. It changed, softened, stopped.

Time stopped is a companion I neither asked for nor have the right to refuse. Time and I, in Caiundo, are enclosed in a tent that flays my nerves. Trapped in a billeting area in the Land of the End of the World, I release the only free part of myself and mentally brave the unknown, fly to a place located beyond any map, and in that intimate empire I contemplate time in complete immobility. The old Aztec shamans were familiar with such flight.

I breathe the air of the drowning man, and there is no anguish, no flailing. I breathe gusts of water. Each desert always confronts me in sight of a river — and there it is. UNITA wants to wait me out. As it knows that animals don't roam by themselves, it gave me a tent so I can waste away in private. When I'm done, they'll come to look, lament, and spread the word.

Exhuming everything that is mine, which is not much: a planet of Aristotelian cosmogony. I live in a flat, square universe erected on four pieces of cloth, with the melancholy vault of a stall without stars. In outer space, there is a satellite with no intelligent life: they brought me a chair.

I sit down and read *Atlas,* by Michel Serres.

"Le livre que j'écris est plus la chair de ma chair que ma chair elle-même."

I sit down and read *The Portable Paul and Jane Bowles.*

The first is excellent, the second a treasure. I can't stand either of them.

I sit down. I get up. I sit down. They come to see me, talk a bit, apologize, and leave. Offering the greetings and sympathy due a cripple.

Two bodies were found crushed against the rocks of the rapids three kilometers upstream, already blue from putrefaction. In the UNITA areas there is no crime, there are rapids. The case therefore merits investigation. I was not authorized to go, either to the crime or to the rapids. But it aroused my interest. They went to check whether the bodies were people or animals. They returned with a categorical answer: On examination, it proved to be goats. Blue goats. Goats pass daily between me and the sun. I have yet to see the blue species; it must be the backlighting.

Reading, rest, reflection, exercise, music. Nothing appeals to me. Oxen also go by—without speaking to me. At sunset they levitate against the silhouette of the barbed wire. I survive by discipline, in a religion of unimportant gestures, an effort at attachment to life: the metallic arch of cold water on my back, under the outdoor shower; washing my hands before eating; brushing my teeth before going to bed; shaking my boots well before putting them on. Through my skin I reassure myself of my body. It must be the prisoner's way. I now understand what Joãozinho, one of the FAPLA helicopter pilots, told me about Sufi priests.

"They go days without being heard or saying anything. Afterward they tell you they were meeting God."

Memorable that pilot, who loved the mountains. The priests are called pir, Joãozinho, and their journey is called zikr. The silent zikr.

The repetition of the name of God, dozens, hundreds, thousands of times until the body dissolves into that silent repetition and enters into union with the Almighty. You and God, in a single body. Zikr. The qawwalis of Pakistan have the same objective: chants of devotion until they attain mystic union. The passion of Punjabi Sufi poets merged with the melodious ragas of northern India. A memory, Joãozinho: a qawwali can spend hours, an entire night, drawing triangles and circles in the air. A melodious zikr.

Nusrat Fateh Ali Khan hasn't died yet. For me, that will happen in Lusaka, four weeks from now.

Joãozinho spent five years in the Frunze Military Academy in Kirghiz. Ten years after his return he learned that he had left a daughter in central Asia. Joãozinho thinks about her, the child he never knew, as he leans on the counter of a warm luncheonette in Luanda, which is nothing more than an open container in the middle of a square. He is the bartender.

It happened accidentally, his last year there. Gulnara, Joãozinho's love. They made all the arrangements for her to have an abortion. In the end, no. Angola languishing in the snow.

Zikr.

Joãozinho fought again in these skies. He told me he killed in order not to be killed. He suffered an accident in Bié, on the runway, when his hydraulic system failed as he was testing the landing gear. The helicopter fell like a rock, from forty feet.

By the position of the stars, I calculate my parallel and verify that the clinical death of my watch has a psychotropic effect. My existence in Caiundo?

It is the consistent cold of night's end, which corrals me sleeplessly in the cubicle of the tent and which I attempt to deceive with an autistic reflex by compressing my extremities and torso into a tiny zone of heat (my own).

It is the heat of the day, as sudden as an attack, an injection of torpor that parches the canvas and fills all my tissues.

The very fine sand, refined, visible only in its accumulation on every side, in the boots, in the black nap of the chair—coat hanger, on the glossy covers of books (from the friction of my fingers), on the floor of the tent. Where did so much sand come from so quickly?

Lunch, dinner, more lunches, and once again more dinners of canned sausage and plain spaghetti with pinches of salt stolen from the kitchen that they don't want me to use. Fruit, of which there is none, not even in Menongue. The angry water and the river, this one here whose name I don't know, and the Cubango, into which the Nameless will empty, seventeen kilometers to the south, both of which I am forbidden to swim in because supposedly they harbor crocodiles.

The news collected from neither interest nor necessity (what use is the present when time itself has ceased to function?).

Anna Karenina, a radio serial Sunday mornings, on the BBC. Radio station is expressed better in Mbundu than in any other language: *ondja iépopero*, "talking house."

My existence here? I don't waste time. It is wasting me. I haven't seen myself in a mirror for several days, and the absence of that face swells resentment inside me. In Kavaleka, also in Cuando Cubango, there was a French humanitarian organization that worked with a concept that interests me: phantom pains.

Kavaleka is the village with the highest concentration anywhere in the world of mutilated individuals per square meter. Phantom pain happens to anyone who suffers an amputation of a limb and continues to feel pain or itching in the missing leg, hand, arm.

Two French technicians were introduced by an element of the Unité Coordinatrice de l'Aide Humanitaire to a large group of the mutilated at the end of a session clarifying the demobilization of the more than two thousand amputees from Kavaleka. The amputees listened to the young couple elaborate what most of them were feeling. The couple spoke in French, but there was a very fluent interpreter, from one of the language schools that UNITA set up in this unlikely province.

Then the amputees saw the magic machine: a box that supplies a current to electrodes that in turn, connected to the nerve branches of the amputated member, neutralize the phantom pain. Those interested were invited to come next morning at 8 A.M. to receive the blessed shocks in their stumps. A huge line would form long before that time, and the French team spent three days applying the treatment and teaching the use of the machine.

Seven hundred handicapped people applauded the therapists when the device was presented.

Jubilation in a mutilated country: the phantom pains disappear; it just takes a machine, which comes from outside and needs only batteries to operate.

Zikr. Eight days here. The car that can take me to Cuangar never arrives. I don't believe in the name of God to repeat it. I repeat my own name, two blasphemous syllables. I have long since forgotten the others. Amnesia prays with me, asking—a trifle—for a car to take me back to who I am and what I love. Amnesia devours all the names, beginning with the most precious. The acts by which I survive have replaced beings and affections. Wife, family, love, objects, voices, friends, projects, desire, fury, places, ideas. A pregnancy in Lisbon and a sonogram lose definition. Everything retreats: the rest of my life exists in time, and I have ceased to belong to time. It's not egoism, it's a capsule.

In the "house" of Alok, the Indian major who heads the Caiundo team site—three tents, two vehicles, and a water tank—there are evenings of cards with the humanitarian personnel. Alok is not a Muslim, and in India he commands Sikh soldiers. He believes in the powers of meditation, which he himself practices daily, sitting cross-legged on a carpet. Caiundo is a good place to meditate. Alok explained to me that the mind has the power to invoke the vital energy stored in every human being. Moreover, it can materialize that energy, give it physical existence, with potterlike movements of the hands that mold a ball of energy. A ball that grows larger and larger as concentration, will, and meditation increase. The soul in a marble.

"I can direct that mass of energy, invisible but palpable, wherever I want to. If someone is quite ill in India, I can have my vital energy go to him and help him survive. The energy of my mind goes anywhere. Distance is unimportant. From me to you or from here to Delhi."

I realized today that I've hit bottom, and I was ashamed. There are two kitchens, the UCAH's and the humanitarians'. No one is generous to excess. At the entrance to the humanitarian kitchen I found Chicha, the chimp belonging to the Spanish nurse Yolanda, gnawing on an apple. My first impulse was to steal the fruit from the animal.

Fruit would taste good. A chimp shouldn't have what I can't have. It's humiliating.

The name of the organization in Kavaleka was Pain without Borders.

Augusto Amaral invented a table to calculate time when he went blind temporarily. He had an operation for cataracts in 1994. At eighty, he was convalescing for the first time in a hospital bed.

"I wasn't happy."

He would be. He reflected at length while he was unable to see. When light returned, he asked that calendars be brought to him, and he studied them. The calendars are hundreds of sheets of paper that Augusto Amaral took home with him at the end of each of the forty-one years he worked in the office of the Benguela railroad (since 1952, after a short time with the company in 1930). Some of the calendars are typewritten! Other sheets have service orders written on the back, or emergency procedures.

Augusto Amaral came to several conclusions, which he called his system:

1. The years repeat themselves every twenty-eight years.
2. January 1, 1900, was a Tuesday.
3. February and March are always the same, as is November.
4. There are other months that are also always the same, according to whether it is a leap year or a common year:

a) in a leap year, August is equal to February and September is equal to December;

b) in common years, January is equal to October, February continues equal to March and November, April is equal to July (but not to January), and September is equal to December.

With these rules committed to memory—he has a prodigious and restless brain—Augusto Amaral can, for any date in the century, tell on what day of the week it fell. He has perfected a system of counting on his fingers.

1. The first step is finding out if the year of the desired date was leap or common. Another rule: uneven years can never be leap years; and not all of the even years are.

2. Next, mentally calculate which multiple of twenty-eight (and therefore which "twin" year of 1900–28, 1956, 1984) is closest to the year of the desired date.

3. Counting is from left to right, with the fingers fanned and the left hand turned downward and the right hand opened upward. On the fingers, count by seven, starting with Tuesday—the ring finger of the left hand (the left thumb is Friday, the right little finger is Saturday, and the ring finger is Sunday).

4. Advance one day of the week for each finger and each year. Knowing that January 1, 1984, was a Tuesday, you can determine on which day the desired year began (for example, if January 1, 1984, was a Tuesday, then January 1, 1986, was a Thursday—that is, the forefinger).

5. Every four years (the leap years), advance two fingers.

6. After finding the first day of the year in question, count on the fingers the following months: three fingers for each thirty-one-day month and two fingers for each thirty-day month.

7. For common years, February and March are the same (rule 3); therefore don't count February and advance three fingers

36

of the thirty-one days of the following month. For a leap year, however, count one finger for February.

It's infallible, and with training the automatic movements accelerate the calculation. A parlor trick, infirmary mathematics that made Augusto Amaral the Human Calendar of Lobito.

"We're here speaking the dialect of the PAM! I speak the dialect of the PA-A-am! I want food, the pula gives it. The white man of the PAM, yah! He's there, with us lined up, and him in front with sheets of paper and writing: displaced, displaced, displaced! The white man is god! You even see it in the Bible. It's the pula that rules. I'm mutilated. Look at my leg: it won't bend!"

With exaggerated distaste, someone told him to shut up. A male nurse of the Angolan Red Cross, extremely affected, who peppered his speech with "ooh" and "good heavens," hands placed as if he had a cramp in his chest. I wanted the mutilated man to go on: his rancor was clairvoyant.

Even before the departure, cigarettes and beer were circulating freely in the coach. There was time for everything to ferment and spread as it circulated: departure was set for 6 A.M., but, eight hours later, the passengers were still waiting. Elvis diagnosed the mutilated man, who had impressive muscles:

"That guy's high as a kite."

Then Elvis got into an argument with a bleary-eyed inspector who appeared from time to time announcing himself as the conductor. He took advantage of Elvis's absence to try to open one of the youth's bottles. He was caught.

"Don't open it!"

"I open and close. I'm doing my job!"

"Your job is just to ask questions. You couldn't be a soldier, you'd die. Don't you know there's acid in there? It'll blow up in your face. Hey, don't you understand Portuguese?"

"Look, I have to inspect everything. What's going on in that cabinet? I'll let it go, just give me a cigarette."

There was a disturbance in the other cabinet.

"Give me a light, make it fast," said the conductor on his return, looking as if he had just got up: he was wearing a brown jacket, pants with black checks on a white background, and a flannel shirt with similar pajama checks.

"Now? I don't have it, you just told me to clear out."

"This car is for the guys. Riffraff goes back there with the bedbugs."

Elvis wore a white wool cap with a pink tassel and embroidery that read ALEXANDRA. He was with a friend, Chiquinho. They are the living image of the Angola that does business wherever it can. The two Kaluandas came from the capital months ago to a village deep in the jungle of Namibe, Caitou, north of Bibala on the Bentiaba River. Choosing the spot on the map was no problem: Chiquinho's brother is head of police in the locale, and they emigrated in order to do business with the Mucubals of the region. They buy red wine in the city of Namibe and trade it for livestock — cattle, goats, chickens, rabbits — or mupeque oil, which in Luanda costs a fortune.

"It's a beauty product. The girls use it to straighten their hair. It turns very dark. Really, really black. It's like motor oil, which they also use — yes, they do, there in Luanda. You look at a bottle of mupeque, and you think it's twenty- or thirty-weight oil. In Luanda, a liter costs you twelve bucks. Here, you'd need a million."

The main business of Elvis and Chiquinho is sacrificial cattle.

"Those kotas, when they die, they have to kill I don't know how many head of cattle. Big cattle! But they don't eat it: it's just to remove the horns. They throw the rest away."

No Mucubal eats sacrificial cattle, so they sell the animal cheap, sometimes for four hundred thousand kwanzas. The same head, in Namibe or Luanda, goes for eighty or ninety million.

"There's times we even arranged for them to come kill the animal in Namibe, or in Dinde; they only take three days to bring them in a herd. They arrive, they keep the horns, and we keep all the meat."

Even the nonsacrificial animals yield a profit.

"A bundle. A head of cattle is worth fourteen million, and you don't even have to pay in money. A twenty-five-liter drum of red wine costs us seven and a half million in Luanda. Fifty liters comes to fifteen million, and that's enough for two or three steers worth eighty million. Sometimes we buy a goat for a demijohn of canhombe."

In the caves of the port of Namibe I witnessed the production of canhombe: two old metal drums, a copper tube, a fire beneath the drum filled with fermented grain. It's a still. There is no regulation of the manufacture of alcohol, so now and then canhombe kills. However, as they told me in the caves, "Fortunately, it doesn't happen that much; what happens more is canhombe leaving you blind."

I didn't try any.

Chiquinho and Elvis had dollar signs in their eyes.

"Ten liters, which is two demijohns or three million, is traded for a young bull, something larger than a calf. In Luanda the bullock can bring us twenty-two or twenty-five million. Up there, with the Mucubals, you can also trade twenty kilos of sorghum for an ox. That twenty kilos may cost us only ten million."

Oil is even easier money: "In Luanda, a beer bottle of mupeque (three bottles don't even make a liter) sells for two and a half. As for red, we buy a five-liter demijohn in Namibe for 1.925 million and sell it in Caitou for a million a liter..."

The pair from the Red Cross looked at the young businessmen with respect. The girls who were traveling, two sweet things from Bibala, also looked at them, though with different eyes.

The departure. Elvis was lying on a sack with closed eyes and a sick expression. He had an infection on his leg, now several centimeters long: a simple boil that had burst and was left without dressing. I cleaned the pus for him.

"Good people, good people. He speak the Red Cross dialect, yessir!"

He's the more expansive of the two nurses.

"Heavens! Listen, listen: let me sit down..."

He sat between Chiquinho and Elvis and, as he did so, rested his left hand between the legs of Chiquinho, who smiled disconcertedly.

The train stopped in the middle of the desert, and out of nowhere food vendors appeared. A young woman announced to the entire car that she had to relieve herself, so she was helped down the stairs to the ground, where she squatted under her colorful capulana. Seen from above, she looked like a bird protecting itself from the wind. As she descended, she almost tripped over the inspector, who'd been drunk since morning.

"You can piss out there. But don't fall all over me!"

The inspector, staggering outside the coach and holding a tattered, filthy red flag, narrowly missed being sprayed by a young man who hadn't bothered to leave the train.

"And you, don't piss on me! I forbid it!"

Salted fish began circulating in the car. *Mulamba* is the term: chunks of fish, dried and salted, to last for some time (Angola has no refrigeration). Everyone ate it. The recess of the car's ceiling, visible because there was no paneling, became crusted with salt and fish. Ju made things worse by acquiring a beautiful fish that she fondled for a long time, holding it on her knees the way ladies hold hand luggage. The fish cleaned itself on her pants.

A well done mulamba keeps for two or three months. What happens these days in Namibe and Tômbua is that the market has been invaded by bad mulamba hastily made by street vendors. It lasts only two or three days.

No one seemed to care. Above the enthusiastic chewing, in the stench of salting and the pouring of beer without labels—there was always beer—the car took on an air of gaiety. In no time the bottles were rolling on the floor to the rhythm of the mountain curves. To better drink the beer and ward off hunger, the group had bought canned mackerel—the entire supply of the two boys who were on the train to sell it. Every bit as disgusting as the mulamba. Red Cross found an enormous pot into which were emptied several cans. The meal became easier with the vessel passing from hand to hand. Anything left over would be sold in Bibala. Ju and Didi were vendors.

It was Chiquinho, behind his hustler's mustache, who began the afternoon discussion.

"Mucubals aren't afraid of dogs, because dogs won't bite them. If a dog comes up, a Mucubal says, 'Boo!,' and his breath stops the dog in its tracks. The Mucubal can pick him up and put him on his back, one leg here and the other there and one hand in his mouth, and the dog just sits there, without closing its mouth. And if a dog does bite a Mucubal, its teeth fall out, all of them!"

"Oh, our Lady of Fáahtima!"

"She must be tired."

"Who?"

"Our Lady of Fátima."

Red Cross drooled, holding a handkerchief, casting a look at Elvis, enthralled at the provocation.

"There's a Mucubal there, respected by all the elders in the region, named João Comprido. They're tall, very tall, João Comprido stands 1.9 meters. When he comes into our cubicle, he's fine, seems normal. But the muadiê is a sorcerer. If he's drinking with others, he can put them all to sleep and drink by himself, and when you wake up, you don't notice anything and all the wine is gone! João Comprido will die well. He already knows the date. And he's already chosen the sacrificial cattle, they're ready. But he won't die. He tells us: God in heaven and João Comprido on earth. When everybody else is gone, he'll still be around."

Ju, a woman with a for-rent smile, garish makeup, and a wig, disagreed. She was obviously feeling the effects of the beer.

"Mucubals are weak, that's what I heard. The Mucuissas are better."

"The Mucuissas live among the rocks. They go into caves when it rains. They eat lizards. You know what a lizard is, girl? Mucubals are strong. They don't joke around. The other day, over in Caitou, João Comprido told a muadiê to light a cigarette in the fire. There weren't any flames, just a few embers. He told him: Don't play with fire, you'll get burned. When the muadiê bent down to light the cigarette, his face got burned all right, all sooty, he doesn't know how."

Confusion. From Mucubals to sorcery is no distance at all if you're not a Mucubal. The car filled with laughter and uneasiness.

"Over in Luanda, I didn't see it, but they told me about it, in the home of a muadiê police official, they cast a spell and the furniture danced."

Elvis and Chiquinho, the only ones besides me who hadn't drunk, plunged into the subject.

"That's right! The chair and the table, the sofa with the beds, one crazy dance!"

"The chamber pot emptied itself. The broom and the water jug, the refrigerator and the stove. The stove turned on without anybody's help..."

Ju, naturally, had a rejoinder.

"Near the Bibala woods, they told me a husband caught his wife with her lover and got a spell cast on them so they'd stay stuck that way, glued together by the lover's dick. They went out in the street like that!"

The blasé nurse, who sported a narrow mustache in the middle of his lip, a thin line beneath the nostrils, sighed.

"Such backwardness! I got up at five this morning to catch the train, and since then it's been nothing but waiting. No breakfast, no lunch, and there won't be dinner!"

His colleague stood up in the middle of the car and took off his sweater.

"I want to look elegant."

In Bibala, everyone disembarked: the spells, the anecdotes, Ju's bawdy riddles, the fish juice; Didi in front of me leaning out and gazing upon the desert, the lip that nibbled at the back of her hand where

43

her chin rested; the boxes of medicines, Red Cross's sighs. Elvis and Chiquinho also sighing.

It was calm when the train pulled out, penetrating the majestic wall of the Chela mountain range: the step from the sea to the plateau. Over a thousand meters vertically, after the canyons of the Namibe Desert, with a silhouette like the rocks in John Ford's westerns in Monument Valley.

Late that night, in the mountains, the shortwave radio told me of the death of John Stewart. On the rails in Moçâmedes, Texas.

Prophets flourish when reality becomes scarce. Joaquim Augusto Junqueira, however, dreamed bigger than other prophets. Though speaking no Angolan language, he understood that war, not just Angola's, was a problem of communication. At a forced stop, his hands in his pockets and his words clotting in the cold, because we had no fire, he revealed a secret: he possessed the key to peace. A language of reconciliation, new and universal. For now, it is spoken by just one man — him. Standing in the middle of the road, late at night, is Joaquim, the father of Quinese.

Like other noble ideas, Quinese has a bastard origin. At school, Joaquim "felt the need to take tests without much preparation and always cut class." He and a Portuguese friend, Mendonça, created a system of codes using squares and crosses. It was complex enough for the message to be written on a single sheet of paper but also secret enough that the teacher couldn't accuse him of cheating. The code grew more sophisticated and even came to include sounds that made sense only to the two bad students.

Joaquim's parents never spoke with him in their native tongue, Mbundu, and they wanted to educate him in a Portuguese school "with nuns and priests." His training in foreign languages took place in Eastern Europe, where he traversed the map of proletarian internationalism in education: he left the former People's Republic of Angola for the former Czechoslovakia, the former German Democratic Republic, the former Yugoslavia, and the former Soviet Union. Still later, when the war of the worlds ended everywhere except Angola, Joaquim saw places like Great Britain and Scandinavia. Today, he "thinks" he speaks six languages: Czech, Swedish, English, Vietnamese, Russian, and Serbo-Croatian, with "a tiny amount of French" and less Italian. He had more girlfriends than languages.

In the former Czechoslovakia, where he studied general machinery repair, Joaquim first heard of Esperanto, a language created for the unity of peoples, "more powerful than English." Esperanto failed, Joaquim observes, because it was a language of adults and "a tree that grows crooked can never be straightened." Quinese is different: a new language for children, for his son, his nephews, all children. Joaquim believes that by extending it through his friends and neighbors, Quinese may "one day, a hundred years, five hundred years from now," reach other borders.

For this purpose, he fashioned Quinese to be an easy language throughout the world, incorporating sounds of Europe and Asia but not omitting the sounds spoken in Africa. "A language based on all the inhabited universe, that is, our Earth." Since "there is no harmony where various dialects exist," the first challenge of Quinese is to superimpose itself upon the diversity of expression in the Angolan territory until it becomes the linguistic vehicle "in a single word, in a single language, to create an experience, a self-sufficient society without problems or with only those conflicts that are easily resolved."

In the country of Quinese no one will say, "You're Mbundu" or "You're Kimbundu," "You're this or that," "You think you're better than I am because you speak Portuguese." A "long, very long-term" project, therefore: not for two years, even five hundred would be utopian, but a thousand years is enough. An inheritance that Joaquim is leaving for the future of Angola and on which he worked for years, since 1986, studying parallels among the structure of Indo-European and African languages. He perfected "the right formula, the appropriate structure," developed a grammar and phonetics for his new tongue, and, finally, put together a "Portuguese-Quinese Dictionary."

Quinese ceased to be a schoolboys' plaything, and "it doesn't owe anything to other languages." But it was once again in the classroom that it proved its efficacy: in a technology lesson, the Czech professor caught Joaquim scrawling unknown characters and reprimanded him for not paying attention. The Angolan said that he was paying complete attention. Sent to the blackboard to prove it, he reproduced faithfully everything the professor had explained, using his notes in Quinese.

The Quinese alphabet "is composed of between thirty-eight and forty letters, in order to distinguish many things," preventing, for example, "sounds with *c* and sounds with *s*, sounds with *k* and sounds with *q*." Joaquim includes in his language phonemes that "meet the needs of almost every language," especially the difficult sounds of Kimbundu, Mbundu (the language he would most like to learn), Quioco, Ganguela, and Portuguese. "Strong sounds."

Joaquim is not merely an inventor-philologist. For years he has been writing two books. The first resulted from agony: seeing the world ruined by conflict, "especially in the bosom of the family." Joaquim sought within himself a conciliatory doctrine that could resolve each conflict at its root. After three years, this catechism of understanding came forth under the name *The Vague Term*. This first work, he explains, will also be the last, because *The Vague Term* will comprise at least five hundred pages, including verse, prophecy, advice, and a philosophical history of the origin of the present existence of life and of its future.

One of the prophecies opens *The Vague Term*: "Whoever or whatever possesses in its physical-biological makeup a structure similar or equivalent to mine will thereby be my like." Joaquim refers to stones, trees, sand, cars, the sky. "From the most distant star, as someone said, to the ground on which we walk, we are made of the same matter, we are alike, if not brothers." *The Vague Term* expounds this prophecy in a proverb: "Tread upon the ground not as the ground but as a brother."

At the beginning of each chapter, each poem, there is a theory; after comes a philosophy, accompanied by a prophecy that indicates what will happen if a concrete problem is not resolved. Such a book gravitates toward poetry. From the beginning:

If someone from euphoria
From spite or cowardice,
From excess of euphoria
Or from mere sympathy
Rejects the prophecy
Despite modesty,
It will be pure hypocrisy
Which I would bear
And never decline.

Joaquim accepts whatever is said about *The Vague Term.* "But my book will live, because it has strength." Like the sounds of the African languages that he doesn't speak and that make him a foreigner on that road where we find ourselves.

In his file, in his head—in our unplanned conversation—*The Vague Term* is "a kind of Bible, not one to replace the other Bible but to show the truth." The other one isn't false, in the opinion of Joaquim, who came within a hair of being a sacristan, which was his dream, or a priest, which was his mother's dream. "But there's a lot of fantasy." Joaquim, like the silhouette of the globe, is the sum of hyperbolas, and it is always about the world that he speaks. "The world was not made the way they think it was made in the Bible or the way science explains it, but in another way, which I put in my book."

The creation of the world occurs "in the second chapters." Joaquim wrote this part while inspired, in moments when he was alone at home because of romantic disillusionment or an emotional problem and went into a trance. In the trance, he picked up a notebook and began writing. He doesn't believe in the original void, the total darkness at the beginning. Or in the spirit of God moving over the waters. By the same token, he denies that man came from the water. He believes in a different birth of life, in which spirit and mat-

48

ter cohabited but in which there was solitude and the absence of everything. "In other words, the world would not progress if it were not homogeneous, if there weren't certain factors that I can't explain now but that I explain in my book."

He speaks of "multicombination and division of the molecules of life," which must be the factors. It's difficult for him to explain now, here, because there is no trance in which he can write. There is only cold and the wait for the fourteenth truck in the column, which ran out of fuel somewhere on the road without anyone's noticing it, because the fourteenth was the last truck and no road in the plateau lets you look behind.

But everything is in the book. When Joaquim writes, he doesn't believe it is he himself writing but something within him. It was the trance that wrote the amended Bible. The same creative process — a fever was the pseudonym — produced the other work of his, *The Enclave of Sovereignty*. *The Enclave* is "an easier thing," which took place when he was in the throes of cerebral malaria.

Joaquim has traveled far, to other dimensions. As if the world divided itself and unwittingly, at some moment, some mechanism of universal equilibrium was activated and he, nearby, in the orbit of that chance event, was dragged to the other side.

That side was an emptiness. Joaquim moved about in absolute darkness, following the light that was his only hope, until he began to sense a strange presence, something that followed him and kept watch over his steps. He finally came to a world of crystal inhabited by beings that emanated light. Wise beings who divined his deepest doubts — the causes of evil and injustice, the suffering of humanity, the unimportance of life — and took him to a tribunal, in a large council room.

"We know that you have many concerns and that you wish to resolve many problems of your world. Listen: You must not be selfish and think of what you need. Listen for the questions you should ask to help your people and your world."

Joaquim felt fear. Fear of asking the wrong question. He was about to ask the reason for so much suffering when he fell into a deep sleep.

He saw his birth and the day he was born, saw himself walking in the first neighborhood where he lived and, later, playing with the children who were still children after he had grown up. He awoke suddenly and asked the question that came to him:

"What is the origin of things?"

Note: It was not he who asked but a voice emanating from the place where he stood, a voice from the past, inside the dream. It was the only question that demanded to be asked.

"What is the origin of things?"

The crystal beings answered this and other questions. Before each question, Joaquim went into a trance and reviewed his path. In the end, he discovered that he had died after all and that he was merely reliving his journey on earth, beginning with the place from which he had come. This was what he should have realized from the first moment, when the crystalline beings greeted him.

"Welcome to Essence, may you be welcome, Similar."

The perception of his own death filled him with panic, and he tried to flee. He ran blindly without succeeding in going anywhere. He returned, weary, to his room in the world of crystal. He plunged into sleep once again. The next day, when he awoke, he discovered that he had turned into crystal. The room had also changed along with him: when he had arrived at the Enclave, he was given the only room with wood and marble, with chairs and a bed, but now it too was completely crystal, like the others. These are the last pages of *The Enclave of Sovereignty*. Joaquim joins a group of friends and tells them he had a nightmare: he lived on a planet called Earth, had a strange color, dark and opaque, and was submitted to a trial. They all laughed, "because everyone goes through that." He was the similar. The earth was only a passage to death, an evolutionary experience for the species.

The Enclave of Sovereignty is finished "theoretically." Joaquim plans to rework a few scenes until the volume gains consistency and reaches at least 250, 300 pages. "All that's left is to adorn the book, increase the chapters, and change the situations in keeping with the criticisms I've been receiving."

Joaquim, mute inventor and unpublished author, doesn't know which work will be the first to make it to the public. It may be *The Enclave* or *The Drunken Playwright*, a completely different narrative that, according to him, is the story of his life. It begins with Joaquim living in the home of a friend where he has strict orders about the time to be back. One night, he returns late, and his friend's parents refuse to open the door. He has to sleep outside, in the rain and cold. At daybreak, he arises and decides that from now on he will pay for his own glasses of beer. The "drunken playwright" makes his living by telling stories to others, selling plots for beer. "It's nice," but it can't compare to *The Vague Term*, Joaquim's most serious book, which he will not publish until he considers it perfect. And perfection, in things psychedelic, is just a matter of time, even if it is a long time. "A Bible capable of challenging the other one, by creating small disagreements, but able to set things right."

Joaquim's mother wanted her son to be a priest. He would have acquiesced if she hadn't gone through a prolonged state of mental disturbance. Joaquim continues to study the Bible, because he believes that God is love. "There is no god that does miracles, there is no god beyond the stars. God is us when we're honorable." Joaquim is a "nontheist." His parents were Catholic. His mother was very affected by the death of her first child. "She was quite intelligent, despite being illiterate," and one day she told him he would have no moral position to humiliate, deprecate, or offend others if he himself was not predisposed toward being humiliated, deprecated, or offended. She died four years ago, and her passing caused a great change in Joaquim, "that double personality of a suffering figure who when moved emotionally is another person."

He abandoned Quinese around this period, in 1993, leaving it in Luanda when he began changing cities frequently. "I hope to resume it someday." It's only a beginning, "someone could do it better," but a beginning is not nothing; even Creation had one.

UNITA's billeting sites are in remote locations, in open spaces where a government air attack would easily destroy the camped guerrillas, as the movement has several times acknowledged. The site at

Chitembo was installed in the farthest corner of Bié. When we arrived with the column of the International Organization for Migration, late at night, the logistical area had too few tents for too many functionaries. I shared a tent with Joaquim and an IOM staff local, included in the team that is going to demobilize the three thousand soldiers quartered in Chitembo. "Souls and spirits write." Joaquimese, the anti-Babel, fell asleep reading the Bible.

Recapitulating: in the beginning was not the Word but the crystalline solitude. The Word remains for the last poem.

"It's my dream to create harmony. Harmony hasn't existed since man became man, because there is no single language. Many have done things they would never see come to pass. Like the man who said that one day man would fly like a bird, and today the airplane exists. He dreamed, and they said, 'Insane!'"

"Aristoter."

We cross the river again in the jeep. Fording. This time it's more risky. It's at night, perhaps midnight. Of Abel's two aides we see only the flickering of the flashlights with which they alert us to the deeper parts of the river. Of the water, we perceive only the noise of the rapids. On the other bank we can make out only the silhouette of the treetops against the oil-black sky.

We're going to make it, it's there. It's been hours that it's there. We should have gotten there days ago. There's nothing there. Just where is there? We don't even know where here is.

Advances of minutes and mechanical breakdowns for hours. Delays in which one could fit the Creation of the World and the seventh-day rest. The filter. The radiator. "The box." The water. The drive. The wheels. The punctures. The fan. The oil. The leaks. The devil putting sand and rust into every part of the vehicle. Push. Pull. Wait. Despair. Think: despair is the most futile of reflexes on roads where there is no turning back.

Mines ahead, behind, to the left, to the right. Mines inside us. Mines in our sleepy, exhausted eyes, trembling and worried, trying to stay awake. Seeking out objects of death whose characteristic is that of never being seen—they wait their entire life and are born for only a second to die with you.

Move by day. Move by night. Eat cornmeal or eat nothing. Save the last can. Boil tea gathered from bushes. Cook in black pots in the earth plowed by tires. Eat the last can. Eat with your hands from flaking enamel plates. Fantasize about fresh water. Salivate salt. Shiver from the cold an hour after the moon rises. Suffocate from the heat an hour after the sun rises.

Dream about a bed.

Wake up with rats.

Go to sleep with fear.

Disdain tears.

Avoid dogs.

Defecate in front of others. Bathe in the river, swim during the crocodiles' siesta, keep away from snakes, dry your body with your hands, extract the shudders from your bones, cover your skin with filthy clothes. Vomit your own smell. Sleep in the open air, sleep on the alert, in transit, in abandoned houses, on mattresses of straw and lice, on blankets with holes and mange. Listen to the wind beneath the divan. Listen to the sound of leaves laughing as they scrape the cement on the ground.

DANGER MINES. Do not touch anything, tread on existing tracks, walk backward retracing your steps, the same steps, exactly, or—

Yesterday we came across two huts. Until this moment, no one else has passed our immobility. Possible location: between the river and the place of the oxen. The place appears on no map. Nor do we. There was a mother and a child. The child had no face. As a baby, when both were sleeping by the fire one night—the only means of keeping wild animals away—the child rolled into the flames. The fire ate his features as violently as acid.

I think he was looking at me from behind a tree. I'm not sure if he was turned in my direction. Difficult: the child had no hair, only a featureless helmet. People, like animals, inspire panic in him. He ran from me.

The savanna fleeing around me.

We are going to get there. It's just ahead. It no longer matters when.

The river robbing me of the places under the soles of my feet. But it's just ahead.

The jungle is loose inside me.

Abel and two helpers. Me and Colonel Nunda, my shadow, and his own shadow, an aide-de-camp who travels ragged and barefoot. Lieutenant Colonel Fogacho, in the middle seat, with his Sharp recorder. Brigadier General Kalutotai's little shadow. A cargo of sacks of flour, and lying on them and on the cloth cover of the jeep, three more people, including a baby in arms. My crate of useless provisions: crackers, two jars of preserves, a Cape red, a small bag of salt.

We make our way through the river and the night. Two lights signal us from farther and farther away. Or else we're straying from the lights. The signals are unclear. Something in between loses focus. The water has gotten into our feet. The baby won't stop crying. I try to stay awake. My body yields. Any noise is simultaneously nuisance and prod. I try to keep on the surface, while the river and another litany drag me to inevitable drowning. We live by attempts. Nunda's adjutant tries in vain to pronounce the name he chose for his son.

"Aristoter... A-ris-to-ter!"

"Vorgan! The radio station of UNITA," says an echoing voice in the middle of an endless sampler of morning crowing and five melancholy notes played on an electronic organ. The tape may be the original, from 1976, because it has the ring of twenty years of age and wear. The crowing would be imperceptible if I didn't remember that on the cassette is the Black Cockerel.

Since Huambo I haven't been able to tune in the Voice of Resistance of the Black Cockerel: "Now that the terror MIGs no longer cross our skies..." It was, incidentally, a lie: the government's MIGs, for the first time since the signing of the Lusaka Protocol in November 1994, resumed taking off from their base in Lubango when I was there, two months earlier. Not to bomb Huambo this time but Brazzaville. The war again went into maneuvers, with an FAA offensive in

55

the Lundas against UNITA's diamond-mining areas, despite the fact that in Luanda the two parties continued making gestures of peace in the Joint Commission and despite the existence, since April, of a Government of National Unity and Reconciliation. Vorgan resumed its biting editorials read by a voice whose hatred makes the skin crawl.

UNITA is boxed in between the Democratic Republic of the Congo and yet another meeting of the Security Council (which will approve new sanctions against the movement). It is not an ideal time to be the sole foreign visitor in Jamba. For years, anyone who came to the bastion on foot was a guerrilla or a prisoner. They would always arrive together. What exactly is the reason for my being here? To visit Vorgan? Is this the road to Mozambique? A delegation headed by the governor of Jamba came, welcome to the bastion, with many men in dark glasses and carrying walkie-talkies speaking in code with their backs turned. I was taken to a room after all of them sat down and was subjected to a friendly but patient interrogation, until the delegation had satisfied itself. Later, one of them returned with a briefcase from which he took a sheet of paper for me to fill out. "Personal information." One question sat especially badly with me: "What languages do you speak?" Spanish, yes, but not Cuban. The biggest gem came at the end: the date, such-and-such a day of such-and-such a month, signed in "the Free Lands of Angola."

I am assigned a roomy hut divided into four parts, a square and three parallel rectangles. Two rectangles, to the left and right, are the bedrooms, each with two beds. The middle rectangle is also divided: a vestibule with a chair and, in front, the frugal bathroom compartment. The hut rests on clay, over which slowly creep lizards and shadows as day wears on. I notice this because my days are slower than theirs. The interior doors are cloth, and the thatch is lined on the inside with black plastic. The outer door is wood and displays a sublime color, an Indian green that is not from there (colors have a geography, and this one belongs to the sea; could it have come in a caravan? in a Boer cart? or in a shipment of print fabrics?). Scattered in the sand are four more huts and a half-submerged jango. This is the District of Cooperation, or the International District.

I am alone or, when I'm not, watched at a distance from behind tree trunks with a single forehead eye. I observe the vow of silence but once could not contain myself and waved at the thin man who passed holding a radio. He ran. People are told to be fearful for reasons of security. I sit down again, still dominated by an extraordinary sight: a man with two solar batteries hanging from his neck, one against his chest, the other on his back, joined by a wire to the radio in his hand. A bit of science fiction. There is no electricity in Jamba, not even a generator. The future without fossil fuels will be a comical ecology, but the rich countries have yet to find that out.

I photograph the green door. But it is already late afternoon, and since this morning and since yesterday many hours of light have gone by untouched in photos that I could only think about. Anyone who photographs a door or anything else has dishonest intentions. It's best to leave the camera alone. There's an animal in the lavatory; the metal bowl I normally use for my ablutions gave it away.

I am penned up like some rare specimen in a zoo; the only freedom I have is to bare my teeth when curiosity brings the onlookers too close. I eagerly await people, but they almost never come, because the head zookeeper has afforded me the hospitality appropriate to dangerous animals. He prefers to take no chances, and I know that somewhere else they are pondering whether or not to let me leave, and if so, whether or not to accompany me. The decision may take several days.

They wake me with two buckets of water, one hot and one cold, left by a little man who comes and goes without his feet touching the floor (I don't have the door key). They feed me twice a day. In the morning, coffee and stale bread. At noon, rice with sugar, sometimes soup, and occasionally a small goat bone and a soft drink. On a day that was special without my realizing it, a bottle of red wine was opened for me. The meals take place in a large hall used for parties, at a U-shaped table at one end. The man serving effaces himself in the insecure formality of gestures (turning over the upside-down plate, nudging the soup dish so I can be one spoonful less hungry). There are no signs of anyone in the pantry. Where the food comes from and who prepares it is a mystery. Lepers must be very lonely people. Even I am no longer certain I don't bite.

I chew my condition of quarantine man in the empty dining area. I imagine the great days of extraordinary rallies and conferences. There are old portraits of Savimbi in his beret with the three stars of the FALA commander. "My fate, your fate, and the fate of the Angolan people are one and the same." In the more recent photographs, Savimbi invariably appears in elegant civilian clothing. "The death of a revolutionary is confirmed when he isolates himself from the masses." Other posters show the sunrise in red rays on a green background, the UNITA flag. There is as much dessert as there is appetizer.

For the rest, I rummage through my crate of provisions. There are no more preserves, and I've used up the last can of sausages. I don't drink the wine, because they say the plane could arrive tomorrow morning (it hasn't come for twenty-one days) with José Martins aboard; I'll drink it with him (I met him in Luanda, he gave me a piece of rubber hose to use as a tourniquet). I think rats have been in my crate. I'll give the small bag of salt to someone; here it's like so many ounces of gold as a seasoning, and in any case I lost my appetite many days ago. I have small bags of tea; water is heated for me. I practice Ganguelan drawings in the sandy floor, with sticks. All of Cuando Cubango is sand, more shifting than my shadow. I don't feel like reading. I listen to endless hours of shortwave, my ear glued to the radio, and come to believe that somewhere humanity is on the move. Fela Kuti died. In the garish colors of emotion, Lagos commemorated the passing of the funeral cortege.

Seen from outside, UNITA is one and indivisible. Examined from within, there are three: in Jamba, Bailundo, and Luanda. None of them forgives the other two: tell me where you're located, I'll tell you which Savimbi you are.

It all began with a cigarette. Fogacho lit one, but if he hadn't, the result would have been the same. He didn't ask permission. General consternation reigned in the vehicle.

"Bad manners, Fogacho! Very bad. You didn't ask permission."

"Not even when there was a woman on board!"

"A Luanda upbringing, that's why. Flea-market manners, that's what you have."

Fogacho replied with alcoholic impatience, tripping over his lucidity. Listen: in Luanda people aren't like that. It's a large place, and no one spies on his neighbor's veranda. In a boîte, women or not, cigarettes for all.

"Everybody smokes if they want to."

A charge from the rear: the four from the fifth column are unforgiving.

"Look at fancy hotels. A wallet doesn't mean good manners,

Fogacho, it's just a wallet. To find a stolen wallet, look in a cabinet member's pocket."

"It's the money they take from the people, those comrades. Cigarettes, girls, the government. I saw it, I know about it, I was there, and never again."

"Those mulattoes don't know what war is. But having fun, they've made a science out of that. They study it till late at night, those brothers, they go abroad to spend their fellowship money on fancy underwear for discotheques. Sunday, at the beach, that's where they know how to fight."

"And those naked girls! That's what's really immoral. An honest woman has no protection in a city like that."

Fogacho was condemned. As a FALA officer, he was integrated into the unified army under the Lusaka Protocol. He was one of the UNITA commissioned officers in the FAA: lieutenant colonel. He left the forest for the city a year ago. Now he was headed for Jamba, overland, to find his wife, his children, and two vehicles that were still there. But no one makes it to Jamba overland. Not even a local lieutenant colonel. Or rather, especially a lieutenant colonel who changed sides. Fogacho got stuck at the same stage as I did, Caiundo, and the stubbornness of a foreign journalist offered him on a silver platter the only chance for a ride.

"There's nothing but treachery in Luanda. Those dictators stroll in their governments, eating off our oil. They finance totalitarianism with oil. As long as they have oil, we won't get a whiff of pluralism. We should have taken the war to the drilling rigs. When the rigs blow up on them, that's when they'll understand."

"Our brothers Salupeto and Jeremias are still there. They weren't buried. That's what the government side does. They summon us and grab us. They're treacherous. The brothers are there, frozen somewhere. They never even returned them to us..."

"That's what's going to happen to you, Fogacho. If I were you, I wouldn't feel safe. I'm not trying to scare you, just a friendly warning."

Anything was a reason for throwing darts at Fogacho, sitting in the front seat of the pickup. In back, with me, were two young intellectuals of the party, Abreu Silipa and Richa, and the fiancée of somebody or other in Jamba. There was also another young man, discreet, brusque. Prejudice is insurmountable: in Luanda, enemies are everywhere, ours and theirs. Including those of our own who were put there by our leaders.

"I'm there, we're there, working, chosen by Bailundo. It was the directorate that did the choosing and assigned me. Are you listening? It wasn't by accident. It was the president's office! My papers are in order. The cars in Jamba, everything."

The guffaws had been going on for hours. Into the early morning, Fogacho had been babbling, disconnected words, childish sounds, nodding off to the laughter from the rear seat. The beers at dinner began to take their toll, making Fogacho the laughingstock. Even without the beer the lieutenant colonel reeked of comedy.

The pickup encountered only one command post, where a UNITA soldier confirmed that the fiancé's car had been by two days earlier, in the opposite direction. Fogacho awoke with a start and began prattling about that post, which he had confused with a different one hundreds of kilometers away. I told him to quiet down. Laughter from behind.

"What's so funny? What?"

"Nothing, lieutenant colonel. Mr. Pedro is a good friend of yours..."

"What work gets done there in the FAA? Have you brought back our brothers Salupeto and Jeremias? What freezer did they stick them in? They say they're in a chamber at the Elf. That's what you ought to investigate while you're at it..."

"Let's go! But our job is the FAA. It's the deputies who make politics. We're forbidden. A prison offense! The deputies who get thirty-thousand dollars a month, they're the ones doing the talking, in the Assembly. In the democracy."

"What the government wants is to pour alcohol into you till you're harmless. Drown you in an ocean of beer..."

"That's not so! I don't drink. We don't drink! I scored seventeen on the test at officers' school. It's advanced studies."

"And are you satisfied, Fogacho, with seventeen? I wouldn't be satisfied with less than twenty!"

"Look at Ben-Ben's grade, the poor guy. They gave him whiskey so he wouldn't see the preparations for war, and now he's there and part of UNITA, but he's finished. They're going to kill him, the Old Man already said so. That's the way they do politics, the murderers. José Eduardo ought to be condemned like the Nazis."

"What's going on? Is this a car or a cell meeting? I'm with a bunch of intellectuals! Not all of Luanda is like that. You don't know what you're talking about. We're meeting the conditions set up to implement the protocol. Peace will come, and I'll be in the middle of it and you'll be proud of me."

Fogacho finally gave up. Four sober men against a hangover, no contest. During the night, the twelve hours of travel were punctuated by frequent stops along the trail. The pickup blew two tires. Time is needed when the path crosses mines. You look for wood in the sand, on tiptoe—as if a mine explodes only from the weight of an entire foot—to illuminate the tire and unstiffen the hands (the temperature has dropped to freezing).

Fogacho was a foreigner. Inside Angola itself, from Bailundo to Luanda, he had changed countries for good. In UNITA, which has always fanaticized purity, there is no such thing as dual citizenship. Fogacho went and would not return. Besides that, the city is a seduction in itself, after twenty years in the bush. Fogacho had changed without knowing it. In Mucusso he became irritated at the cassettes they gave him to listen to.

"Hey, isn't there any of that music from Luanda?"

"You don't like Sah'lomon?"

He complained even louder when he had to borrow dollars— from me, because his comrades in arms wouldn't extend credit to him—upon realizing that he had only kwanzas in his executive briefcase. Millions of useless kwanzas. None of these lapses escaped the pathological radar of the little brothers.

"The lieutenant colonel didn't come prepared...He brought money that's no good in the interior of our country."

Sobering up from the cold, the lieutenant colonel asked for a truce with the four young cadres, refraining from another cigarette.

"I won't smoke. The smoke bothers you, so I won't. No need to gripe. Enough! Fogacho doesn't smoke."

One last jab in the discomfort of the journey:

"Now we're on the way to our Jamba. The Jamba of elephants. The Jamba that you helped build..."

"It's just for two days. Then I go back. I don't want to stay longer. Not in Jamba."

"I think that's a good idea."

It was the woman who ended the skirmish. The cassette player was repeating, I believe for the thirty-fourth time, a Lucky Dube full of political anthems. I bought it in Mucusso from a guerrilla who makes a few dollars trafficking music across the Cubango River.

Your mother didn't tell you the truth
'Cos my father didn't tell me the truth...

In the plastic bag, which has the abandoned look of the man who is holding it, is a small notebook:

Name: Benson Naluli
Category: Songbook
Class: *Buk Yalipina*

Benson is the "homeless bluesman" of Mongu, and his compositions show more talent than much of the music heard on Zambian national radio. He lives off what people pay him to sing. He's the city's walking jukebox, and he is blind. The notebook, very well organized, is written for him by others. The pages are divided by vertical lines drawn with a ruler. In the left-hand column is "No. of the Song," then, in a wider column, "Name of the Song," and to the right, "Price of the Song." The customer selects, listens, and pays. There are dozens of songs, in English and Lhosi, almost all of his authorship. The prices vary greatly: from fifty to five hundred kwachas. Number 1, in English, "I'm Nothing to the World," is Benson's classic and his statement to the world.

I'm nothing to the world when I die
And all my bones will get it right

I can't remember the day to die
I'm sure the grave
Is in my room to stay
I will never say good-bye to the world
I can't remember the day to die
I'm sure the grave
Is in my room to stay

Five hundred kwachas.

Benson doesn't know when he will die; he knows only that the day it happens, "I'll be forgotten, my name will be forgotten, and all my songs will be forgotten."

A man withered by age, the singer carries a guitar with strings made from electric wire. They are tightened with a ballpoint pen. The sound box has a hole in the bottom, which hurts the resonance. Benson solves the problem with chewing gum: there's a huge wad of it, chewed and dried, sealing the opening, a patch that the musician adds to whenever he can, because the gum, when it dries, has a tendency to flake and drop off. Benson once owned a guitar given him by then-president Kenneth Kaunda, but it was stolen. The hole in his present instrument was made nearby, at the bus stop: a driver backed up without looking and ran over the blind man, who had to spend some time in the hospital.

Benson doesn't have a song about blindness. The closest one recounts the misfortune of a blind man married to a sighted woman: she betrays him with the friends that come to the house, and when the blind man asks what's that noise they're making, the wife replies that it's a passing dog or someone asking for a light.

Five hundred kwachas.

He wasn't born blind. He lost his sight at the age of four after a long illness, but his parents were very protective. When he grew up, Benson composed a tortuous country-style song to thank them.

That one is only two hundred fifty.

He was too young when he went blind to have any memory of light. Of the sun he knows only what he's been told. The rest he sees through his skin: the sun is a heat, the night a range of shivers, people voices.

"Today the sky is clear, and afternoon's on its way."

Love for Benson is great sadness.

Should I follow you Jenny
Where you go, my sweetin' love?
For I know that you are mine
When I remember you darling
When you come into my dream
For I know that you come back to me

Jenny, I love you
That I never forget you
When I remember you darling
When you come into my dream
For I know that you come back to me
Jenny, I love you

This one is marked at two hundred fifty.

The Mbunda people of western Zambia consider themselves part of the majority group on the other side of the border, but it's more complicated than that. One of Benson's favorite songs, the one he sings if we ask him to make the selection, is about the authorities' attempts to expel Zambians "of Angolan origin" or, more recently, refugees, of whom there are hundreds of thousands in the country. It's in Lhosi.

Yesterday I received a letter from the Government of Zambia
    saying that everyone who doesn't have a national identity
    card will be deported.
Don't chase us like dogs!
Now they have to tell the Mbunda people who don't have
    national identity cards that they're going to be deported.
Later they'll sleep at the airport and tomorrow be taken back to
    their country, Angola.
Don't chase us like dogs!

They are worried about their cattle.
They are worried about their crops too.
Cassava trees in the forest, finjer mealege too.
In the plane, they carry corn, sorghum, and rice.
They tell them that everything they take with them will be sold
    and the money will go to the Government of Zambia.
Today we'll escort you, accompany you.
Don't chase us like dogs!

Five hundred. More, if you want to give it, for the translation.
A total of two thousand kwachas. The discount is no charge for recording it.

Do the blind see anything?

"A woman's face, smooth to the touch."

"The damp smell of rain, learned by ear."

"I remember a blue car, it wasn't mine. A bicycle that was, a house."

"The road home."

"I had a plastic radio and a red comb."

"The bush calm, and suddenly fire lifting me off my feet. The flames from the bomb racing over me, yes."

"I'm really in a dark life. Forgive me, but...nothing."

"Peace is our reward."

Forgiveness, the reward of the leader who ordered them to fight.

"I stopped seeing when I lost my eyes. Now I follow his voice. I can't make a sentence out of his face, but I can make a word: strong, tall. Isn't that right?"

They fought for their land, hard and a long time, until they made of it a land of guerrillas and no other crop. Then they began to be born from it, men with aerial roots, roots in the ground, in the trunk bone, in the nerve sap. Roots instead of legs, fertile in the ground that mutilated them.

They appear, tall, with no thickness, from the fog of the plateau, from the depths of the cool perfume of eucalyptus. It is in the morning that they emerge. They come, testifying to nightmare and miracle, hugging the silhouettes of the trees, merging with them, walking on their roots, bones, trunks, stilts, crutches: a new species, half man and half plant, half living and half pretense. They are now the vegetables of the land that this land has become.

It is morning, and they move toward me. The smell of leaves stings the nose: I take advantage of it, I weep, dissimulate, succumb. The first fleshwood tree has reached the place where I stand, and it paralyzes me. I grasp the living treasure that he has left: his hands.

"The world goes on, even if it is in a different way."

In Bonga there are over a thousand of these men returned to the land, all of them mutilated in UNITA's war—more today, because others have also come, from Knimbili and Montalegre. They will be photographed in order to be demobilized, which for most of them means little.

"When I realized I'd gone blind, I thought: It's all over. But I was a Christian before this, and that's how I knew a man can't do away with himself just because he wants to."

Bonga, where the forest of trees and men occupied with destructive virility the half-dozen ruins of war, is out of harmony with the beauty products that also came from here. The colonial village that once was Bonga grew up around a brilliantine factory based on eucalyptus oil. What's left are bonfires, rags, and a fine rain, ingredients that, however combined, hold no interest for industry. In the ruins of houses and bodies, Bonga turned to the forest and to the amputees. Only trees inhabit trees. Brilliantine is a style that will not come back.

There is a carpenter who makes the artificial limbs. He practices horticulture on the tragedy of others: he grafts where war pruned. His raw material: a water pipe made of galvanized plastic, a strip of rubber from a tire.

"The pipe is cut and heated in the fire and adjusts to the measurements of the amputee. The cavity is then cut and affixed to the kneecap, the tibia, or the fibula. A piece of wood is molded, and onto it is attached a rubber foot."

In the only house with a roof, to the rhythm of a pestle, laughter, and the crackling of coals, a thousand men come to pose before the camera, seated with a sheet as background: without legs or without arms, without eyes, without eyebrows, without teeth, without ears or skin, one with no nose, another with no face at all. The survivor without a face is a horrible facade scraped clean as if by a blade. I pray he will not speak, because his voice must be like an apparition. The photograph will not be a portrait; that is beyond the reach of chemistry: it will be a contour.

Now a man sits down who has no sense of smell.

"After the accident I underwent treatment that didn't restore my sight but saved my life. I learned to perfect the other senses. But not smell — I can distinguish only onion and eucalyptus."

A veteran with both legs amputated stands atop the roots that fill his pants. One of the legs is a piece of rubber, the name Michelin still visible in relief. He shows me his prosthesis proudly, because I didn't believe he had any: I saw him arrive on a bicycle.

Another amputee is now pedaling that bicycle in circles around me, and his "legs" form an organic whole with the vehicle.

The lids of the old factory's boilers, mounted on the wall, serve as blackboards for teaching letters and numbers. The students are scattered about on planks and hubcaps.

Men remove their limbs and enjoy, they tell me, the gentle breeze on their stumps. They prop them somewhere and wait patiently for the itching to go away. Others, the majority, with neither crutches nor prostheses, drag themselves through the mud begging for attention and food. Some become visible only when they speak or moan, camouflaged amid the filth.

"A man without sight is like a baby, because he lives in a state of thinking, not doing. He becomes something that requires two people. Sometimes you achieve a little happiness, but someone has to give it to you. That's the responsibility of the government."

70

The women sift the manioc for the weekend.

A young female amputee runs toward the factory, quickly because of the cold, with a screaming newborn baby on her back.

I want to leave. The perfume of the trees has become impregnated with poison.

The courage in Bonga is devastating.

The sounds are variations of perfume. In the stronghold of Caiundo I sweep the shortwave in search of landscapes of rescue. The deserts, the cleanest part of us, await me there, at any moment, in the voice of the muezzin who sings to them, perched in a minaret. If I fall asleep to that sound, the dunes will shift within their own undulations. In Kerala, India, an ancient martial art demands of warriors the prodigious elasticity of snakes: turning halfway around in a hole the exact diameter of their body. When I awake from the desert, I'll see the difference in the sand, which has the smell of the wind. The afternoon prayer will be the morning prayer. Warm light will dawn in cold light. The center of the sand has moved, but in these conditions the idea of movement is reassuring.

Hugo interrupted the hypnotic hum of my nap. The jango heard our conversation: photography and psychology, attention and focus, vision and seeing, the sounds I record on the trip, the radio as the sole link to life. Hugo got up and brought from his tent the most unexpected of objects: a photo album.

A breeze flooded the heat of the shade. Intricate photographs: handwriting, details, filigrees, strong textures and vibrant colors. Sundrenched and therefore reserved. Lines and flowers, corrugations and pavements, rust and lichens, grillwork and scrapings—the effects of time on aging surfaces. The proximity of this grainy, almost microscopic world gives life to subterranean species, to humus, bacteria, chlorophyll, corrosion, sediment, mold.

I remember one photo, especially beautiful among the others, of a green leaf captured in extreme close-up, resulting in a striated surface, hypersensitive, with very fine filaments inside the green—like transparent eyelids over blood vessels.

Absolutely elegant and out of context, the photos of the Salvadoran Hugo Santa-María, in Caiundo.

Matos's Unimog is the only possession of this Luso-Angolan mechanic with Jimi Hendrix hair and soot-washed skin, who has lived in UNITA-controlled Cuando Cubango since 1975. The province is his house arrest.

"I've really had to hustle. Otherwise I'd be dead now...Two movements in one place doesn't work. Me for one liberation, her for another. But socialism is communism. We separated. I had to stay behind...Tell them at the hotel in Ericeira, my parents, that I'm alive."

The vehicle, housed in Cuangar, would fit nicely in a *Mad Max* film. A leftover from the war, completely stripped: there is nothing in the cab (no floor, firewall, dashboard), and it has no radiator grill. The road can be seen in all directions: through the windshield, behind the nonexistent dashboard, or beyond the engine (squarely in the middle) in the midst of a tangle of levers controlling speed and drive. The right-hand door doesn't shut, so I can't lean against it; it's tied with cord to the iron bar holding the yellow tarpaulin that serves as a roof. The cab is open in the rear, no glass. The engine, which no longer has any housing, gives off unbearable heat. Only at night, at reduced speed, does it feel good on the body. The space for my feet is occupied by a battery from which extend two cables, attached to the terminals with a simple twist of bare copper wire. The Unimog is without shock absorbers, so at every bump the wires come loose and spit tiny sparks at the chassis.

The vehicle won't start without a push, and when Matos needs to stop, he takes a piece of wood that he keeps by the left-hand door and sticks it into the motor's heart, in the middle of the cab, to arrest the drive shaft in its rotation. There are two headlights: the left one doesn't work, and the right one has a tremendous shake and an enormous glaring eye in the middle. With no switch and no instrument panel except for an odometer, which doesn't work, Matos turns on the headlights from outside, standing in front of the Unimog—a lengthy operation, because he must join by trial and error a mass of wires coming out of the motor until he discovers which is connected to the alternator. The alternator is fed by the battery at my feet, which spills acid that eats at the soles of my shoes. The operation must be repeated countless times, because the wires keep coming off the headlights.

Ten minutes from Calai, late at night, the Unimog stopped running. Suddenly, as if it had a stroke. Matos made the diagnosis.

"Lack of air. Dirt in the filter."

We tried pushing. It barely budged. The sand descended to the river, some paces below, but in the dark it was dangerous to point the Unimog toward the water. On the other side was an open sky of electric lights: Rundu, almost in shouting distance. On the Angolan side, only the barking of dogs testified to our existence. An assistant of Matos went to look for help. He soon returned.

"There's only two huts. At the first they told me if I came any closer, they'd set the dogs on me. At the other, the man was going to come, but his wife wouldn't let him, afraid it was some kind of trick to rob him."

We spent the night in the Unimog, in the open, in bone-chilling cold, under a firmament I already knew by heart. The little I slept was thanks to Colonel Nunda, who shared his blanket with me.

When I woke, the Unimog was moving. I raised my head to see what was happening. It was the river: right in front of me, in all its width, rushing toward my blinking eyes, and Matos was at the steering wheel, bellowing. Where was everybody? I looked behind in panic: the Unimog was being pushed down the sandy slope. If the motor caught, Matos would turn sharply to one side. If not, we would plunge headfirst into the water.

Chairs were brought into the empty room. There were two Black Cockerel posters on the wall and two stickers of Jonas Savimbi. Colonel Nunda, swallowed by the collar of his imitation-lambskin coat, shyly opened his woman's handbag, in white imitation leather, which closed with a clasp of two chrome balls. From it he took a shortwave radio and a broken antenna, which he laid aside, ceremoniously, plus a small wad of papers, which he handed to the administrator. Then he began, offering a greeting that had already been delivered when we arrived.

"We're healthy."

"We're healthy, in general, more or less."

"Yes, yes," parroted the hosts with inattentive eagerness. The colonel, without looking at them, went on:

"Thank you. We, Colonel Nunda, of the Caiundo billeting area, battle of Mavinga, Eastern Front and operations in Moxico, with Major Resistência and Brigadier Olavo, are here on the mission that brought us to Calai, which is to escort the journalist gentleman who is on a journey of exploration to Mozambique, and his wish is to go to Jamba. Following higher orders of Brigadier General Kalutotai, commander of the Caiundo region, and Colonel José Maria, commander of the billeting area, we succeeded in arriving at this position after much difficulty. The aide-de-camp who is with us is one of us and also Lieutenant Colonel Fogacho, whom you already know. He is in Luanda in the Angolan Armed Forces, designated by the directorate with all papers in order and a document from the Old Man on his person and is en route to Jamba to take his wife and children from there to Bailundo..."

"Thank you very much."

"That's how it is."

"We departed with authorization from the directorate, the joint commissions, and the Bastion, for our destination. Transport was difficult, with such great shortage of vehicles that the only one had to be brought from Caiundo itself—Abel's—and left us in Cuangar for reasons of numerous mechanical problems, with the matter unconcluded. We presented the delegation to the administrator of Cuangar, who made arrangements for rest and something to eat, within possibilities. Through our efforts, as a consideration of the authorizations of the directorate that were confirmed to the journalist gentleman and the interests of the movement in the transit of a visitor in these territories, the administrator of Cuangar deemed it advantageous to accept the counsel of Mr. Matos, present here, and use of the Unimog for this mission, for lack of other means. And now we are here to ensure the continuation of the journalist gentleman on his way to the Bastion, where he has been invited and allowed, without further problems. The plan was to arrive at the Bastion on the birth date of the Old Man, but Abel made it infeasible, and upon our return I shall file a report, because that individual, if we let him participate in the process, must serve the interests of the movement. And we wonder if you could prepare a light breakfast for the delegation, as we have not eaten since Cuangar. I express my gratitude in advance."

"Thank you very much."

I spoke next, with the humility of the afflicted. I explained the journey in its conception, its origin and destination, the deadline and the delay, cited credentials not on paper, invoked unproved contracts, sought instructions from Bailundo, Luanda, and Jamba, which had yet to arrive. At the end of my uncertain speech, I thanked them for the warmth of the arrival and requested a quick departure.

"We've lost a lot of time (in Caiundo alone I waited nine days). My desire is to go immediately to Jamba, where I should have been yesterday, by August 3. I've already missed the celebrations. I wouldn't like to stay here another hour."

Stupid. Haste is fatal in places where saying nothing is already saying the wrong thing.

The administrator finally spoke, with petty satisfaction. He wore a sour smile and projected protocol. His square jawbones hung from his high cheeks, carved from wood. His deep-set eyes shone brightly — two sparks of meanness, the sole illumination in that tall, thin body, mature but not aged, topped by white fuzz combed back.

"I welcome you to Calai, where no one comes. It is gratifying for us to have a Portuguese journalist. If you were American, South African, English, or French, how could you understand us? We wouldn't speak the same language, the one that unites us. You're white, I'm black. Skin color isn't important."

Certainly not, except for the type of people who notice that skin has color, mine being the wrong color. And he, despite his ideological zeal, wasn't black.

"We weren't informed of your coming. That's strange. We're going to contact the Bastion. But make yourself at home. There won't be any problem. Do you need anything?"

We hadn't eaten for two days.

"To wash my face."

The administrator's wife brought some water and a clean towel from behind a cloth door. When I returned the basin, I saw that the "living room" where we stood was the only one reasonably intact. The rest of the house, in the penumbra cut by bullets of liquid sunlight (as in foundries), was patched with bricks and blackened by smoke from the fireplace. There was no chimney or window, and the furniture was all chairs, pots, mats, and blankets.

The administrator, speaking Umbundu in a low voice, summoned the UNITA "delegation" to talk outside. Shortly afterward, the youngest member of the welcoming committee arrived. Before Roberto spoke, I knew what was coming. He sat down and opened the usual small notebook. It wasn't yet nine o'clock, and the day had already turned hopelessly sour.

"I'm the municipal secretary of public relations."

"For Calai or for UNITA?"

A bad beginning.

"Calai is part of UNITA. We need a few clarifications about your presence. Merely for information."

"Go ahead and ask. I have nothing to hide."

"The problem is basically a political one...You say you're on a journey, but there are various kinds of journeys, as you know. Is it to gather information?"

"No. It's to meet people."

"But you're a journalist. People give information. A journalist investigates. You're on an investigation."

"No, I'm on a trip. That's different. Working on my own. People tell stories. I've already said I'm not here for my newspaper. I'm not even interested in the peace process."

"But later you're going to write about this and make good money; it's always like that with foreigners."

"I'm not going to, and that's not why I'm writing the book. I'm actually *spending* good money. The fellowship is for that. If I wanted to make good money, I wouldn't be in Cuando Cubango. I'm not here to traffic in diamonds."

"Why do you mention diamonds? Have you bought any stones?"

"Of course not!"

"You're the one who spoke of diamonds. I'm asking why."

"Because, because— Nothing, it was just to tell you I'm not here on business. I'm on my way to Jamba. I'm not asking for anything else. I just want to get to Zambia. *Hame dukombé dikassi logopita ondjira.* I ask for safe-conduct. Like in Europe in the Middle Ages, for heaven's sake! What do you think I am—a spy?"

"What's your interest in Vorgan?"

"I've been hearing of it for a long time. It's not just another radio station. Few people have visited it. I wanted to interview the director. But only if that's possible. If not, all I want is to continue to Zambia."

"Funny, it didn't occur to me you could be a spy. I'll make a note of it."

"I mentioned spying because you suggested it."

"I didn't suggest anything. You're the one getting irritated. You said you didn't want to be in Calai more than forty minutes, which I can't understand..."

"I didn't say that. You misunderstood...or I didn't explain myself

79

well. I'm far behind schedule on this trip. I never thought it would take this long to cross Angola."

"But if it's really for the book, it'll take however long it takes. When you're done, you'll return to Luanda, won't you?"

"I repeat: Luanda is behind me. It was only the start of the trip, because there are no flights between Lisbon and Lobito. From here I'm going to Mozambique and from there to Lisbon. Look, my daughter is being born in October. That's the urgency, okay? By my calculations I should already be in Zaire."

"And what's your interest there? Do you know someone in Kinshasa?"

"Again, I didn't explain myself well: I'm not going to Kinshasa, and I've never been there. I'm going to Lubumbashi and even then only if I have time. I think that part's already in jeopardy."

"Do you have friends there?"

"I don't have friends there, nor do I know anyone in Zaire. I'm going there because Capelo's route took him through Shaba."

"You're carrying cameras, naturally."

"Two still cameras. I'm not a photographer. I haven't taken a photo for two weeks. I haven't interviewed anyone for two weeks! I'm wasting time. I took a picture of Matos, but with Colonel Nunda's authorization. He can testify to that. I don't understand why you're putting me through this interrogation. You're being unpleasant, and I don't like it. If there's any suspicion, say so right now!"

"There's no suspicion. It's just a formality. You're talking too much."

"Because you're asking too much. I have everything in order. I spoke to the Joint Commission and know that Bailundo is also fully apprised. Nothing to hide. Everyone who had to know about my journey received everything in detail. Letters. Satellite communications. Jamba knows and authorized it. I have a fax from UNAVEM verifying that. And now Calai says it didn't receive the information. What is Calai? Does it have a radio? Inform yourselves! That's not how the delegation was received in Cuangar. Who are you? Do you think you're above the directorate? Where's the administrator?"

Roberto drew in his horns and left, furious. Later, the same man who had sent him appeared with a lame excuse, using the underhanded but childish tactic of neutralizing the victim in two steps: first attack in order to weaken him, then come to his rescue to gain his confidence.

"He's been reprimanded. I ask for your understanding; sometimes younger people go outside their area of competence. There won't be any more problems."

There were never going to be. But the nonexistence of problems was once again my being under a sort of irritating and officious arrest, without the power to circulate, speak, or take photographs. I didn't have my backpack with me and couldn't go to retrieve it. They had the entire day to search it (I don't think they did). I was observed sidelong when I sat outside the house to warm myself in the sun. But the panorama had become reduced to pigs and chickens walking through a manure pile, a half dozen huts, some masonry ruins, and, in the distance, on the other bank of the Cubango, Rundu, Namibia. Another country, another planet, a light-second away.

Angola has elaborated in perverse form the concept that information is power. What's seen can be told, what's said cannot be taken back. For a population at war, condemned to serving either of two Siamese totalitarianisms, information can come back as a weapon in the hands of the enemy. That is why, as various Angolans explained to me matter-of-factly, the culture of lies exists.

"Never say what you think. My parents taught me that. And I tell it to my children."

To lie is to survive. Civilians lie in self-defense. Military men lie as a tactic. Politicians lie from bad faith. Everyone lies as a method, in collective schizophrenia. A Nigerian official for UNAVEM confessed that he had been surprised:

"They lie more than we do. And consider that in Nigeria everyone deceives you. It's impossible to get away from it. They get you to trust a business in which you put all the money you have to invest, and then you find out you were duped and are left with nothing. I'm telling you. They make you believe they're big businessmen, millionaires. They install themselves in the best hotel in Lagos and take you to the most expensive places. If you're suspicious, they'll make you think they're with the government: they meet you at the airport, and when they arrive at the hotel with their future partner, in a limousine, there's a pack of reporters with cameras waiting to interview you. None of them is a reporter, but they act their parts, never letting you go, spending their last penny to catch you in the net, and in the end, suddenly, they take you for everything you have or ever will have, and you discover you don't even own the clothes on your back... But it's too late, and you go home barefoot."

In the Angolan emptiness, places are people, and people are what those in command make of them. Calai, as backward, isolated, and poor as Cuangar, proved to be much worse simply because of its administrator. One who arrives doesn't know when he'll leave, and even if UNITA's paranoid suspicion is overcome, time only serves to increase it. Sitting one whole day in the same spot, I was analyzed at a distance. The foreigner in the display case. But no one approached. Everyone knows the rule without its needing to be spoken: everything is forbidden that is not explicitly permitted. This is the inversion of the state of law, a point in which MPLA and UNITA were always in agreement. The sole approacher was the only free man in the village, a street crazy, who showed me a filthy handkerchief and offered to sell me diamonds. He was shooed away, for my protection.

At the administrator's orders, repairs were begun on the all-terrain parked beside the house, with two wheels on blocks. It was "the only available vehicle." Once again, I was invited to repay UNITA's kindness in dollars: it needed oil and fuel, which had to be bought clandestinely in Rundu. A mission for Nunda's aide-de-camp—a very young guerrilla with a more intelligent smile than his, muscles bulging under his ragged uniform, and feet jammed into the remains of sneakers. They ordered him across the river once again, stupidly risking his skin to buy tobacco and beer for the officers, who didn't raise a finger to share with him the little that they had.

The young guerrilla thought he was breaking the rules when, as secretly as possible, I gave him some Namibian money to spend on anything he wanted: beer, tobacco, food, or a gift for his girl in Calai. I surmise the donation was diverted by the others, because he bought nothing for himself. Nine years after the fall of the Soviet Union and eight years after the government abolished the socialist economy, UNITA continues to hold an odd view of private property. The individual is the party, and the party responds by taking care of the individual, a carryover of the bizarre fascist Maoism invented by Jonas Savimbi, who kept his revolutionary vanguard—the peasants—in medieval economic practices. In many UNITA zones currency is a recent introduction, and barter continues to be the rule among populations that never saw a banknote. Chickens are payment for a ride in a truck, T-shirts are exchanged for liters of honey, manioc buys a bar of soap. In the border zones like Cuando Cubango, currency is more widespread, but only American and Namibian dollars are accepted.

In Calai, I was in the company of two monuments to the Black Cockerel's conflicted relationship with money. The colonel who was sent on a mission that would take over a week, in the most arduous zone in Angola, but who set out without any money at all, dependent on the hospitality of others every step of the way. And the desperate lieutenant colonel, his pockets bulging with useless notes, asking me to lend him five dollars for tobacco; Luanda led him to forget that kwanzas have no value in the lands of the End of the World...

Fogacho has the easy impatience of one used to giving orders. Hunger rose to his mouth, and he left, protesting. Score a point for bad manners: they served us rice with sugar in midmorning, enhanced by my last can of sausages. A banquet at the edge of collapse.

I sent the administrator a message on a piece of paper to mark the occasion. The message would have to be transmitted by radio from Calai to Jamba, from Jamba to Bailundo, from Bailundo to Lisbon. It was short: "Dine well. For me."

If it was sent, it never arrived.

On August 4, 1997, when the temple guards were still sleeping off the birthday of the Old Man, UNITA provided me with an unforgettable birthday of my own. In a word, miserable.

Around 1900 hours, the Land Cruiser snorted through the nonexistent streets of Calai, past our applause, disappeared in the direction of the river, returned on the other side, attempted a few pirouettes. These were mechanical tests. The vehicle was judged to be in good condition, and we left. Nunda and Matos said good-bye, because the delegation had completed its mission. Ten minutes later, on the Dirico road, the Land Cruiser came to a halt in the sand with an ominous sound. I put my hand on my forehead and guessed what Moma was going to tell me: "The differential snapped."

We went back to Calai in low gear, taking an hour to cover half a dozen kilometers. Moma was sweating. In 1990 a PKM bullet lodged in his spine; he's been in physiotherapy ever since. He was born in Bela Vista, in Huambo, and joined UNITA at thirteen, when they killed his entire village, including seven members of his family. He hasn't been to Luanda since 1971 and doesn't miss it.

In the dark of night, it was necessary to arrange some transport to replace "the only available vehicle." Moma dropped me off at his own house.

"The television is black and white."

The tiny apparatus, a Giant, was linked to a car battery and tuned to the Namibian Broadcasting Corporation. I watched a debate about water. I had the urge to make tea from the herbs the administrator of Cuangar had gathered for me from his garden. It would be the only meal for more than a day. The lantern burned oil. There was a picture with three painted roses, very tall, covering the nail from which hung the curtain. "Two is for love, three is for divorce." A calendar of the Athens games and a camera on the same hook. And, of course, stickers of the party.

Happy birthday.

It is almost midnight, and I need to salvage the date. In the pack there's a cassette of Marilyn Monroe. I looked for "Happy Birthday

Mr. President." I found better: "My Man," by Billie Holiday. "In Dreams," by Roy Orbison, was next.

I opened the gift and savored it with the tea. It's good to laugh at ourselves when that's the only lucidity left.

Moma came in: we were going to travel in a Kamaz. All I had to do was put up the money for some more drums of diesel and a can of oil...

To get there you have to survive the hellish street of meat where every-one jostles and insults one another as they carry on their shoulders the heads and quarters of cattle — shreds of nightmare slinging blood and flies into other people's faces. Next, the stiff flour sacks on the ground (empty, with women squatting in front of them). It lies far beyond the floor fans with a pilot lamp halfway up their shafts. It is even beyond the kettles swimming with stewing tripe and the baskets of crispy lar-vae. At the end, after the screws and the oil lamps, after the man who makes one-piece sandals from tires "for export," there it is. At the high-est point of the market, after the watch repairman and the man who fixes hoes, is the apothecary's tent.

His wife is in. He has gone to assist in a noisy birthing.

Roots, seeds, fruit, nuts, tubers, a few skinned reptiles, ostrich-egg scrapings, feathers, bones, efficacious powders and excrements, ashes, colored flasks, and small sachets of fragrance.

"Do you feel well, or do you want to take something?"

You work up your courage and make your choice.

Sabongo fruit, two thousand a string, good for various stomach ailments.

Quibaba peel is an important antimalarial, equivalent to cinchona bark.

Abutua, a vine of the plateau: the liquid resulting from boiling its crushed roots, leaves, and small twigs, or a dilution made from the fruit, alleviates gonorrhea and various other sexually transmitted illnesses (and if they're chronic, so much the better); also invaluable for snakebite and as a sudorific for colds.

Humpata losna, a species of artemisia. An infusion of it is used in Huíla as a stomach remedy in the convalescence from malarial fever, and the powder in medication for parasitic worms, especially in children.

Múbafo bark for syphilitic ulcers and scurvy.

Dongos seeds from the Congo for the stomach (also substitutes for pepper in food when there is none).

For a styptic for bleeding in those who smoke liamba, and the world in general suffers from bleeding, encotahote stanches like no other powder. Resinous, with a strong odor, aromatic: obtained by macerating grasses common to the backlands of Huíla. In addition, it yields good results in hemorrhage of the uterus.

The small cachinde candange bush, in a cold or hot infusion, works against headaches, and, using the pleasant aroma of its resin, it takes the form of perfume-based treatment for rheumatism and mild paralysis. It can simply replace incense for odorizing a house, and for that reason the settlers called it wall rosemary.

Cahémbia-émhbia, a mallow for decoctions and emollient baths.

Gipepe seeds, with the same appearance as nutmeg, very common in any market, for various tonics, stimulants, and stomach medicines.

Boiled mucumbi bark against scurvy lesions in the mouth.

The powder of catete bulla, obtained from the tender stems and leaves of that herb, is guaranteed by sorcerers of the interior to work in cases of scurvy-related illnesses (of the mouth). Used whole or as a saturated infusion.

Pemba powder, the ingredient that most pharmacists mix for almost all Angolan charms. Diluted with caseque powder, it is applied in cases of nervous and rheumatic headaches. Pemba powder is also good for facial and body painting, and, for the better-off blacks and the whites in the deeper interior, it took the place of whitewash in earlier times.

Múbafo resin is applied as a plaster to heal wounds.

Mulemba bristles, the aerial roots of a species of fig tree, cure exanthematic fevers, diarrhea (when boiled); externally they are used for cleansing ulcerous wounds.

Mundondo root: this is a vine that, macerated, offers a mild purgative (effective) against coughs and other maladies of the chest. (Boil the leaves and season with oil or butter: it is now a substitute for spinach.) For chronic coughs, there is recourse to musoso bark.

Bark and fruit of mulôlo for astringent decoctions, in cases of intermittent fevers, exanthematic illnesses, and cleansing of ulcers.

Root and bark of molungo against secondary syphilis, used by boiling the root, with the same posology, therefore, as sarsaparilla.

And the great takula powder, the most used in Angolan medicines and in the confection of spells, mixed with various mineral and vegetable products (and for body adornment). Newborns are wrapped in this red "vernix," and it is a vanity of women to have their feet painted on feast days so they will appear to be wearing shoes.

Umpeque oil is for the girls to anoint their body and hair or season good food.

The cold is coming, for which there is no drug. At Chioco, the outdoor market in Lubango, I bought only a heavy overcoat, long and horrible, of faded nankeen with pieces of blood-stained tobacco in the pocket. It seemed to be the warmest thing in the secondhand clothes store, where the things that arrive in charity packages from rich countries are bought and sold. A Spanish beret was just as ugly and cheap.

I know they're near. I know by the swarm of beetles darkening the sky in the distance. The plague of locusts announces itself that way. A black cloud like a winged blanket dragging a hellish shrillness. They descended on us in our first years in Lubango. Every able-bodied person in the house rushed outside to fight them with fire. In open terrain we confronted the thousand wings of Satan. It was an unequal battle. There was no end to them. We lit fires and brandished torches, we exhausted ourselves beating on cans, shaking cloths, and yelling things they couldn't hear because the Devil created them with no hearing. In one day they devastated a crop that had taken months of work. The plants were lost, eaten by a deluge of insects. The noise stayed in our heads, a harvest of hunger, and a biblical terror.

My husband didn't live to see this horror. He died the year they decided on the colonization of Lubango. I went up to Chela on the first trip, with the one daughter I had left after burying her two older sisters. It wasn't like today, a train from city to city. They were caravans, days in oxcarts and camping inside palisades. My son-in-law was in the first group of settlers in Huíla, and I was in the first in Moçâmedes. I'm left over from the first ones to arrive from Pernambuco. We had a sugarcane plantation and a small mill. It was a Brazil for us: that first year was a fever of choosing land and building houses.

My name was inscribed in memory, but it faded with age. One day I woke up: it was gone. It makes no difference: I saw all those who I liked to hear use it disappear with age. The parents from Madeira, the daughters from Moçâmedes, the grandchildren from Lubango. It will be easier like that, they won't know what to call the one who will soon die, and the two-month-old great-great-grandchild won't remember that he saw my shadow. I planted an acacia, those strong trees, forty years ago. I haven't heard a word about it, but I think it's come to its end too; the ridges on its trunk have turned dull.

I planted it on my first anniversary of widowhood. I spent thirty-six years with him in Cavaleiros. It was the first wedding in the settlement, on All Saints' Day. The church of Saint Adrião didn't exist yet, though they had begun working on it. We took advantage of the visit of the corvette from the naval base, because the chaplain wanted to say the Mass on land. We made our vows inside the temporary walls of the fortress. My husband was all I had left of the sea while the priest spoke: there was a roof of canvas and sail, and that was the last time I crossed the ocean. I was only sixteen. I never went back to Manaus and was never able to show what it's like to be born on a river without a bank.

It's approaching. This time I'm not going outside. And it's coming with a sound without shrieks.*

---

*This short autobiography, transmitted orally by two octogenarians I interviewed in Lubango, is probably that of a woman who "was ninety-four years old at Christmas, 1927," mentioned in a copy of the weekly newspaper O Sul de Angola, commemorating the centennial of the founding of the Moçâmedes settlement. In fact, "the first to arrive from Pernambuco" were 170 settlers who traveled on the ship Tentativa Feliz, convoyed by the brig Douro, and landed on August 4, 1849. Analyzing the "Roll of Honor of the Founders" in that edition—which was part of a sparse collection belonging to the Namibe Provincial Cultural Delegation—there are three possibilities as to the woman's identity: Hortense Raquel da Silva (daughter of António Romando Franco and Joana Raquel da Silva, assuming that Hortense was not the sister of Raquel); Balbina Generosa da Conceição (the list includes the couple Augusto Lebreman and Helena Maria da Conceição); Maria or Francisca (the two daughters of José de Almeida Moniz and Joaquina Rosa de Jesus). The woman was a chicoronha—a corruption of senhor colono, the term that came to designate the descendants of people from Madeira. If the autobiography is correct, she arrived in Angola at the age of fifteen or sixteen.

Daniel Libermann's odyssey began the day the rustlers stole Mandela, Chocolate, and the others.

"There are black individuals about whom we can say, That man resembles John Kennedy. Animals are that way too, like people. Even in the corral each has its personality (I never had a Kennedy bull). All the animals are given names: Chocolate, Dayan, Capolo, Mandela. Also the names of countries and cities. I have Andorra, Jamaica, Argentina, like that. Or else traditional names, odd ones, like Chicangona, Sirimovenda. Dayan was baptized by Jerónimo — after the Israeli general."

Libermann's face shone slightly as he spoke of the cattle. Then it faded back into the half shadow of the bedroom. His eldest son lies dripping malaria on the couch; the convulsions rise through the blankets and emerge from his mouth as moans, like exhausted snakes. The air smells of fever, the walls are worn, and the lightbulb is pallid. Libermann has a weary way of speaking. He arrived a few days ago from "a sad story" and is remaking his world. In November 1992 and January 1993, rustlers carried off all the animals from his Fazenda Ali ("Rancho Cotchó River"), eighty kilometers south of Benguela. Besides him, the victimized herders were Francisco Muchila, Albano

Dias dos Santos, Horácio Pedrosa, Tchipindo Nambalo, Ndjamba Ieva, Catchiwe Tchiweka, Maubala Tchiweka, Kachilawa, Mupossela, Nbiavi Chongolola, Chiópio Okaohamba, and Kachiapi Limeke. The ranchers located the cattle, identified the rustlers, and tried to recover what was theirs with the help of the authorities. But the authorities didn't help, because they were the thieves. Libermann spent two years in the semidesert vastness of Namibe, pursuing the animals and fleeing the killers commanded by the Ministry of the Interior.

He arrived a few days ago. He's sitting in his house. That's bad. Libermann loves his herd the way others love people. He loves it as one loves a child. Or a woman. Love for him is a vast pasture. He smiles again as he recalls the makas he had with his wife because he couldn't go a single day without seeing the animals. On the weekend, his friends were going to Baía Azul, to the beach. Libermann took the same road but went in the water farther on, with the cattle of Fazenda Ali.

"I was one of the few people who liked selecting cattle. I never used cattle that didn't have an exotic origin. I used exotic breeds, the ones that put on the most weight the quickest, cattle in which the cow always has the possibility of nursing her calves, unlike the indigenous cows. I had good lines: Zebu-Brahman, which is an Arabic breed; the Arikander, introduced by South Africa, crossed with buffalo; the Mellor; and the Santa Gertrudis, from America, a cross between cow and bison."

The Fazenda Ali, in Calahande, has twenty-five thousand hectares and capacity for ten thousand head. Libermann could therefore house thousands of animals belonging to other ranchers or to businesses like África Têxtil. All told, the rustlers made off with some two thousand head.

It was immediately assumed that UNITA stole the cattle. But in September 1993 Libermann discovered that the thieves weren't guerrillas. Besides the bovine livestock, they had taken goats and horses. It was thanks to the horses that they found the trail, after being told that horses of theirs were in Dombe Grande, an area south of Benguela. There were only two cattle raisers in Dombe: he and Fernando Poentes da Silva. The cattle with Libermann's brand showed up in the hands of the chief of police, the head of a local tribe, and one of the merchants in the area.

An old herdsman later told him that there were more cattle farther south, in the province of Namibe. Libermann and the other cattle raisers spoke with the Benguelan vice governor for defense, who directed them to the municipal administrator of Baía Farta, from whom they were sent to the municipal adjutant for defense. The cattle were quickly located.

"We brought them all, two thousand head, except for the ones that had already been sold by the local chieftains."

What Libermann couldn't have guessed was that one of the government men had been involved in the robbery. The provincial director of the Criminal Investigation Police and Judicial Process of Benguela (PIC), whose surname was Coelho, appointed to clarify the case, was the coordinator of the ring, and on the way back to the city "he quickly mobilized some old men from the zone to claim those cattle and accuse us of stealing them—us, the owners!"

The Benguelan government ordered that the cattle remain in Dombe Grande until it could ascertain who was in the right. Despite the evidence of hundreds of head of cattle bearing Libermann's brand—a brand registered with both Finance and Veterinary—the rancher was thrown in jail, where he was held incommunicado and without formal charges. The same thing happened to Francisco Muchila. After six days, the PIC director showed up.

"Orders have come to release you. You can go get the cattle."

In Dombe, not a single steer: Coelho had ordered the cattle removed.

"They left only the natives' cattle, which aren't branded."

Of two thousand, there were three hundred or four hundred animals. But the thieves had overlooked in their midst twenty-six head with Libermann's brand. When the rancher pointed out his cattle, a mob formed, and someone shouted, "Libermann's with UNITA and ought to be killed!"

Libermann weighed the situation: weapons and ammunition had been distributed; people had instructions to eliminate him; the cattle

93

raisers would have to drive the cattle 105 kilometers to Benguela. "I've always been an owner and don't know how to drive cattle on foot." Finally, "Bring back only twenty-six? I left them."

The next day, Libermann related the incident to the PIC director.

"Don't go back there!"

Four days later, the rancher saw twenty-six head of cattle go past his door in the trucks of another raiser, Osvaldo.

"They belong to the chiefs of police."

He informed Osvaldo. Libermann knew that the only police stalls were between the penitentiary and the rancher Simões: the head belonging to him were there, and now they belonged to the commander.

Another pilgrimage to the governor took Libermann and the other ranchers back to Dombe Grande. This time it seemed they would have justice: the cattle absent from the first return would now be handed over in another location in the district.

They weren't.

"There weren't any cattle at all. There was a written note under a rock. 'Men moved to Namibe. We were advised.' That's when the great maka began with the director of criminal investigation and with the chief of police."

Threats: people often disappear in wartime, for good. The cattle rustlers had been armed by the authorities on the pretext that they belonged to civil defense.

Libermann made a report to Marcolino Moco, the boyish prime minister promoted by Luanda to the secretariat of the Community of Portuguese-Speaking Countries in Lisbon. In March 1995, the third rescue mission for the cattle came from the sky, in two helicopters lent by the national government, and landed in Camacuio, the northernmost district of the province of Namibe. The helicopters carried cattle raisers, lawyers, delegates from the attorney general, and escorts. That day the cattle would not suddenly disappear upon the landing of the owners.

"We're here to look into the situation of the cattle that belong to Libermann and the others."

"That's easy, we can sit down right here and solve the problem."

"Still, it'd be better to order a breakfast."

"Breakfast? What do you want to eat?"

"Coffee, milk, bread? Bread's becoming scarce, we have only bananas..."

"We don't have coffee, milk, bananas, nothing. Just manioc and meat."

"Then make a bit of manioc and meat."

"We'll have to kill the steer, the goat, and the manioc, the grain has to be threshed and ground..."

End of story: cooperation was harder to obtain than food. The lawyers, the delegates, and the escort concluded that conditions didn't allow them to remain in Camacuio.

"Libermann will stay here by himself, and in two or three days... Is there radio contact here?"

"Yes."

"Well, in two or three days, Libermann will contact Benguela, and we'll come to pick them up."

Libermann did not make contact. From that moment, he and the other ranchers were on their own in the arena. On the fifth day, the first group of Mucubals appeared, "some nomads of Kenyan origin, here for the grazing, they do nothing but raise cattle. They asked: 'So, there are problems?'"

"Mr. Libermann's cattle are branded, and we have to hand them over."

The Mucubals disagreed with the administration's agents:

"We don't have anything to do with that. The comrade commissioner decided on the weapons, the comrade commissioner supplied the ammunition, the comrade commissioner received the orders from Benguela to come here, and we will go look for the cattle on Mr. Libermann's ranch. That's why we brought the cattle. We just didn't bring the horses. The cows, the turkeys, the geese, the pigs, we brought them all here. And in exchange that's what they gave us."

The cattle.

"Independently of Mr. Libermann's cattle, there are cattle belonging to these gentlemen. They were there in the area, we couldn't bring just Mr. Libermann's cattle. We found everything, we brought everything. And also, the individuals who are here get their part. Comrade commissioner, so that we can pay, first pay us."

A huge maka. The Mucubals would return the cattle only if the commissioner—the administrator, as he came to be called when the party ceased to be one and united—also returned the agreed-upon part. The business was full of thieves and accomplices, and only the legitimate owners of the cattle were superfluous: they had to be eliminated. The first attempt against Libermann, the most obstinate of the ranchers, was plotted the following week at a summit among the administrator, the local leaders, and the Mucubal chieftains. The Camacuio captain alerted him.

"All of you can be sure that within an hour or two you'll be hanged, because the administrator has already issued the order."

Libermann, fearing for his life, went straight to the administrator.

"Sir, the man from civil defense (which in your area should be called the militia) says they're going to kill us."

"No, no. That's just to kill blacks and—"

"And what am I?"

"Ah, yes... But it won't be Mr. Libermann."

"Well, you know where we're staying. Bullets aren't selective. You're going to kill me at night, and there's absolutely no lights in this area. I'm with those men in the elementary school. How will the bullets hit Libermann and not the others? The men and I are coming here to sleep in your palace."

Libermann did just that. He wasn't armed. He hadn't brought his BI. He hadn't brought his wristwatch. All the men went to the palace, with their blankets and clothes. They entered. The Mucubals, when they arrived, found the encampment at the administrator's house. No one commits a crime in the home of the man in charge.

They were saved.

The next day, Libermann decided to change his route and go to

Lubango. Camacuio belongs to Namibe and to the governor of that province.

"His name is Joaquim da Silva Matias. He was a classmate of mine; we were students at the Jaú lower seminary in Huíla and then at the upper seminary of Cristo-Rei in Huambo. We were together. Baltazar Manuel, who was governor of Huambo, was also a classmate of mine, along with many others. But the governor of Namibe is afraid of you all and of the district administrator, who has more power than the governor himself. I'll talk not with him but with the governor of Huíla, Kundi Pahiama, who besides being governor is a general. He'll listen to me: I'll tell him what's been going on."

"What's your problem?" asked Pahiama.

"I went there by helicopter. I didn't take with me any means of transport. It was for three days. I took no money, not even food. I've gone hungry. And they sent the Mucubals after me to kill me. The Mucubals admit they sent them. Mucubals don't manufacture ammunition or AKs, they don't manufacture RPG7s or mortars. And they have all those things and more. PKMs and more."

"And what do you think should be done?"

"In my view, the only answer is to arrest the administrator of Camacuio."

Lubango, capital of Huíla, has military jurisdiction over the southwest provinces. Kundi Pahiama supplied food, two Kamazes, two Toyota all-terrains, and sixty men for Libermann's group. The administrator, Kalitoko Capela, with the rank of major, was arrested and confessed to having stolen the cattle. Capela, however, incriminated the chief of police in Benguela, Oliveira Santos, who had been transferred to the place he least desired — Huíla. Oliveira Santos had a history of bad relations with Kundi Pahiama. He was called into the governor's presence.

"So then, Oliveira, you steal cattle."

"I have only thirty-three head to pay for. They're the ones I ordered killed to be sold in Luanda. The rest are with the provincial director of Criminal Investigation and his gang. They're the ones who put the cattle on my ranch, and they're the ones who know what they did with the cattle. Libermann should go talk to them. It's not my concern. If I'm ordered to pay for thirty-three head, I'll pay."

"Libermann, what do you want to do?"

"If I was after money, I wouldn't raise cattle. Let Oliveira pay for thirty-three head on Fernando Borges's ranch"—the largest cattle raiser in Angola—"and I'll go look for them later."

Counting those thirty-three, Libermann recovered sixty animals of the 287 that died or were sold, and he was not allowed to bring the calves or the bulls that no longer had his clearly visible brand. Around three hundred were lost. After the robbery from Fazenda Ali, the cattle were split up: two hundred or so went to Namibe and the rest in cargo planes to Benguela. Of thirty-six horses, Libermann got back only seven.

"It's not even worth mentioning the young cattle."

At the beginning of the great expedition, twenty-eight ranchers left in search of their cattle. Only seven made it to the end, under Libermann's leadership, and those who held on recovered almost their entire herds. Many gave up, succumbing to the hardships of the mission. There were days with no food. The hostile administrators instructed local merchants not to sell anything to Libermann.

None of them died, but others died because of them. On the day of the first attack, five herdsmen were killed. Carlos Costa, head of the Dombe Grande sugar refinery, "who's lived here longer than anyone," came across the flock in late afternoon and was fired at, so he turned around.

In 1992, Chiópio Okahamba, "an elderly person," was surprised by robbers as he and his sons, Kihuta Kahemba and Katoko Buinda, along with an uncle, Nhave Chongolola, were grazing the cattle. Old Chiópio managed to flee, but the others stayed behind: first they were bound and beaten on the spot; then they were taken to an area known as Nailowe, where "all the hostages were coldly and mercilessly murdered and their corpses left on the ground."

One afternoon Chiópio found his cattle in the possession of several individuals, including one named João Dalivila, another one called Bombó, and "a well-known chieftain with strong ties to the administrative authorities" in Camacuio, by the name of Maluwa, "chief of the Macubals." Dalivila was identified as part of the Nailowe gang of killers but merely had to return two head of cattle, because he had already sold the rest. He was held in Benguela but, like the other individuals in the ring, was released by order of the head of the PIC.

As for Bombó, he appeared willing to point out the other robbers to old Chiópio. He led him to the Benguelan border with Namibe, to Mamué, where Chiópio was bound, beaten, and held captive and mistreated for two months. When he succeeded in returning to Dombe Grande, old Chiópio gave up the hunt for his missing cattle and withdrew into silence.

Kachiapi Limeke, a seventy-year-old man from Dombe Grande, suffered the biggest robbery in November 1994. He too was bound and beaten. Three of his nephews decided to "patrol in order to locate the cattle that were, after all, the heritage of the entire family." They located the animals in the possession of Bombó and two more individuals, Bepessala and Kakinda, who had a bad reputation among Benguelan cattle raisers. "But, since they were armed men with instructions to kill, they quickly executed Kachiapi's nephews, who were Katoko, Caliua, and Felo Liangolo."

In the two years of pursuit through Namibe, the cattle thieves also killed an old ranch hand at Fazenda Ali and a woman who ran the cantina. She distributed the food "to the men who took care of the horses, cattle, pigs, and goats. The ranch is twenty-five thousand hectares, the herdsmen would come for their food on horseback or on tractors. I don't know what they thought she was. She was seven or eight months pregnant. They must have thought, We're going to take that Libermann's cattle, he must be white, and we're going to open her up because if she has a white man's child, she must be his wife. They cut open her belly. Maria de Fátima, that was her name. They thought I was white and that she was my wife besides being an employee. She died. She was the daughter of my horse trainer, the Cuanhama named Lourenço, who tamed the horses and taught others how to ride. One of the native herders, Cachilehuma, was the lady's husband."

Fazenda Ali had seventy-five workers and several modes of production. Everything collapsed into abandonment, pillage, and vandalism. Libermann still hasn't been able to visit the spot since he returned, because he's heard news that he prefers not to witness firsthand. He works on another ranch, the Mbulo, only eight thousand hectares, that his father owns in Huíla.

"My cattle are at the ranch that borders on old Cahombe's; she's Kundi Pahiama's mother. To steal mine, they'll have to steal hers, and that's just too bold. And there are other people there; cattle are considered the natives' main wealth and the most sacred good. There are Nyanekas, Mumuílas, Muanas, Cuanhamas in Huíla. A different type of people."

Only Fernando Borges has as many cattle as he, Libermann states. From the sixty head he recouped, he now has 118, but it will take a decade to reconstitute the lines that he had perfected over the years. A trained veterinarian, he considers himself "a raiser. The relationship between a raiser and the animals is different. I may have a pet cow old enough for market because it's not going to have any more calves. But it's a cow that gave me so many fine specimens, good bulls and heifers that won prizes at fairs, and I'm not going to take that cow and have it slaughtered. I couldn't eat meat from that cow! I can't even stand the sight of seeing that cow having its throat cut! I'm going to let it die of old age. It costs me money, but it shows my feeling for it. Jerónimo once had a sick cow that I knew was going to die, but I didn't say anything to him. I took care of it and did everything. When it finally died, it died. The same thing with dogs. I have friends with dogs and I treat them. I'm not going to say to them, Look, it's not worth it, have it killed because the animal has undulant fever and it's incurable. I don't say that. Not with tuberculosis, not with foot-and-mouth."

Libermann's children followed in their father's footsteps. His daughter was only two years old when she got into the car late one night, while the motor warmed up, to claim everything they passed on the road.

"Father, that cattle is ours. Father, you didn't bring rope to tie it up and bring it back to our ranch!"

The youngest son began very early to sort through the animals, moving them with a stick, ducking beneath their bellies, looking through their legs, until he found the one he wanted.

"That one's my bull."

When Libermann returned home, the child immediately knew the absence. Chocolate hadn't come back. Chocolate, his bull.

"The plaintiffs and the other unnamed parties affected have in cattle raising their culture, their wealth, their lives, identities, history, and heritage." The wrongdoing of a gang of thieves and killers acting on behalf of the Benguelan Ministry of the Interior—with the complicity of various officials of the Angolan armed forces—came to the attention of the highest echelons of political and judicial power, from the president of the republic to the attorney general. Daniel Libermann found that this power was useless. His untiring complaints and petitions ended in the same laconic motto: He Asks for Justice.

Both ships are quiet, anchored some distance away, their white sails furled. The lines of the black hulls float sublimely in the infrangible desert light—the intensity of sky and sea is a projection breathed by the land. The ships wait to be filled with the cargo of fish arriving in small boats. The bustle is the same every day, but each day brings a different pleasure to João Tomás da Fonseca. He spends hours seated facing the ocean, watching the shore and the installations. There, on his throne as boss, he can contemplate the ships and at the same time keep an eye on his employees on land. He doesn't have to get up: from the chair he can see every one of them and catch sloth, incompetence, error, disorder, theft; for the least infraction he has a small bell within arm's reach. One touch, and the foreman punishes the culprit. The belvedere of the chalet, he thinks, is the most intelligent work he ever did in this country. Beautiful, the two black birds, *Mucuio I* and *Mucuio II*, sleep in the water...

"When he arrived here, at the end of the nineteenth century, he didn't have that house. At first he lived where those ruins are. The ships transported merchandise to the north of Angola, to Cabinda, Gabon, and the Gulf of Guinea. They took whatever was here, dried fish eggs and shark's fins. They brought raffia and hardwoods... The chalet dates from the turn of the century, and he built it with every comfort, hot water and heating systems. The two sentry boxes on the fence, one was for the guard, the other for central heating. The two pigeon coops in the rear were the bathroom and the kitchen; they had hot water."

João Tomás da Fonseca died decades ago. Mário Faria never met the old man. He did meet his children. He is forty-six years old. His father worked there for almost half a century as manager of the fishery. His mother was a canner and later head of the factory. His uncles worked at the same place. Mário comes from a generation of fishermen.

From atop the sea cliff, Mário looks at Mucuio at his feet: that shore is his life. Without him to tell it, it would be a photograph without a history: a small beach like others, inaccessible, lost in the escarpments where the valleys of the Namibe Desert discharge their brownish waters. In the middle, some white ruins, a delicate building, like a squarish stable, and the eccentricity of the chalet. That would be all.

The Mucuio painted by Mário's lips is another place. The ships of which they told him appear, and the old man at the lookout, perhaps in a hat, perhaps in a linen vest. They are there, it's easy to see them, as easy as watching the weekly distribution of water by the European families (the Angolans drank the insipid local water) at the central fountain, the water that came from the city in ox-drawn barrels and later in trucks, until some died because of the copper tubing. John Wayne — that's his walk — has just entered the square, he advances toward the duel on bowed legs, he's the height of the cold room against whose smooth white side Mário's father projected, in the sixties, on a 16 mm machine, the saloons of old westerns bought in Namibe. The shore took on life: there are even 2.5-kilo cans of merma and tuna, with paper labels, MUCUIO CANNERY, in the hands of an American housewife in the Midwest; this was one of the places that the cannery exported to in the past.

Mucuio was a good, sound fishery: saltworks, flour mill, cannery, salting and drying, small-scale freezing, and shipyard. It had over twenty small boats. Mário recalls in his pronounced Algarve accent that there was an eighty-ton trawler, two trawl nets (just for fishing for cachucho and choupa), and two installations that needed a minimum of four boats to carry out so-called Valencian fishing. The boats kept the nets in deep waters and raised them twice daily to take out the fish. The nets would remain in the water for months at a time and were removed only for repair—a task for the south of Portugal.

Fish gave birth to people in hostile spots like Mucuio. The first commercial fishery in Moçâmedes was founded by a Portuguese from Algarve, Fernando Cardoso Guimarães, in 1843 (following an agreement with the native chieftains in 1840 for the establishing of settlements). A year later, Queen Maria sent a thousand fishhooks to Moçâmedes, because she had been told there were many fish there. The neighboring fishery to Mucuio, in Baía das Pipas, received its charter in 1854, and by 1857 there were sixteen fisheries in Moçâmedes, with forty longboats and 280 slaves, plus four more on the beaches in the north (as far as Lucira). The major leap forward would come at the end of the following decade, with the immigration of people from Algarve—who made the journey in their own boats. The first, in 1860, was a native of Olhão, José Guerreiro de Mendonça. The newcomers from Algarve adapted better to fishing than those from Pernambuco did to agriculture (it was the latter who founded Moçâmedes on August 4, 1849, with the arrival of the ship *Tentativa Feliz*). Agriculture put down roots only in the fertile desert valleys like Bero and Giraul, thanks to the sea: American whalers discovered they could use that coast to replenish their supply of fresh produce, which made commerce (of ivory and wax) also possible on the most remote coast of Angola.

Fishing in Mucuio gave rise to a village: more than five hundred Europeans, some one hundred Angolans living in the *compão* (the squarish building), divided into contract workers and volunteers, and on the sea cliffs, a hundred or so *cubatas*, or thatch huts, with more workers. The community disbanded in 1978, when the fishery was looted and abandoned.

Mário returned in 1984 with authorization to put the fishery on a new footing. Many of his worker friends began reappearing. New cubatas are being built, work has been done on the compão (including tearing down the wall), and the salting-and-drying component is functioning. Mário's pride and joy is the boarding school, where the fishery educates thirty street children—the homeless of the desert! There is another school with eighty pupils, the workers' children. A small miracle for an inhospitable coastal town in a ravaged country.

Mário still practices in Mucuio an ancestral technique for preserving fish—the only one feasible in a place where all infrastructure has been destroyed. The fresh fish is gutted and soaked in brine tanks for days, three or four if it's a delicate fish, more if it's thick. Then it's washed again in salt water and placed to dry on platforms, the strange clothesline that occupies the sand of Mucuio. The resulting product is known as mulamba.

If the salting is done well, the fish lasts for months without deteriorating and with no loss of quality. This allows holding on to it when the market can't absorb the production, which is occurring now. The fish isn't selling, because there's no money and because of the illegal commerce, which is growing faster and faster.

"In Namibe and Tômbua that's what you see. Day before yesterday, in Tômbua, just the trucks that I oversee, there was about sixty tons of mulamba. In one day! Those sixty tons are, at least, a hundred fresh fish. In Tômbua we estimate about five hundred or six hundred tons a month of illegal fish, with the heads on. It goes into the illegal circuit and doesn't pay taxes, doesn't pay anything, and without the least bit of hygiene or quality, nothing."

Great quantities of fresh fish head up the plateau daily to Lubango. If there were a consumption policy, explains Mário Faria, part of the fish would end up as meal, oil, dried, canned, and so on. There is no such policy. What happens is that the population of Lubango can't absorb the fresh fish that comes in, and part of it goes into the salt-and-dry system in the city, clandestinely and without preparation. This is done in an effort to save the fish, but, mixed with the hurried mulambas of Namibe's street vendors, the result is simple: the interior of Angola, to which the product is channeled, consumes rotten fish.

Mário doesn't speak of fish as fish. Fish is taste, it's species, it's pleasure, it's wisdom. We stroll around the fishery, between tanks of brine and packages of anchovies, amberjacks, and croakers, as if we were visiting a museum. An oceanarium of flattened species.

"You see the different colors of the mulamba? One of them is made using the classic formula: a month in brine, well impregnated, gives a different look from fast mulamba. Ours lasts thirty to sixty days if it's transported in appropriate containers. This fish is the sarrajão, which has all the requisites for good canning and for fish paste, a nice clean paste, white, pretty, a fatty fish. What was sometimes called tuna is another species of scombrid, like the sarrajão, the merma, the judia. If we bring sarrajão fresh from the sea, we remove the bones and cook it with potatoes and tomatoes, it's wonderful with onion. We have to salt it, because there's not a single canning factory operating in the province."

A love like that is cultivated through the stomach. After all, mulamba was a fisherman's preparation. From the factory one can return to the kitchen—and go back a century and a half. Suggestion for a stormy afternoon:

"It can be a mulamba of swordfish, mulamba of croaker, mulamba of bumper. It's the way you open the fish, first of all. The fish is cut open from the back, along the spine, and usually you take off the head if it's for mulamba of croaker or bumper. Then it's put in very light brine, with little salt, so it won't pick up much flavor. It's left there for several hours, then dried for a day or two, it's fast. Here we eat grilled fish, which is called mufete—the bumper is grilled without removing the viscera; the whole thing goes over the coals. The head's the best part of the fish—the same for kalulu, with palm oil. When we make a grouper, a croaker, a pungo, a guemba, the so-called noble fishes, we always leave the head on."

The lookout is designed with a cage of windows that extend the field of vision in all directions. João Tomás da Fonseca leans back once more in his creaking chair. On the armrests of the chair, his arms embrace the lookout and continue, outside, in the two pincer-shaped cliffs, as if the rocks were an extension of his hands, of his power. His rocky embrace encompasses the shore, the sea, two ships. The sky is not yet his, but he plans to have it one day. Mucuio, this seashore, is his life.

Henri Valot left me at the Rocha Pinto Market, one of the two most dangerous in Luanda, where I arranged transportation for the first leg of the journey. Henri, a Frenchman who spent his teenage years in Brazil, is in Angola as a human rights official. I carry two gifts of his. Michael Serre's *Atlas* and his own map, precious, continued in the first letter to Luanda, written in October 1996 in a city in the interior of Angola. In a "cursed province." Something worse, ominous, new. Henri has served missions in Cambodia and Mozambique.

A different story, here.

"On my table, in disarray, are scattered Karl Maier's book *Angola: Promises and Lies*; two Motorola radios, UHF and VHF; a Canon Bubble Jet printer; two rolls of film, 125 ASA; the *African Charter on Human and Peoples' Rights*, in Portuguese; reading notes; a thousand-piece jigsaw puzzle; Klimt's *The Wait*; and finally, another book, Gilles Perrault's *Le secret du roi*. The musical background tonight is that cassette recorded by Carlos, 'Selecciones del Mundo': among those appearing will be Cesária Évora and Transglobal Underground, Deep Forest, and the great Mexican singers. We inhabit a vast apartment, comfortable and devoid of furniture; a second floor in a small city where furniture is rare. Nonsense in the middle of Africa; it is in fact difficult living in an apartment where running water was cut off several years ago. There is a regular lack of water, so we go down to the nearby river to fill our cistern. It's then necessary to haul the water to the second floor, back and forth with buckets, which often ends in a battle, and then our efforts of a Saturday afternoon are wasted in an instant, the city's precious water on the steps, surprised neighbors in doorways. We try to move, to find a house with a well in the yard.

"The maid knows how to cook with coal; we taught her to use gas. She learns very quickly.

"Little by little the city is dying, the streets burying themselves, the walls cracking, employees working in ruined buildings, leaving their posts at the time of distribution by PAM, the Programa Alimentar Mundial, or World Food Programme. PAM is unfair competition, say the few merchants. It feeds 90 percent of the population in the government-controlled territory. PAM would like to end general distribution but doesn't know how. We are still in emergency times, there is no talk of development, the 'situation' doesn't permit it, it's necessary to come to the aid of the less fortunate, those who have lost everything, who don't know to what or to whom to turn. Settling of accounts in the downtown area of the city, the airport taken over by UNITA, hunger beginning, an urban center that can no longer be provided for, hunger that continues today. A little five-year-old man, Quinzinho, appears at my doorstep every morning, hungry. I like him, I give him what he asks of me, what he needs.

"It's terrible, hunger. Quinzinho says it, shouts it, in tears. I bend down, sit beside him, listen to him, remind him that there's a place he knows where UNICEF feeds people. I accompany him there, but the place is closed, the food stolen. We returned disillusioned, went to the market, where I bought bread, sardines, crackers, candy, soap, bananas.

"Morale is unstable, mine and the Angolans'. To the banal formulas of politeness — 'How are you?' — they invariably reply, 'Normal,' 'More or less,' or 'Very bad.' Permanent crises, ruptures of confidence, interrogations about the reason for our presence. Being a human rights observer in Angola . . . Several times I've performed impossible, undefined, or ill-defined functions; this one is, beyond any doubt, the worst of all. To observe is to appeal, properly understood, to the senses, to sight above all; to speech, to the encounter. I speak, therefore, at different levels; I adopt complex strategies of approach. The reactions of my interlocutors are completely irrational; some are enthusiastic, favorably disposed from the first moment the question of human rights is introduced; others close themselves off, suspicious: does human rights evoke for them juridical imperialism? The intervention of universal claims?

"Maître,* a signatory of the Lusaka Protocol and former minister of foreign affairs of Mali, is a small, rotund man with lively, sometimes sly eyes, a devilish politician, African diplomat, unparalleled negotiator, obviously a legitimist (the government, however corrupt it may be, is still the sovereign government; to attack the Angolan government is to risk the fragile authority of the young African nations). The reports of observations, written in French, are transmitted to this 'special representative.' Maître has declared himself sensitive to questions of human rights; he contributed in 1980–81 to the drafting of the African Charter. Besides this, he reads my reports carefully and in his awkward, almost infantile handwriting makes notes in my texts.

"My readers, francophone Africans, prize the written French language. Isolated in Luanda, the capital of the country, at the end of June, I was asked to write the speeches Maître would deliver at a seminar on human rights. Jean Genet revisited on Angolan soil, that theatrical inversion of black and white. I therefore transformed myself into a white black from a small black man in charge of a fleet of white vehicles marked with the UN insignia. Those who know MPB, and in particular Caetano and Gil's *Tropicália II*, will remember the song 'Haiti,' whose words play with skin color. My career as black was spectacular and brief...I remember a book by Erik Orsenna: François

---

*The title by which Alioune Blondin Beye, special representative of the secretary-general of the United Nations in Angola, was known. The mediator of the Angolan peace process died, in the execution of his duties, in a plane crash outside Abidjan in June 1998.

Mitterrand is said to have written in the margin of his first speech proposed by the new black of the Elysée: 'What do you take me for?' It was more or less the question that Maître made me ponder after he had read one of my texts that ended with the following words:

"'The Prince, the King, the Old Man, or even the President of the Republic all have the same obligation, the same duty vis-à-vis the people: along with the natural dignity of every human being, the leader must exercise with dignity the responsibility vouchsafed by his people. And this responsibility is foremost and without doubt the protection of the essential rights of his people.'

"My career as black came to a rapid end. Which was good; I was sent back to the interior and to my human rights.

"On certain Sundays, Hotel Romeo (that's the Human Rights call sign) calls Alpha Whiskey, 4 Alpha, 42 November, and we leave for Pungo Andongo. Two hours of travel by land to approach the inselbergs, large rocky formations. No one knows where they come from. It's both a tourist and historical location: the kingdom of Ngol was led by a queen, Queen Jinga. She fled from the coast when the Portuguese arrived, and plunged into the jungle to discover, four hundred kilometers inland, these majestic royal stones. She installed herself here, with her husbands and her amazons, and marked the rock with her tiny foot: there is a mark, religiously preserved, and it pleases me to think that it's the foot of a queen with so much power that she succeeded in leaving her mark on the rock.

"The other tourist spot is Calandula, a miniature Victoria Falls. Getting there is more complicated; the road is mined, and the falls are in UNITA territory. It's therefore necessary to invent the pretext of a verification mission and propose to the Russian pilots a helicopter flight through the falls, which they generally accept. The helicopter descends into the falls; it's impressive. Sergei lets me act as copilot, and thus my observer role takes on its full significance.

"Cursed province. To accept such an assignment, in a place like this, you have to believe in fate. Forces, hidden but certain, brought me here. I have made friends here, and often I have injured myself running into walls. I have found here a young, tenuous love."

At afternoon's end, announcing the official night that will cover the ever nocturnal city, a sinister tolling, without temper, rings over the Cangalo district. Pedro Sebastião, catechist of the ghetto of the mutilated, bangs on a metallic ring hanging from a cord. It is time for catechism, and Pedro Sebastião, holding the bible in his arms folded at defective angles, goes once again to teach divine laws to the children of the mutilated of Bié. To begin, the first:

"Cuíto's misfortunes come from the war. God didn't order it this way."

It's easy to explain the map of the Battle of Cuíto. A gesture is enough, made from the veranda of the palace. António da Conceição Gonçalves, Tony, vice governor for the economic sector, makes this gesture, and I take in the destruction where he maps the struggle:

"Cuíto is a mass grave. There are people buried everywhere. In the churchyard, in the church itself, in those gardens, on the avenue, in houses, in yards, in buildings. I don't like to talk about it. I lost parents and children. Be careful with roofs. They're still falling."

The vice governor's gesture encompasses the urban perimeter and, farther out, the bare prairie. In five fingers of emotion there is room for eighteen months of war, of which nine have been under

UNITA siege. The axis of combat was Joaquim Kapango Avenue, which crosses the small city from north to south. To the west was the UNITA-controlled zone, to the east, that of the government. In the neighborhoods there were pockets of infiltration, so that all fought against all from every side to every side.

In the center of the city, in Independence Square, the building of the provincial government belonged to UNITA, and just a few meters away the National Bank was the FAA's. The next battleground was the Bishopric, behind the bank. And, in the opposite direction, crossing Joaquim Kapango, the Gabiconta Building, at five stories the tallest in the city, was the fortress of the government's troops.

Olímpia fought there, desperately.

"Somewhere along the way I asked for a weapon. I expected death, but I wanted to die fighting. If this building fell, Cuíto fell, and the war in Angola would be a different one."

Olímpia wasn't from that building. Her apartment is in the first building as one comes in from the Huambo road, at the south end of Joaquim Kapango. The place had no relevance, as all the structures were equally demolished. The movie theater and the gymnasium, the church and the seminary, the school and the orphanage. The Hotel Cuíto. The motionless cars in the yards along the avenue, where today families live who have no house to go to.

Armored vehicles fired with their cannons set at horizontal. Houses fired at houses, their targets twenty meters away. Within sight, hatred in the whites of eyes. Snipers on both sides took positions in strategic spots, killing anyone who came out and preventing others from helping those who fell. Mines were placed throughout the city, in houses, in the rubble, in walkways, in soccer fields.

A French officer in the mine-clearing operation, trained in Cuíto, told me up to that time, July 1997, he had encountered seventy-one different types of explosives.

"We often joke that with a bit of work we'll come across the other seven hundred—there are close to eight hundred types of mines recorded in the entire world. There's a lot of publicity about the former Yugoslavia. Too much. All the organizations are there to help.

Here the war was different from any I'm familiar with, Cambodia, Afghanistan, Bosnia. In those places the weapons are conventional. Here, mines are of every type. There are even homemade mines. Those we don't count. The material here is as sophisticated as it comes, produced by—everybody: Israelis, South Africans, Chinese, Koreans, Russians, Americans. It's a kind of university for us. And no one's ever heard of Cuíto."

Some of the weapons aren't buried. That morning they called the Frenchmen from the Mine-Clearing School, who were probing at the airport at a mine wrapped in a cardboard box. Some days earlier they had removed from a house a crate of mortars that the former tenant left there since the war.

"The children here play with air-to-surface missiles, which are a little more than 25 cm in length and can take off their hand at any moment because they didn't explode on impact. One child was blown to bits by one of those things a short while back. It's absurd. I don't know how they're going to rebuild this city."

But they are. Without help from Luanda, Cuíto insists on staying on its feet. It's the only place in Angola that I saw with that spirit. How to face the future when foreign experts visit the city and conclude that the only solution is to raze Cuíto and build another in another spot? In Bié there's not the money. There's just the stubbornness of special people.

Martinho, the driver taking me to Cuando Cubango, sets the example, a man who fought constantly in the two years of war.

"People, desperate, risked their lives, under enemy fire, to find the parachutes the government dropped at random over the city. We would haul back the largest amount of sand possible so we could later pick out the salt. I once carried thirty kilos of sand through the Cunje minefields and, once I got it home, managed to extract three spoonfuls of salt. Tablespoonfuls."

On a back street, three men are lining a coffin with white silk.

A policeman exercises with an axle from the Benguelan railroad, on the terrace of the Gabiconta Building.

The Okangalo ("little street vendors") take advantage of the few minutes of electricity to rehearse at the provincial cultural center. They play "The Hunt" on a red guitar.

What you see in Cuíto
I'll never forget
People looking for food
Dying
In search of water
Dying
And people buried in backyards
Children on crutches
Dead women
                    with live children on their backs

In Olímpia's wall, one hole is larger than the rest. It was where an FAA sniper stood. He shot at the neighborhood, gave himself away, and pulled his trigger for the last time. UNITA fired once. It made the hole, corrected its aim, fired again. The man's head was blown off by a 60 mm mortar shell. An indelible stain marks his death.

"I don't know what it is about people's blood. We've tried cleaning it, but it won't come out."

In front of the Gabiconta there was a sports center. The roof no longer exists, and iron girders cast a grid of shadows on the body of a soccer player washing himself as he squats over a red basin. Juliana is hanging clothes at one corner of the upper stands. A plush animal dangles crucified from the wire.

A family on the avenue lives in the yard in front of the ruins that form its residence. They showed me the dwelling: a Chevrolet Apache that doesn't run.

On the top floor of the Gabiconta, the building that has resisted best, one sees written in orange paint: LAST STOP.

Alma my soul, my soul, my soul, a small train, Alma my soul, climbing the mountain range, my soul, my soul, wheezing, Alma my soul, Alma my soul, engine and two water tank cars, my soul, three cars of merchandise, Alma, two passenger cars, Alma, Alma, Alma my soul!

I'm in the last one. There are two compartments, one general, the other closed. Between the two, in the small corridor that connects them, is the space that used to be for baggage. In the rear, a cubicle that was once a bathroom.

We make our way in total darkness. An idea of how dark: in the compartment I can't see my own knees. There is nothing in this train besides metal. The coach is just as it came from the foundry. What doesn't exist: doors, windows and their molding, seats (there's a board), wood, flooring, all the paneling of walls and ceiling. Not even shapes, because there is no light on board. Fear. Ahead, the only illumination: the engine's headlight.

Until Bibala, at the Chela foothills, the train was full. People lying on sacks of salt in the general, with three railroad employees in their own spot: in baggage were two amputees, lying curled up; six passengers in private, including me; more people and more sacks in the lavatory and in the corridor.

They all got off, and daylight left with them. Furtively, we gained altitude on level curves, a meter at a time, circling the vertical wall of the Chela Mountains. At almost two thousand meters, the cold was enough to kill the unprepared — cold like this, merciless cold, I hadn't expected to find in Angola. Nothing in my backpack could protect me from it. This cold would never end. It came in blindly through the windows and left through the doors. There was no refuge, and I could feel my bones fusing into the car: everything was metal, and the metal, like my bones, stored up the cold.

Much later, at a mountain stop, the train was once again beset by passengers. I saw them, one and all, without a scintilla of light: they materialized in their hurried speech, in the gravel echoing their rapid steps, in the labored breathing of people with only a few minutes to get the greatest possible number of sacks of coal on board.

I continued almost alone inside that cage, a black box open to the firmament, to the less black blackness. There was no moon, but neither were there clouds. A mole surfacing inside a planetarium would see the same sight. There were mountains on every side, as high as the lowest stars. Somewhere else in the compartment was a young man. I knew he was there, because he tossed and turned and snorted from the cold. The sound of the wind, the engine far ahead, and the wind seemed to lash through this car and the others when, in a slipping that lasted for seconds, the wheels glided frictionlessly on the tracks.

A pluperfect silence: no one knows what it hides or how long it will last. The darkness makes us a train of the clandestine. From time to time, in the middle of the car, the railroad's agent, Mr. Cambuta, turns on a small tricolor light (yellow, green, and red), on a table set up for him, to note down arrival and departure times, delays, and other events of interest. In the heights of the Chela, passengers in the front of the car light a candle and then a small fire. Nothingness takes on shape, a sad, unstable, poor shape.

The young man became desperate with cold. I could hear the chattering of his teeth. He was like me. I took the old — white! — bath towel from my backpack and wrapped it around his head, with the edges falling over his shoulders, as if he were some exiled Arab. I counted the stars, lost track of time again. I gave up looking ahead on curves to see lights. One day we would arrive.

We arrived in the middle of the night. The Lubango station, the railroad's headquarters, was a failed shelter, completely dark, far from the city, without taxis or a telephone to call one. Hundreds of people stay there, spread out along the tracks, shrouded in blankets and one another, to await the dawn.

I covered the distance into the city on foot — making a few detours to avoid the dogs — and, half unconscious, reached the two Romanian guards at the UNAVEM gate. It wasn't easy to explain the situation. I had a card from the United Nations but couldn't take it out: my fingers were no longer obeying.

They took me to the transmissions barracks. The Romanian sentry knocked several times. Finally, a voice sounded inside.

"Who is it? What do you want?"

"Pedo Mendsh..."

At the door, smiling as always, appeared First Sergeant Pratas.

"Get in here, man! You're frozen! Have you eaten yet? Take this bed. Take an extra blanket from the other one. You must be starving."

The rest of the barracks had woken up, and the sergeant quickly explained things, condensing twelve hours of travel into a totally understandable formula:

"It's the journalist."

The lights were turned out. The sergeant, amused, said from across the barracks:

"One of these days you'll kill yourself, Mendes!"

Afterward, even with the delays, but always at the appointed spot — Terminus, the beginning — a whistle will release the engine's impatience. The wagons of English pine will move in ever shorter spasms. They will shake the faded posters of carnival, folkloric Portugal scattered through the compartments. The Valdevez Arches, Vila Franca de Xira (a wait for cattle), the Convent of Mafra. Portinho da Arrábida with its rows of beach cabanas. The leather of the seats still resists. The yellow metal has been stolen.

The train starts at kilometer zero, and the rose-colored cardboard tickets are dead leaves from another era. Their destinations still bear the old colonial names: Nova Lisboa, Silva Porto, Teixeira de Sousa, hundreds of kilometers ahead, tens of years into the past...

Terminus. They told me that on the other side of Africa, on the other coast, there is or was another hotel with the same name. That's how the journey is: the direction doesn't matter, and any course ends inevitably in the same place. Destiny—the first, the last, the only station. Before departure, the end has already come to pass. From sea to sea, from one Terminus to the other, the engineers launched a car filled with magic and deception.

The Lobito Terminus, built by the CFB in 1932 as an expansion of the Pensão Lobito, looks new. It was already considered a victim of the war when UNAVEM restored it to serve as its logistical base in the city. The Frenchman used his connections: he sent a fax to Luanda advising that I was doing a story on human rights, and he reserved a room for me. I wouldn't have one as good for several months. But bad luck left its mark on the negative: after the first photograph in Lobito, the horizon line fractured with a sharp sound inside the Nikon, and the blue went out of focus in the eyepiece. The second negative was washed out, and the rest of the roll unusable. That left the Olympus.

I phoned Lisbon, and it didn't seem to be my day.

RDP, Antenna 1, Francisco Sena Santos:

"Good to hear your voice! Where are you?"

"Lobito."

"Al Berto died. We're dedicating the magazine to him. Forgive me for breaking it to you like this."

PÚBLICO, photography section, Luís Ramos:

"The mirror's only to let you see what you're photographing. Just take it out."

A casualty on the way to the train, right by the station, where the acacias are white from being crapped on by albatrosses belonging to a species I can't recall. Bad news travels faster than anything. Received at long distance, it's even more hurtful.

abandoned I go along the path of winding cities, alone, I look for the thread of neon that shows me the way out

The sea is to the right of the rails. To the left hangs a nation of the displaced, holding on to the fringe of sand by their fingernails, clutching the misfortune that befell them, because war has cut off their return to the forest and they will weep and bear children on the coast their parents never saw. The demobilized, the mutilated, and the jobless emerge from the ghettos that contain them. We go through Chongorói: they attack the train, tossing their crutches and sugarcane stalks aboard before running on prostheses and hopscotching to gain momentum to jump onto the moving cars. The legless, lacking that ability, look at us in fury, condemned to remain behind, and ask for one last favor from the gravel, inches away from being ground up by the train's enormous wheels.

At the Catumbela cemetery men are playing cards, and clothes for sale are spread out in the dust. Romantic music of Rádio Morena brings smiles to the young women who adorn themselves with the light of the Atlantic, insolently beautiful in the outskirts of Benguela. The young soldiers and policemen nod sleepily among the fare collectors, high as a kite on marijuana.

"Those are the ones who die!"

The train will not go far—the railroad operates on only thirty of the fourteen hundred kilometers of its route—but the departure has all the ceremony of great distances. First class displays more atmosphere, because an older car was chosen for it, from 1928. It has a red lantern and a door that, when open, displays a wake of tracks among the cane fields and palm groves of Catumbela.

The journey has begun. From outside comes a final shout.

"The dead stay behind!"

The line has closed, but the regulation is maintained: passengers wait for the train at the Terminus; then they get on board with a punched ticket in their pocket.

it was a path of the Holy Milky Way. wild palms, lost wells, caravans, sleepwalking nomads, cities of sand and ash, in the afternoon they put him into a strait-jacket, tied his hands behind his back. *

They are heading toward the border—and beyond.

---

*Both quotes are from Al Berto, *O Medo*, published by Assírio and Alvim.

AFRICA HOTEL

"I am in moral pain."

From the Corto Maltese Hotel in Angola there remained a clock that today is kept in Luanda. In exile, it waits for its owner.

The reason Stamatis Kalokouvalos fled his country is obscure but is presumed to have something to do with politics, perhaps with the Turkish question. Stamatis frequently bet on the wrong side — in politics, in business, in gambling. That's why he had such a grand life. Born on the island of Poros — the Kalokouvalos house still exists and is classified as part of the historical patrimony — Stamatis left Greece at an early age, in the 1880s, and the oldest credible information places him in Algiers and later in Alexandria, Egypt, at the time the poet Kavafis was inspiring the city. There Stamatis bought his first hotel, both a means of survival and a kind of dilettantism, obviously, because by vocation he was a journalist and by choice an activist.

He continued to work his way down the map, in pursuit of the diaspora that was his clientele. The journalist was a correspondent for Greek newspapers but wrote about Africa mainly for the continent's Greek émigrés, who were quite numerous in southern Africa. After Egypt, he based himself in Elizabethville, in Katanga, intoxicated by the promise of easy money. He wasn't lucky.

Stamatis went on to South Africa, where he continued to write for Greek newspapers. It was at this time, the turn of the century, that he spent long periods in the north of Mozambique, a territory then in the early stages of British colonization. In Beira, he made friends with an obscure poet, a surveyor for the Mozambique Company, Manuel Mendonça de Oliveira. What little is known about the man speaks favorably of him: "A person of fine upbringing, disciplined, zealous in the execution of his professional duties. Nothing in the time I served with him is to the discredit of his civil and private record," wrote his chief of service. This statement is part of the administrative proceedings that pitted Oliveira against the governor of the territories of Manica and Sofala, Pinto Basto — or Pinto Besta, as the poet wrote in one of his formal petitions. Also responsible for the Beira Meteorological Observatory, Oliveira was reprimanded and punished by an eight-day unpaid suspension for a measuring error that he did not commit, in August 1906. He resigned in September, as a matter of honor, despite the difficult financial situation of his family in Lisbon, aggravated by the fact that the company owed him half a year's salary and a paid leave in the kingdom, to which he was entitled.* Oliveira, a mystic exiled in the Indian Ocean, became acquainted with and a follower of Buddhism. He died in Quelimane, of fever.

Stamatis, not fond of Great Britain, got too deeply involved in the Boer War and the political crisis that preceded it: writings, essays, rallies, speeches, controversies. When the war ended, he was hunted by the victors and would have ended up in one of the terrible English concentration camps for prisoners of war if not for the help of the Greek community.

The journalist managed to leave South Africa, this time for Huambo, with forged travel documents. He began a new life with a false identity: his surname changed to Dáskalos. This was what he was called in the political meetings among the South African Greek com-

---

*According to the documents, numbers 1–19, relating to the surveyor's defense and to the dispatches of Governor Pinto Basto and the director of agriculture of the Mozambique Company

munity: "master." At the consulate, he founded a new family that would come to have its name linked to Angolan nationalism—the poet Alexandre Dáskalos was his son.

In Huambo, Stamatis opened a hotel—known simply as "the Greek's hotel"—and was also owner of a tobacco factory, a bakery, and a good part of the city's real estate. But wealth was short-lived, because the journalist-hotelier squandered it at a casino that, in the 1920s, operated in a hotel in Granja, where settlers, truck drivers, and contract workers gathered. They played roulette. He also worked for the railroad, a painful period for someone who hated the English.

Only one marriage is recorded for the Greek. He fell in love with a woman twenty years his junior. She was from Goa but had never been to India. Registered as a teacher in the Colonies ministry, she requested placement in Goa, where the family of her grandfather, who had come to Lisbon as a doctor, was located.* She ended up in Angola: they sent her to Bié, and when she showed up there, they sent her to try her luck in Huambo because the position was already filled.

Zaida Matilde was devoutly Catholic, of a very austere Catholicism. She arrived without a husband. Stamatis-Dáskalos met her when she was twenty-five, with a daughter and leading a younger brother of fourteen by the hand. Her strangest characteristic was telepathy. They were the widow and orphan daughter of Manuel Mendonça de Oliveira, an obscure poet from Mozambique.

---

*"We, the Director and Council of the School of Surgical Medicine of Nova Goa, make it known that António Joaquim Guilherme Nunes de Oliveira, son of José António de Oliveira, native of Nova Goa, after having attended the Surgical Medicine course of study in this school, sat for the necessary examinations as stipulated in the regulations of 11 October 1865. He was unanimously approved, with honors in all classes, and awarded nine firsts corresponding to the nine disciplines of his five-year course of study and with honors in the ceremonies held on 22 May 1868. Therefore, in accordance with Article 151 of the Plan of Organization and Regulation of Surgical Medicine Instruction in the State of India we confer upon him the present charter in which we declare him entitled to exercise Medicine and Surgery in accordance with the aforesaid regulation, with all the privileges and prerogatives thereunto appertaining. And we ask all authorities and scientific bodies, both domestic and foreign, to so recognize him. —Granted in Nova Goa, on 17 June 1868."

Lubumbashi, August 21, 1997

An unpleasant type of carbonated currant, grenadine, soils my thirst-soiled mouth. I'm not going to turn around now, but behind me I can see the youth's impatience making semicircles. He is under fifteen, with a uniform and machine gun as big as he is. He prowled about the table when I began to write. He's the guard on duty. He must not be from Shaba, perhaps he is not even Zairean. Rwandan, most likely, just like those who searched my car on the Goma road in November. A small Banyamulenge, a soldier before his time.

Noteworthy: order reigns in the chaos of the Congo. The only attack to date was the tunnel of formalities at the border: two trips to the *santé*, where orderlies examined boxes of vaccine as if they were counterfeit banknotes, and one small irritation (my own) because the Zairean visa they gave me in Luanda was fake. I paid a hundred dollars for it and sixty for another...

The greenhorn Kabila, with the universal gestures of childish shyness, went to say something to an old white man who arrived with a Zairean woman wrapped in cloths. This is the garden-esplanade of the Park Hotel. A cloister around a gigantic cactus that reaches to the second floor.

A band is over in the corner observing—the orchestra!—and soon begins playing easy-to-digest standards. The musicians are wearing jackets of bright red fabric: the grenadine band.

They take me to the sawmill of the Portuguese O. Fernandes—or to the rest of his prison. In 1990 the state wanted to pay ninety thousand to indemnify him. He won't accept less than three million. He'll never get it, and he knows it. He'll never leave, either, something he also knows. A classic African:

Young, white, single, with a bright future, he arrives from Puto in the fifties—on the Benguela line—to work in a business. Earlier he taught in Angola at the São João de Brito School, which belonged to the Agricultural Company of Angola, in Boa-Entrada, Gabela. In Angola he was a teacher, or as he puts it, "I began counting grains of corn, if you like. And gallons of gasoline. And screws" at the general warehouses of the Indigenous Services sector of the company. In Elizabethville he found "the best hospital in southern Africa," Muchengue, and also says that "racism here was accentuated, the blacks couldn't go anywhere, only those who had a civic card—very few in number—could enter public places."

Fernandes had a bakery rented from the state, in Mweka, and later in the same region busied himself with jungle exploration, palm oil, and the sawmill, subsequently opening another one in Elizabethville. He had 460 employees, a school in Kasai with six teachers for the workers' children, a small dam that produced the energy he used, trucks, motors, tractors, cranes, cistern, and so on. He goes down the list—the past, as for old Teixeira, seems to assault him in the form of an inventory.

Treacherously, silently, the orchestra has begun to take its place. They are all seated now, including the keyboard player, his instrument atop a table with a green tablecloth. I haven't yet determined the tune, but it must be some "Girl from Ipanema" or other.

He lost everything on November 30, 1973, with Mobutu's Zairization speech. "All I kept were the debts that I spent six years working to pay off." He became an employee of the Zairean firm that acquired it: the Lusitana (!) Sawmill became the Scierie Kamaraba ("locomotive"). In 1974 he was arrested in Kananga, accused of having diamonds, gold, and ivory in his baggage. He spent three days in a holding cell full of people, all of whom did their business right there. "They put me next to a crack, by the door, so I could breathe." The police interrogated children by placing sticks between their fingers and twisting. Out of fear, he gave the name of an Ecuadorean jeweler who was looking for someone with a good reputation in the city—the capital was the other man's. Fernandes became managing partner of the scierie, where he continues today.

A classic African.

There's a video club on the terrace. For the week of August 4–10 the offerings were *Intimate Decisions*, *Fireproof*, and *Cold Revenge*.

I ate at a Greek restaurant with two Portuguese families that work here—I think that today I was in one of the only two textile factories that operate in all of Zaire. I take away seven meters of cloth with the latest novelty in prints: a pattern in the colors of Democratic Congo and silver medallions with the likeness of Laurent-Désiré Kabila. Things are calm but still aren't going well: the Katangans have had enough of the Rwandans who installed themselves here. Now that Mobutu is out, they want them to return to their own country. The Rwandans stay here because of the mines; it's said that the money from Shaba is going directly into bank accounts in Kigali. They have also begun merging and nationalizing the businesses that might prove profitable. The Portuguese predict there will be war tomorrow between yesterday's allies.

An enormous man leaped from the bar to the esplanade carrying a cellular phone. (The wired network is inoperable.)

"J'arrive dimanche!"

A garçon passed by, small, of age, covered in a vest and sadness, his left foot limping, the same side in which the tray in his hand wobbles.

One of the Rwandan commanders is staying in this hotel. He doesn't stand on ceremony: he wears the dress uniform of the RPF. He comes and goes surrounded by lackeys who hold his cell phone and executive briefcase and open the door for him. They alone use the elevator. The headquarters of the ADFLC is just across the street.

With its lethargic caresses, the grenadine band has finally lulled almost all its instruments to sleep. They now purr imperceptible melodies. The cell phone has become furious, perhaps at his wife.

"J'arrive dimanche! C'est pas possible de rentrer avant. J'ai du travail ici. J'ai des chocolats pour toi et une cassette vidéo."

Not even a good-bye kiss. He hangs up.

Teixeira arrived in Elizabethville in 1954 and saw a bathtub for the first time in his life. The Portuguese city where he was born, in the Minho area, had never afforded him such a luxury — and it was a city! Even the shower came into his life only once he began playing soccer in school. He arrived in Elizabethville on the Benguela Railroad, on one of the special trains for Belgian settlers.* He traveled in a sleeping car. At twenty-three, he did something else for the first time: he slept between white sheets "so clean and starched that they slid off."

The starch, the same used to stiffen collars, made the sheets cool.

Teixeira's first car was a coffee-colored Vauxhall, easier to drive than the bicycle he had in Portugal. He bought it for five hundred francs and sold it for eight thousand. He had others: Mercedes, Peugeot, Pontiac, Volkswagen. He had everything. Teixeira is a mechanic.

---

*In the 1950s Lobito was the main port for passengers to the Belgian Congo. At the beginning of the decade, the Belgian Maritime Company inaugurated a weekly shuttle between Antwerp and Lobito, where the passengers heading for Katanga disembarked. Only after that two-hour stop did the ferries return to the port of Matadi, in the Lower Congo. The Antwerp-Lobito service took fourteen days.

He worked for Congo Motors, the General Motors subsidiary in the Belgian colony.

Guimarães already had bakeries, but in this mechanic's story there was not yet money for orange drinks and cakes. That came about in Elizabethville. Soon the heat demanded more: *mazute* ("diesel") was drunk, a generous mix of cola and whiskey, at afternoon's end at the Café Sport or at the Palace.

"It helped you bear up better. It went down without your noticing it."

It was hot in the Belgian Congo. Paradise is always hot, or Eve wouldn't have run around nude: in Elizabethville the man from Minho discovered swimming pools, the almost daily dances "right and left" on the esplanades with beer accompanied by mustard-soaked French fries, and the movies at the RAC theater. Teixeira, who came from a house with no inside walls and where everything was wood, had never been in a pool. He didn't know what a Thé Dançant was in wet swimsuit. The country from which he came had embedded poverty in his body.

"It was planted inside me. Where did I take a bath? Only at the fire station from time to time."

"Boga! Boga-Boga! Boga-Garoupa!"

"Boga-Boga-Boga-Boga-Garoupa, Boga-Boga-Anchova, Sardinhaa Abrótea-ao-Garoupa!"

"aBoga-Boga-Boga-Boga-Bogaaa! Boga-Boga-Boga-Anchova-Sardinha-Abróteo-Garoupa, I'm calling!"

Sea calls to desert. Desert does not answer. I imagine the difficulty of the radio: a featureless ocean and an unlit coast. Anyone would get lost, even the radio! Day will come, surely, the sun will find us, even here. Maybe the currents or the schools of fishes will drag us to the bay. It's our only hope.

"Hey, Chico, good morning!"

Finally, they reply from shore. What if it were a shipwreck? They don't ask about the boat; first they want to know about the fish.

"Middling mackerel. We were held up because of the hydraulics. We have a problem with hammerheads, which are very small. One boat's *Figueras* and the other *Ferrol*. It's short. Doesn't distribute the rings."

Four ANGESP trawlers pull out daily to work. The others are anchored in the southernmost corner of the port. They wait at the end of Rua do Tômbua, by the fish-meal and canning factories, elongated, abandoned buildings with brick chimneys taller than lighthouses, lined up along the shore. They are threatened by dunes, because a small thicket of Australian pines that prevented the sand from advancing was cut down. Tômbua is just two squares and a narrow strip of ruins extending southward.

The canneries were converted into courts where the children of the town mingle with the displaced and the demobilized from faraway provinces that those from Tômbua know only by name. The displaced find themselves flung here in the Namibe desert by the combat going on in the rest of the country, without money or the energy to expend on the long return north. They look at the strangers inside shacks, through fishnet doors and past the sentries of great junk heaps—trawlers of rotting wood, boats beached amid mud and rats, where the bedrooms are the pilot's cabin and broken masts are used for drying clothes. Some speak in distant tongues, like Kikongo and even Lingala, confirming the same scattering of the jigsaw puzzle that one observes in Lobito, where now it is peasants from the plateau who haul the nets onto land.

João de Sousa decided to cast his nets because he saw "a small mist, just a small mist"—an imperceptible scrawl left on the roll of paper by the needle of the sonar probe, which tells the depth in fathoms and the presence of schools of fish under the boat.

"Then we turned—we're here—we were about to suck up that bunch of mackerel down there, eight hundred kilos of mackerel, and then the big hose busted—no, it didn't bust, it came undone. And we were ready. During the night a cold wind wouldn't have let us work. So here we are, trying to fix the hose. Now we're heading to land..."

Before decolonization, Porto Alexandre accounted for more fish than all the other overseas ports combined. There were close to a hundred fishing boats registered. Currently, ANGESP can't keep its dozen trawlers all working at the same time, because even if the catches were sufficient, it would be impossible to convey them to the interior. It is Spanish capital to ANGESP, in a joint venture, that assures continuation of fishing in Tômbua. The long relationship between Madrid and Luanda can be traced back to 1977, to the impounding of two Spanish boats and the time when a third of Spanish shrimp came from Angola. In 1981, the two countries negotiated the construction of thirty-seven ring-net and drift-net vessels.* The largest Spanish shrimper, *Gabrielitos*, which fished on the Angolan coasts since 1978, owned twenty-two of those thirty-seven boats, originating in the Galician shipyards of Vigo, Ferrol, and Figueras. João de Sousa, boatswain of the *Garoupa*, the *Mero*, the *Anchova*, the *Sardinha*, and the *Boga*, is controlling, in Spanish, the speed of the engines: "Para, listo de Máquina, despacio, poca, media, toda..."

"You there, Boga!"

"You read me, João? Go to work, later on land I'll talk to you, over."

In one of the empty factories is the coal market. It's at the square of the tiantónios, as they call the men who make a little money carrying crates of fish or sacks of coal on their backs. The filth has charred their expressions: the tiantónios seem to share a single face, covered with an ancient film of soot and fish fat, which runs down their necks into greasy sweaters, sticky pants, and bare feet treading on ashes mixed with the dust of the ground.

"It worked, the hoses didn't break, they just came loose, so we're putting the hose back in place. We'll stay here, one night's nothing, now a little fleck of dawn's showing. Lots of wind. Lots of seals playing. We cast off. We have mackerel, six hundred, seven hundred. Haul it in to the cannery or leave it where it is?"

I waited at the door of the rudder housing, seated, with the hammering of the engines in the heart of the boat, the Southern Cross

---

*The friendship stemmed in part from two visits by President José Eduardo dos Santos to Madrid, in 1982 and 1984, where the two governments signed a voluminous package of investments in different areas. The confidence of the PSOE in the MPLA resisted even the oil shock of 1986—when the price per barrel fell from $40 to $16—with a discreet bet by Felipe González on Angola, when even allies like the USSR were cutting back credit to Luanda. It was Spanish cooperation that in 1991 financed the creation of the Rapid Intervention Police, the "ninjas" who the following year won the battle of Luanda—just as it was the PSOE that guaranteed the largest part of the funds for the electoral campaign of the MPLA and José Eduardo dos Santos in 1992.

twinkling at the height of the slight undulation before dawn, the slow rhythm of the dropping of the buoys, the cadence of the hoarse whistle of a fisherman on deck.

I awoke a short time later, curled up, fallen backward, wrapped in canvas, with my head inside the small cabin with radios and life jackets. Someone was vomiting.

No, it was the barking of the seals, their craziness: hundreds, thousands forming an irregular carpet on the surface of the sea, barking in whirls and leaps, as if the sea were frying. João de Sousa went crazy too at the sight of this circus: the seals gathered to feast on the fish caught in the nets.

"Look at those jokers! They eat the fish, kilos every day. They eat and shit, eat and shit! A mess. They toss the fish and catch them, and fight over them."

The glow of the moon was on the seals until the sun made its way finally from the Tômbua side to break through the clouds and cast jets of light across the water. Only the morning star remained in the sky, and on the eastern horizon, the edge of the sea lined with white cliffs. The day arrived faster than the closing of the ring of floats—the two ends are raised by a pulley until the net is nothing but a sack of fish to be hauled on board. First you have to shoo away the last of the seals. The sailors yell and bang iron objects against metal of the trawler: the most stubborn ones are pried off with bamboo.

"The *Abrótea* got three tons, but that's all. Lots of wind."

"What about the rest of the boats?"

"Nothing."

"No sign of bumper, it's all mackerel."

"Is it down? Did it go down, or did a rat chew through the wire?"

Boatswain João de Sousa did not take me to the Bay of Tigers. We returned with the mackerel. On the way back, there was fried mackerel for breakfast. Only the coffee wasn't nauseating. As it entered port, the boat was surrounded by children floating on small pieces of cork or polyurethane carved in the shape of a boat. They came over to the *Garoupa*, hoping to get the fish that fell into the water when the crates were thrown from sailor to sailor, from the deck to the pier. The small fishermen-vultures paddle and maneuver rapidly with their hands, fighting over mackerel, shivering from the cold because their legs drag in the water. There is space on each piece of cork or polyurethane for only half a dozen fish, which they then sell in the street for fifty kwanzas apiece.

The day is ending as I wait for a ride to Namibe. A great solitude has come to this desert that lies at my feet, to the small waves that lap at the wooden floating bridge and at the fleet of garbage that rusts the sand. It turns colder.

Carlos, an employee of the cannery, has a vinyl box in his jeep that he received today from the Algarve. In his collection is a LP from the seventies, *Rust Live*. I don't recall the band.

Two sailors have finished their maintenance chores on the *Garoupa* and come over to listen to the shortwave, the BBC in Hong Kong. The timing is right. Englishmen and Chinese, at a distance that depresses me, are celebrating the transfer of an extremely beautiful bay.

"It's over."

"Over? It's midnight there. The guys have already had dinner — they're a day older than we are."

Brigadier General Kalutotai, lord of war in the Caiundo region, can order me back, allow me to go on, or see to my disappearance — nothing is easier in this province, they warned me in Menongue. It wouldn't be a crime. In the Lands at the End of the World, lives evaporate on their own. While he decides, Kalutotai can take advantage of my presence.

He interrogated me the first day, in detail. He called Brigadier Osvaldo to write down my entire lullaby in a notebook. Then he spun his web.

"The Movement and we ourselves have nothing against your passage, no. But there is the problem of transport. The Kamaz isn't viable, because it uses seven hundred liters of diesel to get to Calai. The only driver who goes there, Abel, left day before yesterday, and we don't know when he'll be back. The only possible vehicle is my jeep. It's that Land Cruiser on the blocks over there. It's missing the clutch from the gearbox. If you can arrange one, my own driver can take you to Cuangar."

Kalutotai expected me, in the middle of the desert, to dig up a clutch for an all-terrain vehicle — "1947 model, don't forget" — and, right under UNAVEM's nose, hand it over to the general, along with several barrels of fuel, thus violating the international embargo of UNITA.

I went back to Menongue and its two workshops, UNAVEM's and the one run by a Portuguese named Lopes. Neither had a clutch for such an old model. But I located a Land Cruiser just like Kalutotai's in the junkyard of a Catholic mission, in a barren field. It was sitting on blocks, doubtlessly a characteristic of the 1947 model. Behind the shed and the jeep, lying separately, was the gearbox. Intact, massive, heavy, and sealed.

"Go get key 14," the garage owner ordered.

"We don't have it," the mechanic's apprentice answered. "It's in the other car. It'll be here soon."

"When?"

"At noon for sure."

It was 12:15. We agreed I'd come back at 1:30, to give the key and the owner time, but when we returned to the mission, the box was still sealed.

"Key 14 isn't here yet. The car didn't come."

At 2:30, with or without me, a truck from the Zambian battalion was leaving Menongue for Caiundo. It couldn't wait, because UNAVEM vehicles weren't authorized to travel after sundown. The Brazilian captain, a man named Spies, who had given me a ride that morning, was heading back to Caiundo even earlier.

"I'll take the whole thing! How much?"

"Three hundred dollars."

Moreira, one of the "blue helmets" of the Portuguese Transmissions Company, exploded with indignation.

"Three hundred dollars for that piece of crap! For that kind of money you can buy the whole damn car! Tell him to hop a pig!"

Bargaining. In the junkyard lay the gearbox: a strongbox, a lifeline, my passport to Calai.

"One hundred."

"One fifty, minimum. Check with the priest."

A mistake. The priest was about to leave, and I should have let him go. Greed: I ruined myself because of fifty dollars and thirty seconds.

"I can't sell you the whole box, my brother. Take the part you need and leave the rest, which might be useful for our cars. You can take the box to Mr. Lopes and open it there."

We took the box. It was heavy as lead and spread oil like measles. Lopes, of course, wasn't in his workshop or at home.

"He went to look for some woodcutters, on the Bié road. By the end of the afternoon he'll be back, for sure."

For sure! Moreira started cursing. He was on his day off. He had got up that morning imagining it would be a good day. Simple desires, going for a swim in the river. We asked for key 14, and it came. We asked for others, of every size, and attacked the box with them. People came to our aid with screwdrivers, adjustable wrenches, box wrenches, chisels, a pair of French pliers, and the technical-moral assistance of Lopes's Angolan mechanics. We finally called for a crowbar and hammers to disembowel the box. We glistened: the sweat, the oil, the fury, the shiny blood from broken fingernails and battered fingers. The box finally split in two and drenched our feet with greenish oil. We panted in victory. But the bearings refused to come out from the brake, keeping us from removing the clutch.

The combat lasted over three hours—a bachelor's degree in auto mechanics. Fortunately Spies had been delayed in Menongue because of a generator. He waited for me.

"We'll be part of the night traveling. Relax now, my brother. We're going to do everything we can to see the last of you."

The next morning, after an eight-day search, I appeared before Kalutotai to report the mission's failure. The spider listened to me impatiently, then returned to the start of the game.

"But there's one there. Why didn't you bring the whole box?"

"It wasn't for sale, General. Forget about Menongue. The part's to be found only in Luanda."

I don't know which was more frustrating: finding out, after all that effort, that the priest's gearbox didn't have a clutch like the brigadier's;

discovering that Kalutotai had good cars hidden in the bush, waiting for the inevitable return of fighting; or learning that UNAVEM suspected the existence of these clandestine vehicles but officially saw only the 1947 model and the Kamaz with no fuel.

I gave Kalutotai back the broken clutch of his Land Cruiser. I wasn't entitled to a boatman on the way back. Alone, afoot, like a supplicant at the throne of the river, I slowly rowed to the opposite bank. Kalutotai, emperor of these waters, still had not read my future. At night, Spies, who's a look-alike of the actor Rutger Hauer (*The Hitcher*) in reduced scale, offered me mate tea from southern Brazil.

"Capitalism is exploitation. Communism brings no progress. But this country is poverty itself. There's only one law: whoever can, rules, and anyone with sense obeys."

Mozart and the wind glide calmly over the yellow grass that reaches to our shoulders. We walk in single file. London is in direct contact with us, and the savanna ruffles with the euphoric symphony. I grasp the Royal Albert Hall in one hand, pointing the chromed antenna as the sharpness of the orchestra fades and returns. The guerrillas with me keep up the solemn grainy sound of boots on soil. The roar of the river comes closer. We have to cross the current at the spot where the bridge was dynamited in 1975. On the other side a car will arrive. Today is different: we left in the morning, with the sun in front of us, hoping to make it to our destination in daylight. That won't happen, of course. But Mozart, the orchestra in the river, violins sawing the rushes, in a canoe . . .

A man is on the other side of the river. The savanna runs southward, far south of the ruins of Dirico, in the lands where the water overflows miraculously into electricity. A man sits in Namibia, on the mute other side of his life. I don't know him yet, and he sits in the shade, wearing shorts. I will meet him later and farther ahead, always by the river. Among sacks of flour and oil, delving with eagle eyes into a war that taught him to kill but from which he never learned to derive pleasure.

He stood up.

John Van Der Merwe was an exceptional soldier in the South African forces that invaded Angola in 1975. He had under his command a battalion of Angolan bushmen, the Black Arrows, who along with the Buffalo Battalion swept—a verb he likes and uses—the troops of Agostinho Neto and Fidel Castro from Cuando Cubango up to Kwanza Norte. John Van Der Merwe's military career began only shortly before the invasion, in February of that year: Omega Base, the Caprivi strip, Southwest Africa, after nine days at the Hotel Metropole, in Pretoria, after a conversation with a general of the apartheid, the general who created him.

By order of that general he was given four uniforms, a pistol, and a driver as far as Omega. It was at that base that the South African army, incorporating some Portuguese military men and settlers, recruited and trained the Arrows and the Buffalos. John Van Der Merwe's first job was to recover the bushmen who had fled Angola and were scattered along the right bank of the Cubango-Okavango. They were excellent trackers, shrewd combatants, men of uncommon resistance. PIDE had used them extensively, trained at various bases to ferret out the guerrillas, "Angolans older than the black people of Angola, without villages, people of the forest, who eat here and there." At Omega the bushmen were organized into two companies. Their first impact on the theater of war was with SWAPO, where Jamba is today, in the Angolan border zone of Luiana and Nambangando. Operation Sabena quickly followed: a dizzying advance northward in the direction of Luanda.

"We swept everything from Dirico to Serpa Pinto and from Serpa Pinto to Pereira d'Eça, where we had the first hand-to-hand with the MPLA, from August 12 to 14, 1975."

He insists that initially Pretoria's intention was not to invade Angola but to clear out the border of Southwest Africa with the colony.

"It was the ravages of the Cubans, it was the provocation, that forced us to make them retreat. If the objective had been to sweep Angola, we'd have done it in two weeks, four tops."

But South Africa didn't want to come in. Or didn't want the world to know it had come in. The Arrows and the Buffalos would occupy a city and afterward remain hidden in the bush for four or five days before advancing to the next ambush, the next locality, the next destruction: they spent three months straight in combat until Novo Redondo. John Van Der Merwe remembers: there were many acts of cowardice, many impediments. Pretoria both wanted to and didn't want to, while its troops pressured to advance. In all that time, he lost only two men "and one in an accident. He was a sergeant by then."

It was his one hundred sixty bushmen (with five Portuguese incorporated into the structure of the South African command) who constituted the attack force. The Buffalos, the occupying contingent

with eight hundred men, would come afterward, despite having gar-
nered the laurels of the campaign, which is understandable because
the commander in chief of both forces was Colonel Bretemburg, the
founder of the battalion.

On Independence Day, November 11, he was in Novo Redondo,
without succeeding in launching a bridge toward the north because
the enemy fire was coming only a hundred meters from the destroyed
roadway, and in such a situation no military engineering unit can
function effectively. He also remembers that day: five MIGs, flying toward the coast, almost grazed his head but dropped no bombs. The
Arrows, with a column of twenty-eight trucks, couldn't get past the
falls in Kwanza Norte, and in the Gabela mountain range they were
buffeted hellishly by FAPLA 122 mm cannons. But besides that combat front with the FNLA-UNITA combined forces, another one of
white South Africans was advancing on the capital from the east.
From the north, as close as Catete, Holden Roberto's FNLA.

"We were suffocating Luanda. But we lost the war in Catete.
When you advance on a city, you have to have artillery cover, and
Holden Roberto didn't want to bombard Luanda and kill innocent
children. The black man put him in the middle, and from then on
there were disagreements and a lot of confusion. The South African
general took a disliking to him, got on a helicopter to Uíge, and went
back to South Africa. He canceled the operation."

All these facts are from John Van Der Merwe's head. Like the fact
that, with Luanda about to fall, Agostinho Neto and other leaders
stayed fifteen miles away, safely aboard a ship. Another fact for him is
that the war was already lost because of the United States, which ma-
nipulated Operation Sabena from behind the scenes and, in its indecision, wasted precious time "at a stage when Cubans were coming
into Angola day and night." Brezhnev and Kissinger, an agreement,
two withdrawals, case closed.

The column of bushmen set out from Novo Redondo on December 21, relieved by white soldiers (there was a mere score of them in
the Arrows, including the sergeant: officers, panzers, doctors, logistics
personnel...). Christmas was spent in the rear guard. He was supposed

to return to the front on January 5, but on that date the troops from Pretoria were withdrawing.

"I don't know if it was good or bad. It was bad, because Angola has never since been stable."

The South African defeat meant the undoing of another plan: handing the country back to Holden Roberto and the removal of UNITA, because "the FNLA had a completely different ideology: it wanted the whites in the country as they were before; it wanted power but with the whites still there. It proved that several times. UNITA, wherever it appeared, killed, robbed, and ravaged. The UPA massacres happened a lot at the very beginning, in 1961, but in those years Jonas Savimbi was with Holden Roberto..."

John Van Der Merwe and his men returned to Caprivi on January 5, 1976. He was made first sergeant of the battalion and commanded the Arrows until 1978, at Omega Base, as regimental sergeant-major, with disciplinary and operational jurisdiction. Three years of operations against SWAPO, never in Namibian territory—"here in the interior there were no ambushes, no guerrilla nests"—and never in conjunction with UNITA. The Arrows unleashed operations in western Zambia—in an initial phase SWAPO had bases on some of the islands in the Cuando River and on the Zambezi plain—and in Angola, "very deep into Angola." One of the main SWAPO training bases was at Henrique de Carvalho, two thousand kilometers from Caprivi! As regimental sergeant-major he had command functions at the base but participated in many of those operations, because "I was an individual operationally appreciated by my men, and they asked me to go with them. Even the officers running the companies felt safe when I was there. There was a strong tie; either we all die, or nobody dies!"

In 1978 he felt he'd had enough. He asked for transfer to Pretoria, switched from infantry to engineering, and took a nine-month course in that field. That brought him back to Omega: the airstrip construction had been going on for three years, and the army needed someone who could finish the job. In just nine weeks, having arrived as a machinist, he rose to head of the team with an engineer and topographer and got the strip in shape to receive thirteen hundred meters of asphalt.

He "fell in love with it" but didn't last long as a soldier-worker. He was contacted by his old commander General Zangos, who invited — "or almost compelled" — him to go to the Recces, the elite among the elite of South African troops. Six months of training, four hundred men selected from a pool of two hundred thousand: in the end, five or six were chosen, and each of them was a war machine.

The Recces began to recruit Buffalos because of the demands of Pretoria's new military commitments:

"African tactics are different from European. The black man adapts better, he's tougher. He doesn't need food or water. He doesn't fight better — because without a white man, a black can't do a thing, it's not worth the trouble — but he knows the terrain, and when he trusts the white man, he holds his sector."

What the Recces wanted from John Van Der Merwe was to serve as interpreter between the Buffalos and the South Africans and to take charge of their maintenance and their families: supply ambulances and medication, food and cars with civilian plates to move about in South Africa (and guarantee that they didn't say anything they shouldn't en route), military instruction, and so on. That wasn't what he was interested in.

"I gave up, or rather, I didn't give up. I told the commander I wanted to go farther. Or else I'd go back to engineering."

What he had in mind was the parachute corps. South African parachutists are also reconnaissance commandos. Two men are launched by night forty kilometers from Luanda and have to complete their mission unaided, get the desired information to Pretoria: where the refinery is located, how it works, how many soldiers and what type of weapons they use. Afterward, a rendezvous at an agreed-upon time and place, evacuation in a rubber raft, and a submarine waiting offshore.

It was the reconnaissance paratroopers that he wanted. They were the support group. An attack on the general barracks in Luanda; or a prisoner whom it's necessary to evacuate from a cell in the Angolan capital; or a Recces jump from thirty-five thousand feet, so the plane won't be detected. At that altitude, everyone, pilot and jumpers alike, uses an oxygen mask. The jumper knows he'll fall somewhere in a thirty-kilometer radius, unless he's unlucky enough to land inside an enemy camp, but that doesn't happen, because deserted spots are chosen, and sometimes even an infiltrated commando is on the ground waiting for you...

"I did a lot of jumping."

John Van Der Merwe was in the Recces from November 1978 until 1983. It wasn't easy to get out when he decided to, but finally he was authorized to transfer to Windhoek (where he had been briefly prior to Durban), once again as RCM in the construction battalion of the South-West Africa Engineering Regiment (SWAER). That was his operational preretirement. A year later, he returned to civilian life and would have done so earlier if Pretoria hadn't blackmailed him over his legal situation: it was only in 1984, after a strongly worded letter to the South African governor, that he received authorization for residence in the colony of Southwest Africa. The authorization was granted in January; the paratrooper left the corps in August.

"I can tell you: I was forced to embrace that life. But I always fought for something better and was very successful. I was much decorated. They've been here three times to try to get me to rejoin the forces."

Of those nine years, John Van Der Merwe, a pawn in the destabilization policy of Pieter Botha in southern Africa with its "war in the jungle," recalls a formidable army unrivaled in all the continent. An exemplary organization in which nothing failed, nothing was lacking: troops that, wherever they were, appeared at 9 P.M. with a Dakota that dropped food, water, and tobacco; troops that, if they received a radio SOS from operatives surrounded in the middle of Angola, would get a plane in the air and in a few minutes wipe out the enemy.

"And at the end the pilots would say: 'If you need me again, call me, please!' The pilots flying the Impala, which is one sonofabitch of an aircraft. A beautiful plane. It can fly high enough to disappear from sight, or it can skim the treetops. It decimates a column."

He remembers other things, but they take more time to be remembered. The first memory, and the most difficult to speak about, is the day he held a grenade with the pin removed against his chest, so as not to die except by his own hand.

It happened in Benguela after the capture of the airport (without resistance) by the combined force. At the end of the runway was, and still is, a soccer field. The South African column camped there. It was caught by surprise the following day by FAPLA and Cuban troops, with reinforcements coming down from Novo Redondo. Fire from every side, in a circle, at over four hundred soldiers who had the misfortune to lose their artillery by a well-placed shot from the enemy that took out the mortar squad — eight men, two dead on the spot and the rest seriously wounded, the equipment useless. Heavy fire, constantly increasing after FAPLA realized that the South African mortars had fallen silent. The commando managed to break through the encirclement, in a vehicle that made it past four mortars to go for reinforcements — the Buffalos. He stayed and, like the others, could see the end approaching.

"Our gang saw we were lost. Then it was spontaneous: each of us started sweeping hand-to-hand. When they saw us coming straight at them, they began to retreat. I put the grenade in my hand and thought only of God and my family. My last day. We all had our grenades ready and would let them go only if the enemy laid a hand on us: we would die and take one of the enemy with us. We removed the pins and held the levers tight against our chests. We shouted, 'Easy! Easy! They're afraid, take it easy!' And suddenly — we got the hell out of there. Zigzagging like snakes. We swept a couple of dozen of them and left. But a lot of our people didn't make it..."

August 15, 1975. Perhaps the worst day in John Van Der Merwe's life.

"I'm not a killer. You kill only in defense: we're trained for that, it's part of a soldier's life. In combat I carried a lot of men on these shoulders, blacks, enemies, to safety. I saved a lot of people. I never had the urge to eliminate people. And that's why I couldn't take it any longer. I was forced to stay for more years, because they wouldn't give me my papers... I have bad stretches in my past. But killing for pleasure wasn't one of them."

There is a man standing on the other side of the river.

Ben-Ben, future chief of the general staff of FALA and dauphin of Jonas Savimbi, was a mere second lieutenant when he went to the home of João Miranda in Dirico to escort him to his death. João Miranda had been under house arrest for twenty days, because UNITA had accused him of being a PIDE agent, a reactionary, a settler, a fascist. The prisoner did not recognize himself in any of the accusations and objected especially to the last of them.

Born in Bragança, Portugal, in 1945 and living in Angola since the age of eleven, he had family and a story in Dirico. The administration, the police, and many friends in the small town tried to prevent his conviction, but UNITA insisted on linking him to PIDE. The solution was to flee. Covachan, an agent of the Portuguese Socialist Party (later on the security staff of President Ramalho Eanes), a friend from the corps, secretly arranged diesel fuel so that João Miranda could make it to Mucusso.

His wife, Elizabete, and their daughters left in another car in the opposite direction, under the pretext of going shopping in Huambo. The plan was to cross the Cubango by canoe, at Calai. When he arrived in Mucusso and crossed the border to South-West Africa, the South African authorities responded quickly. They communicated with the command in Rundu, which promptly sent troops to receive the family in Calai.

The Miranda family was safe. The commandant of the local police, Inspector Erasmos, installed them in a government guest house. That same afternoon General Loots (retired), a veteran of World War II, showed up, accompanied by a Portuguese officer from Madeira, Lieutenant Silva.

João Miranda was interviewed and informed that at the end of the month he would receive a salary, retroactive to the first day he fled Angola.

The family was later transferred to Grootfontein, in the northern interior of the colony, for greater protection. The Mirandas spent a month in the boredom of the largest base in Namibia, in a tent, without any information about what they were going to do. João had not lived in barracks since 1969: he had done two years of military service when the colonial war in Angola began heating up. Two miserable years in a poor army that gave four days' rations to soldiers who spent two weeks in the jungle, chewing raw manioc and drinking dirty water from puddles, trudging on foot because vehicles were rare. Grootfontein was a great base indeed.

There came a day when an individual appeared in Grootfontein with a work permit in the name of João Miranda and a Hercules C-130, who took the entire family to Pretoria.

A tall blond lady was waiting, along with a black limousine, both from the state; two interviews at the general staff in Pretoria; questions, lots of questions, what did he think of Angola, of the war, of independence, of white flight, of the future and whether the future was a step backward. Everything happened too fast. Without lifting a finger, the Portuguese João Miranda had joined the army of apartheid. His first mission was in the Caprivi Strip, Southwest Africa.

"The general welcomed me in Afrikaans and told me to forget Portuguese, told me to forget the past. I just smiled at the man, I couldn't express myself, didn't have a language I could speak with him. A Portuguese soldier translated for me: 'I thank you because your country has taken me in.' I was received with open arms. I didn't volunteer, wasn't even asked. I was simply inducted. Yoked, as the blacks say. I accepted humbly. I wanted a job. I didn't want to go to Portugal, obviously. My belongings were in Dirico. I had nothing. To show up in Portugal the way soldiers do, with nothing, would have been tough.

"I told him: Nobody can say anything bad about the South Africans; I don't allow it. They've accepted thousands of Portuguese like me. I was lucky enough to go to Pretoria, have an apartment that wanted for nothing, benefits. They would even give me money if I asked for it. I didn't pay a cent for the apartment, four or five rooms, completely furnished—from toilet paper to soap. My wife just shopped, and in those days she could fill the kitchen for 150 rands. Today I pay that for a pack of cigarettes."

João Miranda is sitting on the terrace of his house, in Mukwé, with the Cubango River at his back and Angola beyond the rapids, two decades behind, well beyond the rapids. He once again has a food store, a serious business and his own, as well as a house in Chitembo, to the west—south of the Dirico savanna. He wasted years in that store in Mukwé when it belonged to others and he was an employee of bandits: José Francisco Lopes and Arlindo Maia, the two Portuguese who ran FRAMA, the company that in the 1980s served Pieter Botha's government by putting weapons in UNITA's hands in exchange for ivory, diamonds, and hardwoods.

He is seated and wearing shorts. He is a bit less of an unknown to me.

At the general's order, in 1975 he was given four uniforms, a pistol, and a driver as far as Omega. They also told him:

"Starting now, you're South African. You're going to a new country. At Omega that's the name you'll use. You're another person, not João, just John. John Van Der Merwe."

On his desk are two wired phones, two cell phones, and a walkie-talkie.

"Hello?... Try to get her by radio. I have to talk her. I also need to speak to Michael... Yes, please... No, he's not here. Call him in London!... He already left? Thanks."

Paulo de Sousa's office in Lusaka is a cage of positive stress. Inside is the busiest man in Zambia. The space is modest, and yet how much goes on there: sausage manufacture and advertising layouts, radio magazines and sour cream production, fashion shows and chicken farming, beauty contests and management consultancy, amateur theater, coffee export, film criticism . . . Paulo is all that. At the same time.

Paulo de Sousa was born in Ndola, in the Zambian copper belt, the son of Portuguese immigrants. (His parents met when Paulo's father, who worked for a German beer company, took English lessons from Paulo's mother.)

"So, until we go through customs, we can't do any of the rest? You keep everything safe. Leave it at the door, I'll bring it here when this is over. Okay, thanks a lot."

Paulo's jeep was charged a 25 percent import tax at customs, "but since the car is in a certain sense commercial, I can get it through for 15 percent."

Until the age of six and a half he studied in Zambia. Afterward he was sent to a private school in Ermesinde, where he repeated the first grade because it was his first year of study in Portuguese. Then he returned to Zambia and made the classic Portuguese mistake of wanting to carry on the family tradition: his grandfather had been a blacksmith, his father, too, worked as a blacksmith, so he would be a mechanical engineer.

Two options presented themselves: London or Johannesburg. Paulo didn't like Europe and didn't want to be able to see his family only once a year. He finished his degree in industrial engineering, realizing that he wouldn't be happy in mechanical engineering.

"I am? Thanks. Hello? Nomsa, you have good news for me? Excellent! What time? . . . Ten A.M., all right? Okay, and what are the jobs? An opening for a nanny and the other for a cook. Do I interview them one at a time? . . . No, no, we want a man or a woman for the cook, a woman for the nanny. She already has a maid. Okay. You're sure? Are they trained? We'll see them Monday."

Paulo is looking for employees. He is adviser to the head of the largest economic group in Zambia. It includes everything, from public relations to all the logistics necessary to oil the empire. The Galaun Group expanded, then needed to create enterprises to meet its needs, because the market did not provide those services: milk products, soft drinks, meats, construction, wood, a supermarket chain (the only one in Zambia), seven coffee plantations, and now currency exchange.

It was always Paulo's dream "to be in the arts." In Ermesinde he began with theater and poetry readings, in South Africa he was part of a project called R. A. G. (Remember and Give). It's difficult to do theater in Zambia, there are few amateurs and staging even one show a year is a feat. Paulo's grand plan is to save some of the money that the Galaun Group pays him and take a course in theater at the Actors Studio in New York.

"Hello? Thank you ... So you only made one? Okay ... Brilliant. He's coming by for lunch, and I'll show it to him, so you can have it this afternoon. You're a dear. I'm very pleased."

Zambia "is a small town," and social life is fragmented into groups, in "an almost indirect racism": the mulattoes, the Greeks, the "white Zambians" (with two subdivisions: those with South African roots, "with a colonialist mentality, and those who accept that it was here that they were born and it's here that they're going to do what's best for themselves"). Shortly before returning from South Africa in 1991, Paulo met the organizers of the Miss World contest. After a battle with a Zambian competitor who had obtained the license, he took on the task of organizing the Miss Zambia Pageant. He also got involved with fashion, opening a modeling agency—Splendour—with the first Miss Zambia, Elizabeth. He was the chaperon when Elizabeth represented her country at the Miss World contest. Scandal in Lusaka: "There were ministers asking why a white man would want to help a Zambian woman."

"Hello? ... What's wrong with that chair? No, it's not mine. It doesn't have wheels. Wheels! Do you know where Andrew is? Send Andrew to me."

Miss Zambia had to overcome another problem: in a country where many traditional ceremonies are performed by bare-breasted women, legs are taboo. Paulo had to educate his countrymen about the beauty business and explain that parading in a swimsuit is part of the international rules. He succeeded.

"Yes?...You should have done that at lunchtime, Francis, we're leaving now! Where's Henri? Okay, let him be, you go and make it quick."

Two years ago the Miss Zambia winner was a young woman, "black but very light-skinned," daughter of a white father and a mulatto mother. A new scandal: at the time, the country was boiling over the demand that the president be "Zambian for at least three generations," an absurdity in a country independent for only three decades and one whose recent history is a mosaic of migrations from all of central Africa.

"Hello?...Yes, Evans. No, I'm not, there's someone with me. I'm afraid I don't have an answer for you, I'm waiting for a phone call from the director. Thanks."

On Saturdays, Paulo hosts a weekly talk show on Radio Phoenix in which he introduces himself as a "citizen of the world" to avoid problems: it is still ticklish to be white in Zambia and affirm your Zambian identity. "I'm not black, but I'm African." Some were confused when Paulo appeared on national television screens hosting, along with a black Zambian man, *Sissy's Music Spotlight*. They showed clips and interviews with the support of Radio France International. After more than twenty years of television in Zambia, Paulo was the first white to go on the air as a host.

"Ah, you finally found it? Thanks, I'll write it down here."

When Zambia received on video the premieres from Hollywood on the first flight to arrive from the United States, Paulo also did film criticism for newspapers and magazines in Lusaka. That ended: with the introduction of cable, the government tightened the rules, and the video clubs closed. In 1994, his passion for cinema led him to join, as Zambian executive producer, the team that filmed *Red Flower*, a short subject made by Canadians.

Paulo has a Bemba name (from the Ndola region, where he was born), given him by the models: Chibale. It means "large plate," in the sense of generous, one who always has something to offer even if it's not money. The word has another meaning: hardheaded, stubborn. In the street, where he is greeted by people he doesn't know, there's another nickname: Mr. Zambia.

Lobito, 14 June 1997

"It was when we stopped in Sumbe. For them to take off the luggage, for him to pay. I put the money in his hand, but he didn't come back."

"He'll spend it all, you can be sure of that. I bet he's running around the market right now with two or three girls. The money should be enough."

"It's ten grand!"

The entire car laughs at the old man, who is in a dramatic and comical situation.

"I'll get to Lobito without the money . . ."

It wasn't just the old man's problem. It was equally the driver's.

"If you don't have the money, you don't go. Better get out."

"No. I'm going."

The driver pulled out.

"Stop, father, stop! I'll look for him. Back up, I'll look for him in the market."

"Listen, there are passengers, kota. I'm not backing up. Get out now, or we're never leaving. Make up your mind."

We went a couple of hundred meters and stopped at a gasoline pump. The old man's indecision couldn't resist the opportunity.

"Let me off. I'm getting out."

Outside was a woman who looked like a stuffed sack.

"Is there room?"

There were fourteen in the nine-seat van. No one wanted to trade a thin old man for a fat woman.

"There's room! I see some! Let me on, I have to go to Benguela."

"You'll have to pay for two seats, lady," joked the youth in front of me. The lady got on. Confusion. For any of us to wiggle a little finger, we would all have to get out and redo the jigsaw puzzle of the entire cargo.

"Push hard, lift the bag! Move that basket! Put your foot someplace else! Put my shopping bag back there, please!"

Bags held between knees, backpacks between legs, flour sacks beneath seats, and bowls and pans. When everything was finally in place, there was no room for the driver's helper, the youth who opened the folding side door and called out, "Lobito!," to the passengers in the market and took the tickets at the end of the trip. He had a Zairean accent and an incredible gaze. He refused to be photographed ("Not even if the photo comes out right now and I can keep it, not even"). He sat in front of me, straddling a small kitchen stool, with one leg wedged between the door and the adolescent girl in shorts, the other leg mortised between her legs. Two shy people, five hours in a van with nowhere to put their hands.

"Lovebirds..."

No one got off at Canjala. Through the window came live chickens with droppings on their feathers, a stalk of bananas, and a piece of meat raised to the glass, it had just been cut, still dripping blood. Gruesome, glistening in the twilight. The fat woman made the worst possible purchase: a large chunk of dried buffalo meat transformed the van into a torture chamber.

"Hey, lady, put that thing on the floor."

The road to Lobito is a disaster, among the worst in Angola (rivaling the stretch between Caxito and Quibaxe).

"This road, never seen anything like it!"

"It's a punishment!"

"God our father!"

"How much longer are they going to punish the people? We've been punished enough!"

"Angola isn't worth it! With the money Angola has, it could at least fix the roads."

"This government! The only thing it does is what we don't need. What it doesn't do is what we need."

"You think the government rides in cars? Not likely."

"The thing to do is grab a muadiê there in Luanda and stick him in a truck, not in some sleeping car, in a truck with a driver, and put him on the road, back and forth! Then he'd see what the roads are like!"

The van braked abruptly again, ending up in a back breaking pothole. At every moment it seemed we were about to go off the road, and on the bumps all the passengers braced themselves against the ceiling.

"The driver's going too fast."

"He's not going fast, I've seen fast driving in Luanda. From back here it looks like he's not watching the road, but he is. He aims for the potholes and doesn't miss."

"In '89, at the time of the Gabela celebrations, all of us from Sumbe went. As soon as the week was over, the road was closed. The governor went back by helicopter. We had to wait."

The conversation had shifted from the road to the war.

"In this zone it was incredible! Getting through here was—"

The helper finishes the fat woman's thought by making the gesture of fear with his fingers hanging like a jellyfish.

"They were burning cars. Used to be a lot of cars around, but they've been hauled off to junkyards."

On the south side of the Canjala bridge are painted the words: IT IS FORBIDDEN TO CROSS THE BRIDGE WITH A STRANGE FACE.

"King Cazembe is a very dark black man, good-looking with a short beard, red eyes, very talky with white businessmen who come to his court to negotiate." This is the judgment of Pedro João Baptista. It was written almost two hundred years ago. Baptista, with his companion Anastácio Francisco, made one of the most unjustly forgotten African crossings, because it was one of the most notable. Two semi-illiterate slaves were the first to link Angola to Mozambique by land—and did so on foot.

The pombeiros, usually mulattoes or blacks, represented commercial interests in zones of the Angolan backlands where whites could not penetrate. Baptista and Francisco were trusted pombeiros of Lieutenant Colonel Francisco Honorato da Costa, director of the Mucari Fair in Cassanje, Angola. This was the most active nucleus of attempts to do business directly with Muataiânvua (the Lunda emperor). The feat of reaching Tete, arriving at the westernmost frontier of Portuguese penetration from the Indian Ocean, took time—from 1802 to 1814. But Baptista and Francisco succeeded in anticipating by half a century the "first" crossing of the continent by David Livingstone, from Luanda to Quelimane (1854—56)—surely a bitter irony for the missionary whose passion for Africa somewhat exceeded that for Africans. The pombeiros got there before all the European explorers of renown who often, in the second half of the nineteenth century, made use of, ignored, or, in the case of a few incorrigibles, disdained the delightful diary of their journey.

The two pombeiros broke the tragic series of attempts to penetrate Central Africa and set to right the most recent disaster. In October 1798, the Portuguese Lacerda e Almeida reached Cazembe from Tete, but there the expedition ended: Lacerda succumbed to diseases and exhaustion and no longer had the strength to note in his diary the reception he was afforded in Cazembe, where he died and was buried a few days after his arrival. A decade later, to Baptista's great surprise, "King Cazembe has Teapottes, Cups, Bowls, Bottles, Spoones & Forks of silver, & Porcelain plates from Lisbon, fine Hattes, Bukkles for Shoes, monney in gold dubloones & half dubloones, manifold courtesys of Christianity to remove his Hatte & offer greetings, he has all the Utensils of a white man that have remained there, the late Senhor Governor Lacerda & of other whites living in the same village [. . .] because there is none to carry the goods to Tete."

Baptista and Francisco were in advance not only of Livingstone but also of Vernon Cameron, Hermenegildo Capelo, and Roberto Ivens. Nor are their medals of misfortune any less epic—suffice it to mention that a week after beginning the expedition, they were captured and held for two years by a tribal chieftain, until word arrived to Honorato da Costa, who paid a ransom so they could continue!

It is not, however, praise for their extraordinary experience that matters; it is the record. Baptista wrote a diary that, each and every day he added data about the route, served European knowledge of Central Africa as the invention of a geography through the word. To grammar and science (in its nineteenth-century canons), that word was rough and inexact, but it had the same force as the intimate "songs" of the Australian aborigines, whose territory is created in the very act of chanting it.* The paths, the stones, the rivers, the desert, the lizards, and the spirits of ancestors were always there but were only (re)born as a place when they were spoken.

Being the first who entered and returned to tell the story, Pedro João Baptista enjoyed the most enviable of a traveler's privileges: the primordial virginity of seeing. For him, as for the aborigines who unravel by memory the lines that cross the seeming emptiness of Australia, there was a superlative truth: in the personal map of the foreigner—and it is he who is in question here. Before his telling it, there was no territory, there was only news of it. For that very reason, an arrival is at the same time a creation (the place emerges), a mapping (it receives coordinates), and an archaeology (because all that is presupposes or reveals all that has been). At the limit, as happens with the aborigines' "lines," the traveler *is* merely his account, he identifies with it because from it he extracts his identity; he doesn't exist outside the map; traveler and map are a single entity.

The "song" of Baptista offers a bizarre narrator—a "rarity of quality," he would say; the pombeiro is doubly foreign. He is as foreign to the Portuguese who have him as a slave as he is to the suspicious

*See *The Songlines*, by Bruce Chatwin.

Africans conscious of white acculturation. They sent Baptista to see the Other, and he goes, seeing an Other different from any seen by the European explorers. Baptista is Other, can be strange, an enemy, or mysterious, but he is not exotic; he is a brother and lives in a familial cradle—so many of Capelo and Ivens's astonishments would seem infantile to the pombeiro! Baptista is the bat that an old Ganguela drew for me in the sand of Cuíto Cuanavale.

"Bat." This drawing relates the loneliness of this species: the bat was expelled by the birds because it has teeth instead of feathers and was expelled by the rats because it has wings.

One of the delights of Baptista's diary is his style. Slave of a fair where the greatest enlightenment was that of a backwoods soldier (i.e., scant), Baptista was not a man of letters, nor was he an illiterate. He wrote awkwardly, but saw with genius. Nothing escaped him, as this description of Tete proves: from the confusion resulting from the exile of the court in Brazil because of "great Bonaparte" to the "disunion that in the said Village there was between one and the other," including the uncertainty of who ruled, the Portuguese or the English. This combination produced a sensitive text, very rich despite its roughness of form. The pombeiro invented an anarchic grammar in which direct discourse is interrupted without warning and verbs display no sign of conjugation, punctuation has the irregularity of ragged breathing, and erudite expressions coexist with a lexicon found in no dictionary. Scientific concepts are absent there—the cardinal points of the compass do not exist, but it is apparent that east is meant by "walk with the sun in your face." The rigor of the description is such that it has been easy to identify the locales and geological features seen by the pombeiro. In addition, Baptista's methodical chaos produces parallel, frequently divergent records with results that, ahead of his time, we could call surrealistic.

Baptista and Francisco were well received in Tete. At other places they were offered "young domestics, Black women & children." In "Rios de Senna" Baptista was given "a morning cote of white piqué & a Robe of metal-blue felt with its tinsel buttons, two china plates from Lisbon a pair of Boots." But he was given no more sheets of paper when he tried to finish writing about the route. Nor gunpowder or weapons to defend them on the way back (they refused to return to Angola by ship because they thought their mission unfinished). In 1815 they were accorded other gifts and honors in Rio de Janeiro.

At least Baptista and Francisco escaped the misfortune of the pombeiros from Silva Porto, who in 1853–54 crossed the continent from Barotze to the north of Rovuma, then down to the island of Mozambique. At the end of the ordeal, the authorities disregarded their credentials, took them for runaways, and condemned them to almost a year of forced labor, later expelling them by sailing vessel to Benguela, where they received no compensation whatever.

Baptista and Francisco left the Mucari Fair in November 1802. They arrived in Muataiânvua's Mussamba (capital) at the start of 1806. They left again in May and reached Cazembe in October, where they had to remain until December 1810. The pombeiros entered Tete in February 1811 and retraced their steps in May, returning to Cazembe at the end of 1814. Long delays in the journey occurred in Cazembe both coming and going. Baptista explained at length the context of Cazembe's political rivalries with neighboring potentates and questions internal to the royal Muataiânvua line. Successive military campaigns and the artifices of the Cazembe monarch kept the pombeiros there and may have been the cause of their long stay on the banks of Lake Mweru.

Or not?

By Senhor Doctor Mathias Jose Rebello, of Luanda and Physick Major of Senna, I arranged to deliver this letter addressed to

> Her Most Dignified Highness & Lady Pemba
> Who is the Sister of Cazembe.

> Lady of the Salt Lake, I continue to be perplexed of love and close to ten years have passed in front of the last Visit by me which was in the said country of Cazembe where you are, & therefore I find myself very diminished in lack of your extreme presentness, and I do not know if you are alive or dead, Most

Illustrious Pemba of devotion which I have in my only life &
because this is the name of Your Highness who makes Beauty in
quantity which excells that of five hundred of the most beautiful
women of the valleys of Arângua & loveliness of eyes more than
pearls of coral, the eyes of my Lady of Cazembe stones of
Copper & of panther & in truth marked in ivory.

It has pleased God to take the bird of Zanzibar taught to
sing by Lady Pemba & I respected much said which you ordered
given to me, because it was the echo of the voice & fine words
of Pemba. Long is the shore of sadness caused me by the death
of that bird which has left me alone. Not being able to take
another step, here I will remain in this village called Benguella,
I mean to say in this prison called Benguella, which is filled
with consternation in fevers & great maladies which I find since
my coming here from the Nation of Brasil which is of the same
dominion of Mueneputo, & Brazil is many days away with the
sun always behind the back & there was I sent over the ocean
with companion Anastacio. And those days went by with Your
Highness of Salina in my thoughts so much, water very salty
splashing in my face as we did. And it was at the great Pumbo
Market of Rio de Janeiro that we were presented to Mueneputo
who in our State and Realm has the name of Our Lord Prince
Regent & was sent from the Court to escape being captured by
the great Napoleon. Arrived there with companion Anastacio,
we gave account of the Fair of Mucary of Cassange to Muata-
Yanvo, & Muata-Yanvo to King Cazembe brother of Highness
Pemba, & from Pumbo Cazembe to Rios de Senna, & the route
of the Roads & fortunes on the return to Mucary. And our Lorde
Mueneputo who received us with much esteem, & with great
admiration to see us successful in such a grave enterprise,
conferred on me the rank of captain of Company of infantry &
ordered me to dress henceforth in uniform with Trousers, Shoes,
& monthly salary of ten thousand réis.

I saw uncommon quality in the Court, a kissange elephant
called Pianno which filled the room where the titled people of

the Pumbo Rio de Janeiro wear every kind of dress, Ladies with Cloths from India & the most varied of silks, even red drapes on the windows, & beaver drugget & manifold other tissues, velvet shoes & Gold in the Hair & the tailcoats of the Lord owners of young servants & Blacks. Said Pianno was sitting with a man in front & I heard there from said Pianno the kissange which Lady Pemba played for us when by mystery of the Sovereign Virgin first we saw us on River Luarula the which day I was pleased with Your Highness. The kissange began to cry inside me, Pedro, in the hall of the Mueneputo & the others danced like flamingos & still I Pedro lost no time beseaching passage to this State of Angola, from the power of desiring to be at the side of my Lady, stronger than a herd of rhinoceros pushing me.

I have consumed the small packets of lake salt which you Lady Pemba gave me & which I enjoyed looking at & respected greatly, such that I placed them on a small altar in blue glasses. God the Father forgive me, they melted away like the life of the said bird, bird of Pemba, so nothing of you for me will remain on this Earth, your scent or salt, & I would ask of God only to see you once more. A last time, like changes of pasture in winter, I will one day succeed. My only thought is to winter in your house & your bedroom & I always say that Beautiful Pemba absent burns my ashes & flames like bars of Copper in the chest of I Pedro João. The said salt which I chewed, gray straw salt, salt of Cazembe, from the lands called Cabombo, Muagi, Caracuige which is from the Territories and roads of Lady and Father of the same, is salt which has the same flavor as that which we used when we wintered together.

I succeeded in not lacking a bearer the success of sending to you some small bottles of sands, from the roads and territories that lead from this land Benguella to others, & the said sand I collected for Lady Pemba in hope of arriving anew to Pumbo Cazembe, & it was the collection I made in these years after Brasil, from desert, yellow, peach, gray, red, brown, white & others, more varied in color than the fabrics given to the

Cazembe by the Whites of Rios de Senna. In the Desert, different sands feel different to the fingers, but all of them have the feel of the Lady of the Salt Lake, some sands feel like your hair, others like your mouth, others like the soles of your feet, others the bosom & still another in an isolated bay going from Benguella with the sun on the left, has sand more rough but fragile like the secret Fruit of Pemba, without malice this & Our Lady of Conception be the witness to it.

And I look at me day after day in the two small mirrores of gilded paper which you gave me, & I see me in changement so far away that I told the Black Woman which Cazembe offered me on the road to Casange, told her to divine where Lady Sister of Cazenge is, with help of Our Virgin Conceived she is not yet dead she still awaits her grace, & I spend another day in sweating sickness happy of knowing this divination & send to buy herbs of liamba. For said herbs cool the fire of the Head & tell me the future & send me to the Home of Pemba on the road of happiness, a bird freed by the Jia Dia Pamba. But I awaken in the sickness & the feeling & perturbation from which I am to sucumb & am desirous to quickly escape along the waters of the Bihé to the brook where you my Lady repose.

Your Slave in peace & calm of love,
Pedro João Baptista
Benguella, February of 1822*

---

*The letter never arrived at its destination. After the death of its sender, it remained for several years in the possession of a Brazilian druggist in Benguela who sent it, by ship, to Matias José Rebelo. The letter was found among the estate left by Oitaviana Rebello de Moura e Menezes (d. 1978, Salisbury), great-great-granddaughter of the doctor in Tete, to her family, whom we thank for the kindness of permitting its publication for the first time. A letter from Matias José Rebelo to the great-uncle of Ms. Oitaviana leads one to believe that the doctor received from Benguela, along with Pedro João's message, "a small box with shavings of rhinoceros horns" (called *abada* in the backlands) and "elephant hair" mixed with sand, as well as "small blue flasks." His descendants, however, have no recollection of any such object.

"Does Mr. Norton live here?"

"Yes, he does."

"Is he in?"

"Yes. He's in back there."

"What about the dogs?"

"I'll take you."

The dogs didn't stir, so perhaps I didn't exude fear. The youth took me inside the fortress house. Could he be old Norton's grandson? Great-grandson, surely.

"There he is, in the jango." Sitting with his back to me, the nape of his neck closely cropped, presiding alone over a table made of immense boards, with books lying in positions of consultation, and a bizarre collection of objects. Boxes of German tobacco, very old and very pretty, painted by hand and by rust. Inkwells. Pens, eggs, stones. Flasks with roots, colored powders, small reptiles, tiny bones that might be from a bird, shells. Dead leaves, tubers shedding earth inside the glass. Preserved, the table could occupy a place in the Geographical Society in Lisbon or Brussels. Closer to Norton were two small piles of pink paper, one on his left, the other on his right. He did not move.

"I can't talk to you. I am in moral pain. I can't talk to anyone. Forgive me, young man. I'm in no condition to see journalists or visitors or anybody. I am in moral pain."

I insisted, amazed by the table. Norton rose, and two blue eyes looked at me from my own height: direct, limpid, faded from an excess of living, framed under bushy eyebrows, close-cut hair, and a white beard down to his chest.

"I was born in Benguela and lived in the Upper Zambezi, where I fucked three native women. You know that Benguela didn't used to be anything like this? In the thirties anofelix killed people right and left, in a horrible way: it stopped their urine, until the poor devils died without being able to piss. One day when I was fucking a black woman at the lake where the canal flows into it, which also didn't end like it does today, I discovered where the anofelix was coming from, because I saw some mosquitoes leaving crab holes. I told Dr. Frazão, who ordered digging done there, and they discovered the anofelix larvae. A zebra-like mosquito: it has very long legs and black and white stripes. A great physician, Dr. Frazão."

"The one the avenue is named after?"

"The same. He fixed up the hospital here, in those days. The whole place was infested, and he brought from England, from Fergusson, two fumigation engines. Killed all the parasites. Even killed a couple of men who were drunk. Come here tomorrow. Anytime. I'm eighty-three years old. I smoked, I fucked, I drank. In the forties the tobacco ran out and I smoked South African marijuana — never again! Come back tomorrow."

Tomorrow Norton was at the gate negotiating seduction with an underage female. The girl was trying to sell him a bowl of string beans. Norton made no attempt to hide his willingness.

"How much?"

"Three hundred."

"One hundred."

"Two fifty!"

"One fifty because you're such a pretty girl. All right, young thing?"

Small improvisations are the mark of the true professional. Confused, the girl closed the deal. Norton, his eyes on his fingertips, was massaging his wisdom under the girl's chin, in delicate movements, his eyebrows serene and pleasure heavy on his eyelids.

We went inside with the beans. We sat on the jango. The young thing remained at the door. He spoke to me of women and of the part of Angola he knows best, the "triangle of death."

Norton is in moral pain: he still hasn't accepted the desertion of his fourth wife.

"I was a bigamist. I had four wives. One got baptized, she's in Switzerland or France or Portugal even. Josefa. Later I arranged this one and one more, Maria, and one, Feliciana, died on me. Clementina got it into her skull that she'd leave the house, the children, everything to follow that fanaticism of hers. The Bible is written in parables and metaphors. Clementina followed Mark 10.29–30: 'And Jesus answered and said, Verily I say unto you, There is no man that hath left house, or brethren, or sisters, or children, or lands, for my sake, and the gospel's, but shall he receive an hundredfold...' It's a metaphor, but she took it literally. She left her children. My library I gave to a son who's in Portugal on a UNITA scholarship, but this house with the modern bathroom, jango, bedrooms, dining room, and television, and the residence that she shared with our firstborn—all hers, and she abandoned it!"

The jango is full of shadows. Around us, on the ground where the sun raises dust, are dogs, many dogs, wallowing in horrible sores, gleaming and red. And cats, teasing their whiskers on the stones where Norton's women lay the fish.

Standing guard over our conversation is a young thing, a mulatto with clear eyes of undefined color—there are olives like that, constantly shifting between brown and green. Her legs are bare and quite beautiful. Her hair is light brown, unbound to its curls. Mentally, I curse Norton's ability to contaminate the dreams of others.

"Is she your granddaughter?"

"My daughter," said the old man, overflowing with triumph. "Why?"

"No reason... She's very pretty."

He knows of at least fifty-four children of his. He doesn't know how many great-grandchildren he has. "I even have great-great-grandchildren. This lady alone has eight children by me. That light-haired one there, her mother died and left ten children. She's semi-albino. My youngest daughter is four years old."

"You mean, you were still fertile at seventy-nine?"

"And still am, still am. If I find a new girl, my sperm is still active."

A friend of Norton's explained to me that the old man has a daughter who's a doctor in Switzerland. Every year he sends her a sample of his sperm to be analyzed by a lab. This is his erotic universe: methodical, compulsive, honest, and free of any malice.

"Go get the Flit so I can spray here!"

A son — or grandson? — brings the insecticide.

"The mosquitoes are biting me. Excuse me."

Norton, who is wearing khaki shorts like a Boer farmer, sprays profusely under the table while remaining seated, until he has formed a deadly cloud that ascends his legs.

"There's that other one, Baygon, but this is better, I find. Mosquitoes are awful! This is Deom Super," he says, coughing, returning the can to the row of sprays lined up on the table. In front of us is enough insecticide to protect a plantation.

Norton is the son of a Lisboan from the Rua des Janelas Verdes, Júlio Alves Silva, a cavalry captain who at the end of the last century came to Angola. Silva took his son with him when, years later, he was transferred from Benguela to the Angolan Upper Zambezi, the enclave of Cazombo. It was there that the boy Norton had his sexual initiation and also honed his preferences:

"Luena women are the most sensual, because, number one, they circumcise the clitoris and because they practice moving their hips. The waist sways so much, it looks like they're walking on ball bearings. And they know how to suck, they suck like they have hot peppers in their mouth. The Luenan woman is the most affectionate, and I say that having tried every tribe in Angola — all of them, all of them. I'm proud of it. In Egypt, Libya, Tunisia, Morocco, and Algeria, they removed the clitoris. Now the United Nations has forbidden it. The women from those countries no longer felt any pleasure, but that's not the case in the Upper Zambezi, where they circumcise but don't remove. The clitoris is covered by a foreskin, and they remove that. The woman becomes more sensitive. Later, she starts exercising the clitoris at puberty, and it grows a little. Sometimes there are clitorises so long that they cover the entrance to the vagina—"

Norton makes two Vs with his fingers and places one over the other to form an orifice, through which peeks his right thumb.

"Try to stick your finger on top of my finger. It won't go in . . . Not like that, straight in: it won't go, you see? You have to open the plug, as we call it. Even with spit it won't go in, because you have that blockage. The Luena women won't accept a man who's not circumcised. Traditions, hygiene . . . What about you?"

"No."

"Luena women won't accept you! They check. The man with a foreskin is quick to catch diseases. Why don't you get circumcised? It's a simple thing. I, who have Jewish ancestors, and all of us here at home, sons and grandsons, we're all circumcised. Even among Catholics there are some who practice circumcision. It's biblical, it's written. The race of Israelites is circumcised. I did it voluntarily when I was fourteen."

He went into a thicket and did it with a razor, in cold blood. Sixty years later, he found that the foreskin had grown back over the years and took advantage of an operation for a testicular hernia to make the cut a second time. He asked the Ukrainian surgeon in Benguela to do it.

"They have strong powders that heal, there in the Upper Zambezi. I got my initiation with three women, two were young and one who was an aunt and gave me her nieces. They do that there. Then I was in a seminary and practiced onanism, which is against God's law. Jerking off. The Bible forbids it."

Norton's first legitimate wife was *cafusa*—the daughter of a biracial father and a black mother. The others were black women, and their marriages with Norton were contemporaneous inside the walled enclosure with three separate houses and a single exit.

"All of them, sexually, of the Bantu tribe, that's good."

The best—not the most sensual, Norton emphasizes—those who have a large vaginal "volume," are the Cuanhama and Mumuíla women. They have a wide vagina with capillary profusion, a "triangle of death." Whereas the local women have a small vagina with skimpy pubic hair. But Norton isn't a slave to his preferences. Every bed is a race. He likes white women when he goes to Europe, and in Portugal he especially appreciates women from Minho "because of the whiteness of their skin." He never had a white wife "because I never ran into one. When I came here it was hell. There were very few white women. We had the bilious, anuretic types. You don't know what anuretic is? Retention. It was deadly! It would start in the month of May. We used to call it the month of malaria. We would get *lica*, very tiny blisters caused by heat and perspiration, intense heat. The jango that my father made, the columns split with a shaking of the earth that made us all run outside. From that time till now, the climate has changed. It's cool, it's the humidity."

Norton learned Mbundu in Silva Porto (Cuíto), where he was director of the Chissamba Mission. He speaks eight languages, not counting his native Portuguese: Mbundu, Tchokwe, Luchazi, Luena, Luwale, and understands a bit of Kimbundu and Swahili.

"Très bien, je parle quelque chose en français, when I'm in France. When I'm in Germany spechodeutch, when I'm in Italy parlo italiano, niente maniente. They're the most blasphemous people in Europe, the Italians. They insult God: porco Dio! God's a pig. Tranca Madonna! You know what *tranca* is? Well then. Spanish is the only language that I don't have to learn, hablo un bocadito. I like the muchachitas from—from Andalusia, because they have lots of bush, an enormous mons veneris. If you ever go to Andalusia, take the opportunity to have sex. They're more sensual, it's the Moorish blood, like the women of the Algarve."

It was, in fact, in the Algarve that Norton was taking off his clothes in connection with a matter of hot blood, when four guys approached him. "It was a close call. My driver was the lookout. They wanted my clothes and my money. But my driver came back with a couple of cops, just as I was in the act. The girl had made me take off all my

173

clothes—the plan was to rob me and keep my clothes. How could I complain, later?"

From Portimão Norton has the phone number of a hairdresser's where he once went to bed with seven girls. "He spent money, but those women "left nothing out, from six o'clock on, yessir." He went there whenever he went to Portugal.

"Just say Norton of Benguela sent you, and you'll see. Prostitution in Portugal is on the sly."

Not like in Denmark. Or in Holland, where what's amazing is houses of prostitution with no Dutch women. To find a native bed partner, you have to go to the park where the *cangonheiros*, "drug users," are located, as a Spanish colleague taught him.

Norton was born Francisco Alves Silva, "illegitimate son of Júlio Alves Silva with Isabel Trindade," registered at the old church in Benguela, Our Lady of Pópulo. General Norton de Matos, his baptismal godfather, changed his name to Francisco Norton Silva. It was the general who obliged Júlio to marry Isabel, after a luncheon in the Upper Zambezi with the Nineth Infantry Company to mark the changeover from military to civilian administration in the area. They ate tigerfish, "which they call *pungo* there." Afterward, the soldiers wanted to meet the cook, and Captain Silva brought Isabel Trindade to the table. "They thought her just a cook. Norton de Matos didn't like that and announced that she was my father's wife."

The wife of a hero. Júlio Alves Silva came to Angola in time to meet Silva Porto: they met once in Benguela and once in the bush. Júlio distinguished himself in the campaign for the defense and establishment of the borders of the Upper Zambezi with Rhodesia, assuring that a vein of copper that began in present-day Zambia would remain on the Angolan side. Lisbon decorated him for an act of valor.

"In the end, the English, that's why I like them, took a beating, but they also thanked and decorated my father."

Norton's property, in the old "high" part of Benguela—the São João or Peça District—was bought in 1937 for sixteen thousand angolares. It was full of mango trees. The owner was a Brazilian, and the high walls, which still stand today, were put up because the place was a slave enclosure.

In those days there was an abundance of fish. Norton recalls when the fishermen moved on top of the sea, "really on top, in those big rowboats." Some cataclysm occurred, or a mass flight that brought millions of cachucho to the coast. The beach was littered with dead fish, along with a few still alive. "They made a fortune that day. All the men on the trawlers had to do was scoop them up."

Another unexplained phenomenon took place some years later at the Cinema Calunga, close to midnight, with the sudden plummeting of thousands of quail of unknown origin.

"They perched there, tired or blinded by the light of the theater. Everybody grabbed some, even ladies and little children. If the electricity were only working, I have a video... Agostinho Neto said that we'd go back to oil, and we have!"

When there's electricity, Norton leaps onto the VCR like a partridge. There is no shortage of films in his house. In the library, in a small house next to the jango, are several shelves of cassettes, "with pornography and all," just behind the door, guarded by a .45 Magnum and a .22 long rifle.

There are bibles and programs of spiritual revival, caricatures of Brezhnev and Fidel, books by the nineteenth-century prophet Hellen White. But the dominant decoration is portraits of women — real portraits or clippings of celebrities taken from magazines.

"That's the woman, the one who ran away. Clementina Katanha, a Londuibali, October 21, 1952."

The library has two parts connected by a central door. In the middle of the second is a spacious bed surrounded by books, newspapers, issues of *Reader's Digest* in Portuguese. Laid out in line with the door, it is situated in such a way that anyone coming into the room for the first time will almost inevitably trip against the edge of the mattress and fall onto it. Old Norton is crafty.

"I have apple bananas. Try one."

"Who sleeps here?"

"This is for reading. This time of year it gets cold. This picture is the woman a short time back."

"And this is you when you were young, already with a beard. Is it some kind of vow?"

Norton, not answering, takes some bananas from a stalk hanging in the corner. In the library, cooled by memories, he returned to his moral pain.

Outside, beside the jango, he haggles with a saleswoman in Mbundu, buys fish, shoos away the cats. A young man comes to complain about his brothers.

"This is my oldest son by the woman who ran away. In the Bible it says, 'Love thy neighbor as thyself.' Who's closer to her than me, haven't I been with her for twenty-seven years? Let's go..."

Like certain metaphysical libertines, Norton is unable to control his flesh but lives with his eyes turned heavenward. He was Catholic, then Protestant, and four years ago heard the message of the Seventh-Day Adventists (which is why Hellen White's books have no dust on them).

"Catholicism has strayed from the faith. Your name is Iberian, but you have a Jewish nose..."

"Not Jewish, just large."

"Jewish, by the curvature. Really! You have Semitic blood, for sure. If you were in Germany during Hitler's time, you'd have been arrested! But they wouldn't have kept you, you know why? Because you're not circumcised."

"What are the pink papers for?"

"Work slips. For keeping track of the days of my employees. Here, on the left, expensive employees. Here, cheap employees. They do various kinds of work. I have that workshop outside. I have five cars, taxis, that carry passengers between Benguela and Lobito. Let's move around a bit. I can't sit for very long, because just take a look, look at this thing."

Norton points to his belly, where it looks as if his trunk has come loose from his spinal column, creating a protuberance:

"Rupture. Abdominal rupture, paratesticular."

For over twenty years Tota hasn't seen the only woman he truly loves. He knows that she is well and in Portugal. It was he who saved her, the day that war forced him to give his life for her. Some choices are like that, leaving a man hovering forever over his past: after all, he is still alive. A half-empty bottle of whiskey is on the table on the porch.

"There are two kinds of fall: the violent and the free."

Tota began flying planes in 1973, in a flight club. He flew a Stoll. In those days, belonging to a flight club was the dream of any young adventurer: you paid twenty-five hundred escudos a month and accumulated air time—a commercial license demanded a minimum of four hundred hours.

Tota was one of the best. One day, realizing that something was wrong with the landing gear, he opened the door to see what it was: a bullet in the tire. He managed to land on one wheel, in Huambo. As soon as he touched down, he went off the runway. But that was all. They got jerricans and siphoned out the gasoline. That happened in the two most turbulent years of his life, the countdown to Independence, when he also learned how to make a night landing when there are no searchlights or electricity: you put a car with its headlights on high beam at the end of the runway and other vehicles side by side along the strip, their headlights on.

In 1975, with the war under way, he chanced to lead a civilian column supported by armed volunteers (with stolen weapons). The column was to leave Angola with the pilots' automobiles that were in Rundu and on the airstrip at Cubango. Tota took the column to Serpa Pinto. The FNLA didn't let him continue.

It was there that he was introduced to Daniel Chipenda, with whom Tota formed a fast friendship over the following months, "although in Menongue I didn't like his looks."

Tota stayed with Chipenda, using Cuando Cubango as a base for reconnaissance missions in four small planes that constituted the FNLA air force. With him was the girl he loved more than anyone in his life—perhaps because loving in danger has an absolute intensity, the end always imminent. It was flying with her that he surprised the UNITA forces advancing on the city. He circled around and appeared from behind the enemy troops, flying just off the ground.

"A shot came in the window and hit the back of the seat. It didn't kill the girl because she didn't have her belt on. The propeller tip was shot off by another bullet. Luckily, they weren't tracers."

Tota landed—on just one wheel and without going off the runway—bringing the news of the siege and information about the number and type of enemy forces. Menongue would fall and UNITA would take no prisoners. The civilians had to be evacuated, but to do that it was necessary for a small force to protect their retreat, holding out against UNITA's advance: they would die in the final attack. It was the logic of numbers. Either all would die or some must be sacrificed.

Tota decided: he would die, she would live. The column left and was saved. It was a definitive farewell.

Although the attack on Menongue was an inferno, Tota managed to escape, breaking through the encirclement in the only available vehicle. He reached the eastern border and later the safety of Kinshasa, where Marshal Mobutu gave Chipenda's men no water—in the hotel and at the palace there was only French champagne.

Tota returned to Angola years later, when with the passage of time his involvement with Chipenda had cooled enough so that he wasn't bothered at one of the farms of his uncle, Fernando Borges, the largest chicken farmer in the country. Today Tota runs a farm in Humpata, with cold storage and milking machines, in the heart of the Huíla agricultural belt, studying the evolution of crossbreeding the zebu, or the Charolais and Santa Gertrudis, with local cattle.

A presage of the Yugoslav civil war began to manifest itself in the School of Letters in Lubango at the end of the 1970s. There were professors from several republics who quarreled among themselves in the Grand Hotel of Huíla. A Portuguese from the school suffered a beating. He received shipments of yogurt from a Yugoslav and for this was pursued in the Serra da Leba area. He showed up, torn and scratched, at the home of Maria Alexandre Dáskalos and Arlindo Barbeitos and for two nights could not go out. The couple themselves were no better off. The insanity spilled over from the university and merged with the political climate of terror that was gripping Huíla. Things were made no easier by the arrival in Huíla of a cell of veterans from the Red Brigade — including some women — invited by a colony of leftist Italians in Moçâmedes. They produced wine, grew grapes, and made cheese.

There was one unpleasant accident: some professors from Lubango who had come to Namibe in the Italian pilgrimage were killed by South African helicopters.

They were very refined people, this group of brigade members, from the upper bourgeoisie or even the aristocracy, with established careers, who had adopted radical positions and still espoused the cult of arms. Lubango also received a contingent of Basque refugees from the ETA, as well as elements of Tupac Amaru, including a Uruguayan woman almost sixty years old whose room at the Hotel Continental—where the red carpets had turned gray-moldy because of the flooding—was called the Bataclan, a name taken from the Brazilian writer Jorge Amado's novel *Gabriela Clove and Cinnamon*. Despite the attacks planned at these gatherings, they ate simply, beets with fresh cheese and yogurt made from powdered milk, and they took siestas on the hotel terrace, wearing black sleeping masks. In addition, the collection boasted a fugitive activist for Indian rights in Brazil (which role he still plays today) and a German architect (he now lives in Luanda).

A Dadaist hurricane had installed itself in Huíla. One of the eyes of the storm was a Zairean professor, who introduced himself as Cité du Bois "but not of wood," come from Lubumbashi to Brazzaville and from Brazza to Lubango, part of a wave of Bukango professors who didn't speak a word of Portuguese. Cité du Bois became head of the Department of Romance Languages and had under his authority the Portuguese Rui Teixeira, who was working on a thesis about Ernest Hemingway, and a Romanian woman who spoke Latin as if she had drunk it at her mother's breast.

Cité du Bois wore an orange robe full of holes, out at the elbows, and puttees, but it was in literature that he distinguished himself. He wrote and presented in his classes marvelous compositions like "My First Ride in an Airplane," with the fascinating character of the stewardess, or "The Human Body," which he used for a class in French grammar, beginning with the head, eyes, neck, "the mustache that some use and others do not," and ending with the "ear-cleaning finger"! He also became well known for a composition about his arrival in which he described himself as dazzled by the lights of Lubango; by the women in Western-style dress (including the Mumuílas?); and, in a footnote, by a facet of European culture previously unknown to him: soups of kale, carrot, potato, meat. These were his literary works, worthy of analysis at the university level—he considered himself an Angolan writer whose language was French.

Aiding his prominence among the faculty was the fact of his

constant trips to the Grand Hotel, carrying a small pot to take away the leftovers. He consumed tangerines. He frequently would come into the classroom, remove his puttees, stuff them in his shoes, stretch out his legs on the desk, and fall happily asleep.

The atmosphere was different under the baton of Ambrósio Lecoki, who rose to minister of education and desired to use the university as a springboard to the presidency (there being nothing higher). In Lubango was a friend of the literary historian Óscar Lopes, a polyglot from Porto, who was persecuted by the dean of the college, Henri Lussailasio — the dean would listen to his lectures while concealed behind a curtain. This pressure finally became too much for the Portuguese professor. One Saturday, he lost his temper and suddenly pulled the curtain aside, unmasking the spy. He was forbidden to leave the province, which proved to be very serious, because he was well on in years and diabetic, and in Huíla there was no insulin. He was going to die. (When tragedy seemed imminent, he managed to depart the province in darkness, with his wife.)

There was also a Portuguese psychologist, with polio, who was removed from the Grand Hotel by a FAPLA truck. An aficionado of Rimbaud, he was disliked by Lecoki, who informed him that he would receive his salary but would not be allowed to exercise his profession.

Panda, the head of the secretariat, was from State Security and conducted exams of undergraduates as a member of the workers' committee; she would threaten them with prison and beatings. The curriculum had made-up chairs — History of the Peoples of the Third World, Developing Countries.

Tribalism, not only of the Yugoslavs, was the constant menace. The group of Bakongo students was special: it was known that they carried out rituals of sorcery because there were two castrates among them, the last descendants of royal lines. They had been castrated by rival groups. Into this scene arrived the most beautiful Bakongo woman Lubango had ever seen. The city went wild over Josefina. She went to live in the university residence hall, which was located between the college and the Diogo Cão Secondary School. One of the glories of the district was its flowering jacaranda trees: the dean of the college, among those who were left breathless by Josefina, ordered them cut down lest they be used by suitors to climb into the young woman's room.

Josefina fell in love with someone she shouldn't have, Cachove, an Mbundu fellow student. The college now had its own Romeo and Juliet. To the Bakongos it was simple: With an Mbundu, never, Josefina! As the tension rose, the Bakongos began holding secret meetings and casting spells. And State Security was everywhere, terrorizing the workers — one worker committed suicide in the lavatory. Rumors were flying; a Uruguayan professor and a Cuban who taught philosophy were warned that something was about to happen. There were signs to heed: Maria Alexandre Dáskalos, when she came home, would find her doorstep covered with chicken bones and horns filled with power-bearing materials, sometimes even young goats drowned in a basin and hung from the pillar of the building. Until one day, the Uruguayan, a communist and professor of logic and dialectics who had taught at the best South American universities, went running: he lived in the men's residence hall, and there was no electricity. He had heard a watery murmur, a chorus, and hid under the stairs.

A cortege of Bakongo students passed by, in loincloths only, their faces painted with white chalk and candles burning on top of their heads.

Cachove decided to place the problem of the lovers before the MPLA Youth Organization: he was the victim in a case of tribalism, proscribed in the new Angola. Confusion. Threats that Josefina's family would not be allowed into Angola. The Party in an uproar. She was summoned to the Congo, and scandal erupted. Arlindo Barbeitos, who had stood out in denouncing the college's absurdity, was accused of being an apologist for social democracy, a West German agent, and a teacher of dangerous materials in his courses. His food ration coupons were taken away — and in socialist Angola not having coupons meant death by starvation. The couple survived with the help of the aid workers, but Barbeitos was expelled by Lecoki, Agostinho Neto had died, and José Eduardo dos Santos was now president; the minister's fury was implacable.

These were the times, it should be kept in mind, that followed May 27, 1977, and the purge of the apparatus, of the Party, and of society. In Huíla, State Security and the police had divided during the coup and were carrying out a dirty war with persecution of every sort. The jaws of the Tundavala, a narrow vertical passage hundreds of meters high where the plateau plunges to meet the sea, were not large enough to swallow the members of both sides. (People were kidnapped, taken to the cemetery, tortured, and later thrown from the Tundavala.) In Lubango a political struggle unfolded, centered naturally enough in the university.

It was only a matter of time before Barbeitos and Dáskalos would be eliminated. With the help of friends, the professor and poet fled, disguised as a worker at the German Ngola beer factory. Dáskalos escaped in a plane. The story had an epilogue in Luanda, the night Angolan Public Television broadcast a Manu Dibango concert. When a friend escorted her home after dinner two men were waiting at the entrance to the building.

"Comrades, the elevator's not working."

They went upstairs with the two men behind. On the second floor, a hand pushed against the door. The strangers pointed guns at them—"This is a holdup!"—and thus began a flurry of fists for this, for that, for lots of reasons, because "You're from Lubango and you've got to learn."

Some wanted to kill her, negotiations, to rape her, negotiations. They locked her and her friend in the bathroom. They finally left, and Dáskalos learned later that they were deserters from the presidential guard working as a gang for someone and attacking certain people.

Cité du Bois, although he lost his job, was the one who held out longest against the insanity in Lubango—it was his milieu—after the majority of the aid workers had returned to Luanda, in the 1981 dry season. The Zairean professor had a maxim: he said all one had to do was care for plants, and he would be fed. He locked himself on the veranda and ate flowers.

There is no silverware. The plate circulates around the table in the dark of the room. No one holds it, it flies on its own. No one speaks. Also invisible are the hands that, as the corn meal passes around, bury their fingers in the same white flour, in a sinister banquet of insects born of the night. There was a gasoline lantern, but someone standing in wait extended his pincers over the table, took it without touching it, and accompanied it to the door, extinguishing it and himself in the shadows. All that is left is a gas-soaked rag stuffed into the neck of a beer bottle. The rag does not provide light enough to create people. It can do no more than materialize eyes, occasional teeth. At the table sits the synopsis of six men: eyes and teeth.

Look and eat; measure and watch. I entered and disappeared in the country where the last supper occurs when there is food. Animals normally fall after dusk, when they heed the snare that whispers to them of hunger and thirst. I don't know when my next meal will be.

It is dinnertime in Brigadier General Kalutotai's cocoon.

As we chew the corn meal in unison, I imagine the brigadier general seated at the head of the table. But he may not be. He may have left, hidden among the bats that come and go, restive in the preparation of something that I can't see and that disturbs me — my end? Kalutotai may have left in his place the two threads of light with which he gazes at me from the summit of the table. Such eyes have no need of a body. There remains also the blade of a voice that renders other voices silent. Kalutotai has my life in his hands. For nine days he has been mulling over what to do with it. Today, finally, he summoned me. He has come to a decision.

"Eat a bit of something with bread."

In Cuando Cubango, meat is too precious a good to eat every day, or even every week. Our "something" is a luxury, sauce dripping from a handful of small cubes of meat. The sauce gives the cornmeal a flavor that lightly caresses the tongue, evoking distant memories. The idea of goat is as tasty as goat itself — and no meat is more tender.

The brigadier general lives in one of the small houses razed by civil war and the South African invasion. There aren't more than ten of them, the ruins of them, dwellings of guerrillas, without streets but aligned along a row of enormous trees that shade a history of total violence. Roofs are either nonexistent or made of thatch, windows are boarded up in anticipation of the next battle — in Angola wars come like the days. The furniture has disappeared into the fire, and the rest is installations of tin, mats, holes from bullets and howitzers, clay cooking utensils and dogs, clothes drying and babies crying under the open sky, between walls scorched by nights of eternal cold. In the back is a Kamaz, immobilized by the lack of fuel, and a smaller all-terrain vehicle, an old Land Cruiser "1947 model."

These are the privileges of Kalutotai, UNITA commander in the military area of Caiundo. The name was given to a billeting area that is in fact seventeen kilometers to the north, in a village called Kapico. The locality of Caiundo — an old center for *cantineiros*, bush merchants — was erected on high ground overlooking Cubango, a strategic location, guarding the bridge linking it to South Africa. The bridge was dynamited in 1975 but, even destroyed, continues serving as a bridge. By day, if things are peaceful, the brigadier general sits on the veranda, without moving a finger, or moving only his small crop against his outstretched leg, surveying the straight line that brings the

Menongue road to Namibia. He always sees long before he is seen. Which may be why he's still alive.

Kalutotai is not from Cuando Cubango. He arrived in the province in 1975, in the first UNITA retreat, which populated his rear guard with people from outside—Mbundus and others from even farther away. The brigadier general hasn't seen Luanda since 1972, nor has he been in any of the coastal cities since Independence. His world is the bush, and the bush is his curse. Beds, electricity, paved roads, running water, telephones—Kalutotai detoured into another world where the luxuries of peace have no place. Caiundo is a cell in which canoes circulate and he is commander of his own life sentence. In Angola, the parties—two armies—are not ideological options; they have become simple geographic contingencies: you fight for and vote for the place where you are. With their feet in the same fetters are the guerrillas who, at the end of the day, run out to the field with a ball made of cloth, reproducing in soccer the yells they have learned in war, the only ones they know, when the goal is in sight:

"Kill!"

He summoned me today, after nine days. Abel arrived in Caiundo, and the brigadier general has decided to give the trip a hand: Abel wanted $600 for four hundred kilometers of bush through minefields (I found out later that he originally asked for $1,200!); an hour's "sensitizing" by UNITA brought the price down to $300.

"He's mafia. I had to remind him of some names he hasn't heard for months . . . It's not done that way, in bad faith. The Party is all, and, if private individuals operate, it's because we allow them to."

There were compensations for Abel's mobilization—he felt unruffled in his own Land Cruiser with his road uniform, a Chinese-style UNITA beret. I would pay, at the Namibian border, for two drums of fuel that Abel would bring back to the brigadier general and enough crates of beer to dignify the August 3 celebrations, Savimbi's birthday, in Kalutotai's quarters. Besides that, Abel got even by delaying the departure for two nights, taking advantage of the time to make small deals in the billeting area.

We left by stages. First, from Kapico to Caiundo, which meant fording the great Cubango. Caiundo is an arena in an ellipse of mines. The banks are also booby-trapped. There is only one spot—secret—to go in on the left bank and one spot to come out, downstream on the right bank. The jeep growls like a buffalo whose heart isn't up to the weight of its years, then slips into the water like a crocodile, between the rushes. Skiing into our madness, we pass the triangular red signs with white skulls, known to all. DANGER MINES. If none of us fall overboard, we will reach the bottom of the embankment alive...

Sitting in the backseat, more surprised than panicked and with water up to my ankles, I understand why the crew has to have at least three men. Next to the driver is a helper, with one leg inside and the other outside, so he can grasp the inside of the car with one hand and with the other hold the air filter above the surface, as high as the length of the tube from the motor will permit. The third man goes ahead, on foot (he removed his pants to avoid getting them wet) to indicate with his body the least deep spots. Salvador Dalí would envy this Polaroid: the trunk of a man zigzagging in the river and the jeep following him, embraced by the water, navigating full speed ahead with a yawning hood.

"Everything's mined around here. Caiundo was an important position, and the Cubans left mines all over."

"How do you know where they are?"

"We don't step where people have died. The cattle also do some mine clearing and marking...And we have information from an ex-FAPLA who joined us after the liberation of Caiundo and has been a big help to UNITA."

I listen closely, but there is no hint of irony in the explanation by Colonel Nunda, whose mission it is to escort me to Calai. We make it to the other side, where UNAVEM has never set foot because of the absence of even minimal conditions of safety.

"It's not as dangerous as it was a while ago. Here the mines are already a meter away from the trail."

A shiver runs through me. Then what was the distance back there? In the rearview mirror I see that my lips are as cold as my wet feet.

The second phase of the departure takes longer. Abel orders us out in Caiundo. There is something wrong with the radiator. In the rear of his house, under a jango, he sits in the sand with helpers, next to a small bonfire, for a demonstration of basic mechanics. One of them holds the radiator in his lap. The other bangs on a steel rod heating in the fire and then places it over a bar of solder to cover the hole. The solder won't stick. In any case, the radiator looks more like a colander: it has hundreds of holes in dozens of spots, a distressing beehive of several layers of dry solder.

"It's almost done. You can leave tonight. The food's run out. Do you still have any rice in your crate? I can tell them to make it..."

A lot of time goes by after the meal, when the rag burns out and they tell me to wait in the entrance hall, furnished only with sacks of flour that attract large rats that approach without my being able to make them out. Kalutotai's human insects come and go in the same fashion. I still see nothing but teeth and eyes — the visible part of their skulls.

The canoes have stopped now because no one dares row among the crocodiles. Whether we leave or not, the night will be spent on the darker side of the river. I am unfamiliar with the birds that fill the stars with portents. The sky has a ghostly brilliance, something I've noticed for weeks. It must be the total nonexistence of artificial light below. Suddenly I long for the security of the farewell from Carlos Seixas the night before, in the kitchen. I gave him back the book he lent me in Luanda before I left: Paul Bowles's *The Sheltering Sky*. He didn't have with him Jack London's *The Road*, which I lent him, the first book I read when I landed in Angola.

I stole this from London for my journal: "The hobo never knows what is going to happen the next moment; hence, he lives only in the present moment. He has learned the futility of telic endeavor, and knows the delight of drifting along with the whimsicalities of Chance."

Carlos left me a treasure before returning to Menongue, to Luanda, and — two days later! — to Portugal and his plans to establish a center for research on pastoral cultures in a mill in Alentejo. I take with me a bottle of red wine from the Cape. Shiraz Reserve, 1995, Simonsvlei Wynkelder.

"They gave me this. I'm giving it to you. It'll do you good. A toll. A friend."

The last entry in the journal is also a gift from Carlos. I savored it while Kalutotai's spiders anesthetized me with cornmeal redolent of diesel.

"You won't have any problems from here on. There's no more peaceful traveling than in a country at war."

Mr. Ventura
Director of the Office of Foreigners and Borders of Angola
(DEFA)
Cuíto — Bié — Angola

Dear Ventura,

I hope this finds you in good health. I do not wish you ill, I just don't want you to forget me. You must know, even knowing little, that this is the reason one writes his friends. To say, as you yourself would say: Here I am!

Here I am, then, to say to you everything that remained unsaid when I met you in Cuíto.

I don't have — don't have at all — the bad habit of bottling up matters in my throat. You were in your house, I was at your mercy, and you don't like foreigners. This dislike, in its public manifestation, is a career. In your case, it is a vocation. You managed to be nothing more than an impediment, but you could have become a tragedy. You had the arrogance of a settler and aroused in me the rage of a slave. It is unpleasant to have to swallow such rage. It tastes of gall. You are too young to have experienced it, and I am too young to have inflicted it, but the Party inculcated the idea in you, which you spit out as slogans. Therefore what you did, you did for pleasure. That, sir, is what is known as pettiness. Or stupidity, if it was merely zeal.

Perhaps, Ventura, you're not sure who the sender is. I'll give you a hint: One morning in July a foreigner came into your office to renew a visa. A white man, yes, if you prefer to speak in those terms, since I noticed that, to read a man, you first read the color of his skin and then his passport, and there your reading ends.

A white journalist. Try, Ventura, make an effort, the possibilities are few, Cuíto doesn't get that many foreigners, and you don't recall any of them renewing their visa in Cuíto. (That's why your office, to justify its existence a bit, invented the need for all foreigners to register upon arrival and request authorization before leaving, a rule that derives from your interpretation of the "free circulation of persons and goods.")

No, the bald guy wasn't me, that was Giovanni Diffidenti, a photographer from England and Italy who lived in Angola and put together an exhibition on the victims of mines, *Interrupted Journey*. A man of great generosity, Giovanni, in case you didn't notice. He took the children of Cuíto and of Angola away inside his small Leica, to a conference in Ottawa. That's in Canada, and it was important. Later, without bodies, without wings, they flew to Stockholm, where they were seen by kings and presidents, so the world would not forget them. Emanuel Sapalo, two legs and an eye lost to an antitank mine, for whom "the best war is fought with your mouth"; Marta Mukumbi, 14, missing one leg, who wanted "electricity for everyone, so we could go to the movies, watch television and have running water in the faucets"; old Josefina Vicumga, little Pinto da Cruz, Joaquim Pedro, who lost both arms and his sight to an antitank mine, supported on the shoulders and by the eyes of Joaquim Mafuco... It was pretty, Ventura, it was the only day on which Cuíto won the war.

Everyone around you is a survivor, as are you, but the others have kept their dignity.

I'm the one who came into your dark office with his papers in order, asking for a routine renewal of the visa that you had no reason not to grant immediately.

The one who was subjected to an absurd interrogation, to a battery of questions in an ever narrowing circle, until the spider found the pretext to bite, insisting that "If you're traveling, you're ... a tourist, aren't you? Don't you have a business you work with in Angola? A business that guarantees you the money to survive and return? A business that can vouch that you're not an illegal immigrant? What's your contact in Angola? You don't have one? But you must have one. You have to go back to Luanda. You're going to Jamba? What's that card you're wearing on your chest? UNAVEM? You work for UNAVEM? You don't? Then why the card? The card is only for employees of UNAVEM. You say you're not an employee of theirs. That's a contradiction. Explain no further! You talk too much. You talk too much!"

I'm the one, Ventura, whose credentials you asked to take a close look at because "the United Nations identifies soldiers and observers, it doesn't hand out cards to journalists. But didn't you say you were a tourist? Then how can you be saying now that you're a journalist? Well, are you a tourist? You're lying to authority. That's serious, very serious. You talk too much!"

You sent me on foot to the other side of the city in search of the UNAVEM liaison officer. Halfway there, I was called back by one of your lackeys—"Sir! Sir! The director wants you to turn around"—to be told that the liaison officer wasn't necessary anymore and I should wait a little longer, to be subjected to another round of questions, each more idiotic then the last, I should put on a sheet of paper the entire story that you heard an hour before.

"Write legibly. We have to understand what you write."

"This is the only handwriting I have."

See it, Ventura, the same handwriting that you have in front of you now, your eyes bulging in fury, the same fury I felt when you asked me to write—"In capital letters!"—on a sheet torn from a calendar the name of David Wimhurst, spokesman of the representative of the secretary-general of the United Nations in Angola, and "now your affiliation," the fury, Ventura, that exploded because men in your position have learned to turn the very act of writing the name of one's father and mother into a humiliation.

I'm the one, Ventura, who told you that your questions were insulting, that your suspicion was unjustified and your behavior deplorable, the one who refused to leave your little office "without the UNAVEM card, which you know very well you can't confiscate, unlike the passport, which you also don't want to return. I'm not leaving, call the police, call the army if you feel like it."

And it wasn't necessary to call the police because they were already there, called by you, in the person of the Angolan National Police liaison officer with UNAVEM, who even so insisted that journalists aren't included in the peace process and therefore my card had to be false, the police with whom you left, leaving me in the hands of your competent lackey, who because of me and through your fault also cursed that day because he had no lunch.

You must remember having threatened, "Pretty soon I will lose my patience with him!" With me, Ventura, when you had lost your patience long before, because the victim's resistance leaves the spider furious, until you were suffocating so much from the fury that you stopped talking to me. Surely you haven't forgotten the way you lost control, waving your arms, spewing despotism: onto DEFA, the United Nations, the government, the police, in Cuíto, in Luanda, that day, that afternoon, the next morning, the next afternoon, two days, a waste, a predicament, Ventura.

My biggest bad luck, I want you to realize that you're an incompetent: any DEFA employee can distinguish a visa from an extension of one. You're suspicious: you bothered everybody and his brother to obtain from UNAVEM in Luanda a letter confirming the validity of my credentials. You acted in bad faith: without waiting for an answer, you phoned your superior to say you were holding a journalist with a fake card, to which your boss replied with the obvious instruction to deny me renewal of my visa. You're a coward: when you were shown the satellite message the next day—"I would like to inform you that the Portuguese journalist Pedro Rosa Mendes was issued an authentic

194

UNAVEM press pass, with the number 135, which allows him the use of all the facilities of the United Nations during his trip through Angola on the way to Mozambique" — you weren't man enough to admit that you had given false information to your superior and that you had been the instigator of a gross defamation. You acted like a bastard: when the DEFA in Luanda and the vice governor of Bié, Tony, ordered you to return my documents, you couldn't even bring yourself to stamp the passport, leaving me an illegal on the road to Cuando Cubango. Ventura, you were petty: after a two-day circus, in the presence of a representative of the Ministry of the Interior, who was also dragged into the story, you handed over my documents with ridiculous formality to the UNAVEM liaison officer, Major Espinosa, who, playing his role, placed them in my hand with a smile on his lips.

You personify "what in Uruguay we call the power of the incompetent. Never fear the power of the competent. If one is intelligent, he knows how to use the power he possesses. To use it or not to use it. But beware of the incompetent who holds power. He does great damage."

You don't know, but there was a Brazilian captain, Monteiro, who spent hours decoding the message from Luanda to you, because in Luanda they use *Windows* and in Cuíto it's DOS, and he taught me that "in Brazil, we often say the world will end up in the hands of the incompetent. Because of their greater numbers."

Human genius, Ventura, succeeds in things that you will never attain, but stupidity has a power for sabotage of which I was unaware. I can't find the words to describe it in Portuguese, but Uruguayan Spanish has a term that fits: *cortedad.*

Cortedad is the terror in which your subordinates live, who despise you but who are obliged to pretend they respect you. *Cortedad* is your keeping them in the adulatory silence of elementary school, obliging them to walk on tiptoe, to knock at your open door with their eyes on the floor, to stay their step upon entering and leaving, clicking their heels as if in salute. *Cortedad* is the sadness of your office, a gloomy trunk, your kingdom, with bullet-ridden chairs and desks, where the only rays of light come in through holes of different caliber, from the metal plates on the windows to the backs of your employees.

Cortedad is your concept of professional duty, reduced to the administration of the great power of petty villainy.

They told me you were very nervous and a true believer. Such people make for dramatic conversions. God is your last chance.

Just as the last time I saw you, you aren't looking me in the eye: on that occasion you couldn't bring yourself to do so, today you cannot. It's all the same: I neither shake your hand nor say good-bye. You did nothing to deserve it.

From him who does not forget you.

List of taboos of the Mwata ("husband of all"):

1. It is disrespectful to try to shake the Mwata's hand unless he offers it in exceptional cases.
2. A gift is not handed to the Mwata but placed on the ground in front of him and someone picks it up for him.
3. The Mwata eats alone, and tradition forbids seeing him eat.
4. In an audience with the Mwata, the visitor sits cross-legged on a mat. It is forbidden to place one leg over the knee of the other.
5. To speak to the Mwata, one claps his hands to call the Mwata's attention to one's desire to say something.
6. It is a serious violation of Lunda tradition to mention a death to the Mwata, except through a special counselor; otherwise, one can be subject to payment of an indemnity.
7. To greet the Mwata, men clap their hands and women who are standing kneel and do the same.
8. It is contrary to Lunda tradition to step on a thread of the *muselo* (royal hammock) when it is on the ground. The bearers of the hammock will demand compensation and may mistreat the violator.

9. Visits to the royal sepulcher in Lunde or to other sacred locales are restricted. Unauthorized visitors are forbidden to approach them.
10. Persons with bleeding wounds are forbidden to enter the palace.
11. It is forbidden and a lack of respect to smoke inside the Chipango.
12. It is forbidden to bring a dog inside the Chipango.
13. It is forbidden for any person (including the Mwata's wife) to spend the night in the Chota (Palace).
14. It is forbidden for a menstruating woman to enter the Chipango or for the Mwata's wife to enter the Chota.

Mwata 18, the Avenger:
An Ethnographic-Historical Short Subject

DRAMATIS PERSONAE
Mwata Munona II Chinyanta IV Kazembe XVIII,
known as Kafumbe Kasemenwa Lufu
White Explorer
Secretary in Red Beret
Royal Highness Wife of Mwata
Wallace Son of Mwata

SYNOPSIS

Mwata Kazembe, heir to the powerful kingdom of the same name, vassal of the great Muataiânvua, receives the visits of the White Explorer in his faraway capital. The White Explorer met a nephew of the Mwata who has been pacifying a neighboring kingdom and brings a letter from him to his uncle. The White Explorer has spent too much time in the jungle and has not yet learned to be among humans. He dresses in decadent fashion, is exhausted, and exhibits disjointed behavior. The Mwata receives him and wants to talk with him of other explorers, predecessors of the visitor, who were well received by the Mwata's ancestors and were buried near the palace. The Mwata demonstrates his magnanimity by inviting the White Explorer to have lunch at the palace. The White Explorer meets the Mwata's heir. The film ends with a final proof that the White Explorer comes from a kingdom of barbarians.

SCENE 1

The credits are a sequence of extreme close-ups of surfaces, in ocher tones, in which furrows of clay stand out. On this common background is a succession of crude drawings, childish but geometric, backed by the first sounds, very soft, of a marimba orchestra. The colors do not vary, and they are the colors of the earth: yellow, brown, gray. Later, the viewer will perceive that they are the walls of straw huts in the village.

The film opens in the small square of Mwansabombwe, the Mwata's capital, with a close-up of the legs of a man loading sacks of dried fish onto the roof of a bus; his face is not seen. The camera pans down to the ground, revealing as it does so the vehicle's windows and the bustle of the passengers. The bus, an Indian make, is covered with a thick coating of dust. The details will locate the viewer in time — it is early morning — and tell him that the bus arrived the night before over a dirt road, which indicates a remote location.

Without a cut, the camera floats in a semicircle, in a few seconds taking in the rest of the activity in the square: small shops with cane mats on the ground, jerricans of fuel in the street with bottles of gasoline lined up on top of them, walls painted in Coca-Cola colors, and in the background young men playing Foosball in the sand.

As the traveling shot continues, the field opens to the right, until it aligns with the main street, made of clay, so that the viewer's gaze naturally follows it. There, still indistinct, is the stooped figure of a man, walking; soon it can be seen that he is white.

The camera, sweeping at a height above the people's heads, descends the street. The man is coming up it. The viewer now sees the man's face—glasses, lifeless eyes, the look of fatigue and fear—at the moment when the man stops and gazes at something. Still young, he turns to the left; the camera turns to the right; a gate and a flowering mango tree fill the screen. It is the entrance to the Mwata's palace.

The traveling shot can end at the crown of the mango tree and in the sky, washing out the scene with excessive light. Cut.

Dialogue between the Mwata's assistant, Secretary in Red Beret, and the White Explorer in a reverse shot. Note: in editing, choose the image of the listener rather than of the speaker. The dialogue will be, as far as the camera and the action are concerned, between two mutes.

"This is a palace..."

"Yes."

"It is obligatory to bring a gift for the Mwata. A sign of respect."

"I...I've been traveling for three months to...strange places. I'm carrying a minimum of baggage. I didn't bring anything for His Highness. I didn't know."

"It doesn't matter. You didn't know."

The White Explorer is disheartened. He took a bath yesterday. He no longer smells bad to himself or others. He is wearing what he calls his clothes-to-see-the-ambassador: black pants with a noticeable tear in the knee and a Pierre Cardin shirt, fake but smart, bought on Cairo Road in Lusaka. The camera provides these details, and the viewer realizes through them that any greater ceremony is impossible for the White Explorer.

Secretary in Red Beret has an impassible expression.

The White Explorer looks desperately at his wrist. It's important that the cameraman capture in this shot a faint untanned band of skin around the wrist, revealing one more mishap: the watch band broke.

"Not even the watch..."

Cut.

The White Explorer has the watch in his pocket. Close-up of his hand in his pocket. Cut.

This time the camera shows Secretary in Red Beret while he speaks:

"It doesn't matter. Do you know how to greet the Mwata? Bring your hands together, palm against palm, without making any noise. You'll be seated on the mat in front of him. But you must rise before he enters, not looking at him but knowing that he is walking toward you. After he sits, you sit down again. The letter you bring, do not give it directly to the Mwata. Give it to me, and I will hand it to him."

A shot from some distance, so the two men's entire bodies appear. Brief pause in the dialogue.

The shade of a mango tree. A dog wandering slowly by. The White Explorer in the shade, in a long-sleeved shirt buttoned to the neck, sweating with no gift for the Mwata. He has a tape recorder in his hands.

"Listen ... The only thing I have of any value is a silk shirt. I don't know if it's good enough ..."

Cut. Over the final part of the sentence, edit images of the White Explorer, in a prefabricated room with no furniture, wrapping a pair of boots, along with a shirt.

A man appears at the gate, gesturing that the Mwata has summoned him.

SCENE 2

Close-up of the teeth and ferocious eyes of a lioness. Cut.

Boom shot of a wide chair, so that the wooden frame of the chair occupies the center of the image. Beneath it, like points on a compass, are the head, paws, and tail of the stuffed lioness.

A helmet in gilded metal, well polished so that the words SAPEURS POMPIERS DE PARIS 1897 can be read. A form appears reflected in the helmet. The Mwata is not seen, but the viewer knows he has arrived — the camera has not broken the taboo, even though this fact may escape the inattentive spectator.

Close-up of sneakers, a well-known American brand. The camera moves slowly upward, showing black jeans and a white T-shirt, ending in a jovial face that fills the screen: the Mwata.

"Welcome!"

The Mwata seats himself on the lion throne, appearing in the frame in front of an image that was in the background: above the chair is a print of the earliest kings of Kazembe. The White Explorer and the secretary sit on a lower level, one step below the small cement platform erected for the Mwata. Without cutting, the camera rises and effects a traveling shot revealing the sacred enclosure, a common garden, and the palace, a residence in British country style. The Mwata speaks.

"Other Portuguese have come here. Pinto, Gamito, De Lacerda. They were men of peace. We called them Chalila Mwana Bonbdo Uwali Kuposa Busanga—that is Swahili. They gave us trinkets. Two hundred years ago, as you know. Good people. We buried De Lacerda near here. I shall speak to you of this, but this morning I have business. We will set an audience for two o'clock. Where are you sleeping?"

The White Explorer tries to babble a reply. He looks as if he is about to faint. He is sweating. He opens his mouth but says nothing. He moves into the background, in a framing that reveals the impatience of Secretary in Red Beret, filmed almost from behind. Previous shot: the White Explorer sweating.

"Where did you eat?"

"Where did you have dinner?"

"Have you had breakfast?"

The framing of the Mwata is the same for all these questions, with very quick shots.

A quick shot of the jango, filmed from the palace, with the Mwata standing up from his throne. Return to the previous shot.

"Today you will lunch at the palace. Summon Royal Highness, my wife."

Royal Highness arrives, and the White Explorer extends his hand to her (breaking one more taboo). He realizes his error and brings his palms together, amplifying the disaster because the opportunity has passed. The camera, which has kept the Mwata offscreen, now brings him in view in a discreet pan shot of the three parties, freezing at the moment of the hand clapping and the Mwata's raising of an eyebrow.

"Is one o'clock good for Royal Highness? Then please be here at one for lunch."

SCENE 3

Static shot for some seconds of a meal laid out, seen from overhead, various dishes, a palette of colors, from which aromas can be surmised: chicken, fish, boiled vegetables, oranges, a water basin and soap beside it, on the ground, with a small towel. Close-up of a plate of meat. A gigantic hand dips a white paste into the plate. The camera at ground level frames the room where a man is sitting and eating. It is the White Explorer, his legs crossed. There are photographs on the walls, out of focus. The White Explorer is far away, but the sound is that of someone slurping his food.

A traveling shot of the walls of the room, with three cuts: two shots from left to right, one shot from right to left, from the perspective of one looking at pictures in a museum. The sound of chewing continues. The traveling shot encompasses calendars, black-and-white portraits of earlier Mwatas and of tribal ceremonies, paintings, wall decorations. A lion skin. The tracking freezes at the lion's mouth.

The camera, at ground level, shows from behind two legs coming into the room, which advance into the image, as in a western. The White Explorer is sitting in the background and, turning to the right, looks in the direction of the camera, with food in his hand. His mouth is agape.

A young man enters, approaches the White Explorer and the camera. The camera draws back as he introduces himself.

"I'm Wallace Son of Mwata. I've come to have lunch with you."

The White Explorer choking. His hands are greasy. The dishes: thinking he was going to eat alone, the White Explorer put on his plate both chicken legs and most of the white meat. All that's left for the prince is wings. The camera frames Wallace Son of Mwata sitting down, washing his hands, and slowly, reluctantly, taking a wing.

Repeat, with the Mwata, the same framing as when Wallace Son of Mwata entered the room. The Mwata approaches, and the camera raises to his face. His sober smile reveals an infinite pleasure.

"I hope you have eaten well. Wallace will go with you later to the bus. But now we have to talk a little. I shall tell you of your ancestors who came here to civilize us. Do you wish to record?"

END

Sunday is a day of rest in the Bero Valley (a *mulola*, or dry stream, like others in the Namibe desert that carry water once a year, in the downpours of March). Sitting amid the corn harvest, surrounded by salmon-colored rocks, the clan is smoking and drinking. The soba of Macala speaks to the echo of the wind, in the presence of women of queenly elegance. His two upper incisors are filed to a point, and he has had the lower ones removed. Like the others, he wears wide bracelets that nearly cover his arms; the same adornment on his ankles. He invites me to try his peppery tobacco, which he carries inside a gilded staff — it's used like snuff. He speaks a peculiar form of my language. I know nothing about him. The recorder has preserved his explanation. I thought at first of printing it as conventional prose. But rereading it, I found it to be mystical. Everything is *realrealthere*. Thus spoke the Mucubal:

WATER GONE

the water gone
from the well
— motapump
Mucuval doing bad

water gone
artesian well the government's

river lots of water: rain
pass here
good for the garden
—river pass here just once this year
Angola suffering
will go hungry

cattle realrealthere
that one left
no grass here
came realreal *face*

money where at?
like this
—Mucuval got no money in bank

cachimba
problem is no tube
—the tube is where?
no way to pull the water

we drinking massango
sell in square
good to give strength
—gives you strength

that river got thin
just took a little
can't go there
—it's a mountain

that one's of the hose realrealthere
won't work
the tube realrealthere
came loose realrealthere

corn is there
—all
but problem of water
dried up

animal you kill just a day
eat and that's all
the other year
other year kill four more
or three more
one for people
one for government
one for my son

kill
kneel realrealthere
oh-oh! knife not
break realrealthere
squeeze realrealthere
and it dies
not kill with weapon
there—it dies

José rows my sarcophagus through the islands and rapids. We zigzag along a border: some islands are Namibia, others are Angola. I am lying in the bottom of the canoe, my arms extended along my body, and the canoe adapts itself to it, my head and shoulders fit perfectly into it. A sarcophagus is like that, a custom-made box for the final crossing.

We had to wait for nightfall in order to return to Angola. Because of the UN embargo, the Angolan border is closed in the areas controlled by UNITA, as is the case of Cuando Cubango. In the Caprivi Strip the control is tight. Namibian patrols — with soldiers who speak fluent Portuguese — go up and down the river. They are zealous and efficient; when they see anyone crossing the river, they shoot to kill. They did so this morning, firing on some women who had come for supplies.

On the Angolan side there is no sustenance. Beer, flour, cooking oil, fuel, batteries, tobacco, fruit can be bought in Namibian shops, almost always owned by Portuguese. Everything is carried out in the greatest secrecy, amid codes and whispers, which has its ridiculous aspect because these furtive customers give themselves away at first glance: there is panic in their eyes. They buy with brusque gestures, bent backs, and stooped shoulders. They wear rags and shoes with holes in them.

There is no telephone in Mucusso either. The last time I used one was three weeks ago, in Menongue. There was no way to avoid crossing the river to make a phone call. That takes a whole day. First you have to know what time the last patrol went by and take the pulse of the surroundings. You snake your way through the rapids to the island closest to the home of T, a friend of UNITA on the Namibian side of the river. T's land extends to the river. Whoever is on the facing island has to wait in the vegetation until a familiar face shows up. They order us to come ahead, wait, or return another day, if it's a bad time.

A car was parked at the shop. Whole. Normal. Painted. With glass in the windows! I was shocked. I have grown unaccustomed to everything. The return will be like that of sponge fishermen: a slow ascent, in degrees of decompression, from nitrogen in the veins to fresh air.

The water laps gently at my back through the smooth belly of the canoe. The slap of the oar is interrupted when José takes advantage of a current to follow the river's satiny darkness. Lying there, I have the sky above me, I can plunge into it at any moment. From my sarcophagus, profaned by five cases of beer that I was asked to bring back to Mucusso—with it, it will be impossible for us to maneuver if anything goes wrong—I follow the Southern Cross. What if José makes a mistake in the crossing? There are treacherous rapids, some of which lead to the crocodiles' den. The hippos are farther down. The surface conceals jagged rocks. The crossing takes too much time.

"We're getting there. It's there at that big tree."

There, Faustino is waiting in his Hilux with its headlights off, under a tree that rises above the other crowns.

Compulsive stupidity: risking your life three times to be able to say, "Hello! I'm alive!"

The ferry crosses the Mekong the full width of the room. It overcomes the pull of the current, stands suspended in the thick thread of the water, and, farther on, flies in the first dunes of the desert — invisible but present in the darkness. At the top of the hill, the most tepid hour of the day sails, when it isn't hot. Behind, the arc of the bay stretches, nestling its cold currents and a caress of coastal clouds. The bay, after the last orchestra seat, beyond the lobby and the posters, is reflected in the white facade against which I lean. The ferry on the screen, devoid of depth, stops at the riverbank and will always return there to tell this story. It is the 7:30 matinee at the Cine Namibe, and Indochina appears in the forbidden afternoons of a French schoolgirl in Saigon.

Jean-Jacques Annaud's *The Lover* is an unlikely film for an oasis at the edge of the desert, but it was this incongruity that transformed a banal work into a stunning evening. Marguerite Duras never knew that her adolescence would also hide in a small town in the south of Angola, in a brief respite from the perennial local fare of Rambos and kung fu.

In the outside display case of the Cine Namibe (which used to be the Cine Moçâmedes) they have put two hazy photos of nude bodies, which naturally, have attracted spectators expecting a pornographic feast. The showing begins when all seven of us choose our seats (indecision spread over five hundred empty seats on three levels!) and the candelabras are turned off. The ferry then appears, moving among the dunes and the sea of Namibe to the sewing-machine sound of the projector. The spools have more cuts than a plate of spaghetti, and the other six spectators, disappointed by the work's decency, take advantage of one of the initial breaks and leave. Until the end of the book, only the usher, mute, drinks in with me the throaty voice of Jeanne Moreau and prays before the exquisite face of Jane Marsh. The young face of Duras, before its sudden aging at eighteen. An old image that comes to the screen in the form of a fine rain, precisely like the Atlantic cacimbo that plagued Namibe that night and left me stranded there, anguished, on a small island by the seaside.

He does not yet know the bedroom, nor the bed concealed in it, in the fine darkness, a platonic altar. She has not yet brought him rice with dried fish for breakfast before the rising of the sun, a breakfast he will refuse before daybreak. He has not yet asked for coffee. The room key is still in her pocket, the key to a treasure that she has guarded forever, still in the bottom of the pocket where she fingers the key with nervous strength when he disturbs her without knowing it. The bed does not yet exist.

She will still have to earn the money, coin by coin, accumulate it from her dedication to him, earn it to be able to buy the bed and set up the altar, a snare of love into which he will fall, falling first from sleepiness, injuring himself a little without getting trapped, only bruised. A gentle snare able to provoke the pain of ungratefulness, he thinks, when he senses in this room the chains closing around the steps that he is to take. The minimal pain that she cannot combat: the guilt of discordance, something they both will lament, it being no one's fault.

That bed will be in the middle, always. Bought with the money that she so needs.

She came into Henri Valot's office, and he saw her that first day as he would see her on the last: crying. Abundant tears, all that her beautiful face could yield, flowed throughout the interview.

Her face, according to photographs that he keeps in Paris: the face is her entire stature, a small woman, a figure in silk paper. To him, until the last day, she will be only her face. When she entered the bedroom, she had no face. It is not the most valuable thing a woman has to offer. In other countries, in other religions, yes. Not in Cambodia.

Sokim explained to him that she was a nurse and that she had an eye infection. That first day, the tears were only because of this. Henri told her a nurse's place was in the hospital, she had the knowledge that was lacking everywhere in the country. She then told him of the silent curtain with which he was unfamiliar but had guessed because behind the curtain are all the faces, all the eyes, all the women, all the men.

Sokim's parents died in the Khmer Rouge madness. The children were taken in by Sokim's older brother, Rathnal, in Oudong. The nurse needed money, the family needed it also, which is why she applied for a job with the electoral teams.

(Henri recruited 250 people for the first stage of elections, taking the census. Love stories erupted among those young people, from the same village but working outside the home for the first time. The recruitment was democratic, done across all social strata, because some tasks demanded no special training: monitoring the lines waiting to be attended, or using a rubber stamp.)

He keeps the photos: Sokim and Henri at pagodas. Everywhere. Sokim and Henri, and the smiles of others as they watch the couple's intimacy mature.

He didn't see. It wouldn't have mattered if he had.

He takes out the photos of Sokim, in Paris, where she is not because he left a bed offered him in Cambodia, the empty bed beside which Sokim may still be standing.

The wise men of the village came to Rathnal's dinners. The other professors, monks, elders. Sokim was always in the living room, always in one spot, behind Henri, serving him and no one else, and the others laughed at seeing their love grow. She remained standing. She refused to sit.

One night Rathnal spoke to Henri, said that it was time to marry, to find a good woman, she could be here, in this very room. Rathnal knew of his sister's love: she sent delicate love letters to Henri, in Khmer, translated into English by her brother. Letters in which modesty vied with forwardness, the calligraphy of Sokim's face: set phrases, a few daring ones.

Every day, she would take Henri a basket of fruit. Bananas, mangoes. In the village, she was his friend, demonstrating her consideration by the baskets.

She saved the money she made.

At the end of 1992 the Khmer Rouge abandoned the peace process and attacked several United Nations offices, including the one in the district closest to Oudong. Suvash Chandra Sarker, Henri's colleague, was fearful: his wife had given birth two months earlier, and he wanted to return to Bangladesh. He left the post two months before the elections, leaving Henri by himself, because the provincial chief, the elderly Indian C. L. Rose, decided to leave Henri on his own.

Henri, by himself, in Oudong, had the support of David, a Kenyan policeman, and Captain Anchev, a Bulgarian officer. One night he was warned that the Khmer were planning to attack Oudong. His large house was well known, and he received orders to always spend the night in Phnom Penh. Every day, sixty miles on the difficult Highway 1. It went on like that for several days.

Until Sokim insisted. It wasn't the first time. Henri had not accepted before.

A wooden house, large and elevated, for a family with many brothers and sisters. He waited at the ground-floor entrance. She went to get the key and opened a door.

A bedroom, a large bed, mosquito netting, rug, bookcase. Henri's bedroom. Sokim's savings.

Elections were held, three days of euphoria, and then nothing. The departure. There was a final dinner, a melancholy table, gloomy as a wake, with special foods choking back the dry words. The family withdrew early to their rooms, they always went to sleep early. Henri, in his room, fell asleep immediately. He would leave the next day.

In the middle of the night, a knock on the door. It was Sokim. She was crying as on the first day, but he couldn't see her eyes, because her head was lowered, in her customary shyness, her head in shadow, keeping her from what she wanted to do, from what she had decided to attempt, the final night: she was in a nightgown, at the entrance to the room, treading upon generations of rules and morality that forbade her to be there, like that, for him, she who had waited, walled in by house and rules, for twenty-five years.

She had waited for a man, and she was twenty-five years old. Tonight she must leap over the abyss, or he would no longer be on the other side to catch her.

The face that he knew and did not see now. The beauty of that small, exquisite woman, gentle, frightfully gentle, with delicate Indian features. Many things crossed his mind. He tried to prevent her coming in. She came in.

He lit the lamp, and she lay down in his bed, in their bed, on the enormous white altar unlike any other in the house, because only Henri slept in a bed. They spent hours together. She was small, delicate, weightless in his hands.

The most elegant thing that he could give her made her feel scorned.

She cried at the airport. She offered him a gold chain and a Buddha in black wood. Next to his heart: the small face of a Buddha.

216

Elle est retrouvée!
—Quoi!—l'Eternité.
C'est la mer mêlée
Au soleil.

Those lines...Again, please!

Songdeth was a thousand years old.

In 1992 I arrived in Oudong, some fifty kilometers from Phnom Penh, to prepare for elections. Oudong is the capital of the kings of Cambodia: following the decline of Angkor and the attacks by Siam in the fourteenth and fifteenth centuries, the kings installed themselves there. Oudong was the capital until 1866. On Mount Oudong the kings Norodom and Sisowath were buried in magnificent stupas: the Buddhism of the Cambodian kings was mixed with elements of Hinduism. The kings, until Sihanouk, always had a Brahman at their side.

In Oudong we looked for a place to rent and chose Sum Mol's large house. I was told that a Cambodian prince lived downstairs who would greatly like to hear the French language again.

I went downstairs to introduce myself to him.

An old gentleman with long white hair, thin and wearing a *sampot* (the cloth worn by both men and women), came out of his small house: Prince Norodom Songdeth. He had reddish skin, sunburned, deeply marked, rivers that partitioned his brow. He received me simply and kindly. He explained he hadn't spoken French since 1975. He thought he had forgotten it. We sat down outside at five in the afternoon. I got up from my hammock at midnight.

These nocturnal conversations would go on for a year.

That same night, to my great surprise, I saw many people come by to greet Songdeth, bringing fruit and other gifts. The scenario was always the same: the people would arrive and lie down in the sand in front of us. With a word, Songdeth would free them from this uncomfortable position. He told me:

"I'm no longer anything, not a prince. I'm at the end of my life, but respect for ritual is an essential virtue of Cambodian culture."

Ce peuple est inspiré par la fièvre et le cancer. Infirmes et viellards son tellement respectables qu'ils demandent à être bouillis — le plus malin est de quitter ce continent, où la folie rôde pour pourvoir d'ortages ces misérables. J'entre au vrai royaume des enfants de Cham.

Songdeth spoke perfect French, learned in the best schools. He belonged to the royal family and was the uncle of King Norodom Sihanouk. With the entrance of the Khmer Rouge into Phnom Penh in 1975, unlike the rest of his family he decided to remain in Cambodia.

I suspect an inclination, an interest on his part in the communist experiment of Pol Pot's Khmer Rouge.

However, Songdeth was a member of the royal family: a problem. With the support of Sum Mol, he went into hiding. With this they traded roles, and Songdeth became the *homme à tout faire* of his *homme à tout faire* (Genet, with his theatrical works *The Maids* and *The Blacks*, didn't invent anything). Songdeth hid in pagodas, in the great pagoda of Battambang. But the Khmer closed the pagodas.

Songdeth and Sum Mol were transferred to the large irrigation project at Pursat, where people died of hunger, thirst, and fatigue. Songdeth never spoke of the violence of the Khmer Rouge. He spoke of work, of Pol Pot's dream of taking Cambodia back to the time of Angkor.

After 1979, with the fall of the Khmer Rouge regime because of the Vietnamese invasion, Sum Mol found his family in a wooden house under the stilts of the large house of his *homme à tout faire*. For him too it was time for retirement, the conclusion of his life, in the Hindu sense: the refuge, near the forest, the abandonment of material and spiritual properties.

Songdeth appeared to be sixty, but he was a thousand years old.

The prince was trained as a pilot in France, from 1935 to 1939. After the German invasion, he took refuge in London. His great frustration was not being able to exercise his abilities as a pilot, not having the right to fly missions over German or French soil because of his royal origins. The French didn't want a Cambodian prince to die in the war. He was given administrative duties in the small Free French office in London. Charles de Gaulle's office.

After the war he returned to Phnom Penh and a life as playboy. In the fifties he imported from San Francisco the first Harley-Davidson in Cambodia.

Songdeth was consulted by Sihanouk but made his friendships outside the palace, in the democratic opposition to the monarchy.

Et le printemps m'a apporté l'affreux rire de l'idiot.

Songdeth had weary eyes. He could no longer stand to read, but he adored French literature. One day, to my surprise, he appeared at my house. He had climbed all the stairs, that man who walked so little. The reason for the visit: to see my library. I had some classics of French literature for my Cambodian nights. I hoped to use my stay in Cambodia to reread the works that had left their mark on me as an adolescent. In this small library were the poets of the late nineteenth century (Baudelaire, Verlaine, and Mallarmé), some great novels from the same period (by Zola, Flaubert, and Balzac), and some works of anthropology (by Lévi-Strauss, Mead, Clastres, etc.).

He chose Baudelaire, sat down, and I saw that he couldn't read it. I took the book, opened it to "Parfum Exotiques," and read it to him, slowly. I read several poems that night, until he fell asleep. I left him on my bed and went to sleep on a mat in the living room. He woke me at 4:30 the next day to ask if we could resume that evening.

These nocturnal readings would go on for a year.

We went through poetry, *Les fleurs du mal, Une saison en enfer,* and various poems of Mallarmé that I've always found difficult.

He loved them.

Flaubert had in his home a *gueuloir,* where he would read aloud the sentences he wrote. Novels should, above all, sound good. Flaubert tried every intonation and would even shout the phrases he wrote. I never shouted, but I read with attention and patience *La tentation de Saint-Antoine* and the complete *Education sentimentale* (an immense book, hundreds of pages, dozens of nights). I also read *Les illusions pérdues* of Balzac. Songdeth and I loved two works that are coming-of-age books, in the German tradition of the bildungsroman. I was twenty-five, coming of age myself, those nights in Cambodia. I don't know, however, what those books meant to Songdeth. He always ended up falling asleep in his hammock. We would turn off the generator, which ran from 6:00 until 11:00, and I would go to bed.

The light that allowed me to read was as weak as the prince's eyes. The volts of the generator were channeled through a network of wires. Each wire stole part of the energy: radios, refrigerator... By the time it got to the lamp, it was tenuous, a candle power.

In my office at the United Nations I had fourteen cars, a Land Cruiser and others. And I bought, with a female friend of mine, an old Ukrainian sidecar, a copy of the German wartime ones, Oural was the make. It was green. I painted it blue and white.

One day, Songdeth was summoned by King Sihanouk to the Royal Palace in Phnom Penh. He asked me to accompany him and didn't want to go by car but by motorcycle. I said, "My bike is terrible, it runs hot, you can die at any moment. Let's take one of my new cars."

"No!" And he appeared at the appointed time with a typically French *casquette* and got into the sidecar.

"Let's go!"

On the road we astonished everyone, and the same when we got to the palace, but the guards threw themselves on the ground in front of him and opened the gates for us. I took him to the stairs. A man from Protocol directed him to the king.

I returned several hours later, and Songdeth wanted to take a spin around the city. We did so with heads high, he seated beside me, looking at almost twenty years of absence.

We stopped at roadside restaurants on the return trip. In bars. It was a long journey, the return to Oudong.

Songdeth was a thousand years old.

Sur les routes, par de nuits d'hiver, sans gite, sans habits, sans pain, une voix étreignait mon cœur gelé: «Faiblesse ou force: te voilà, c'est la force. Tu ne sais ni où tu vas ni pourquoi tu vas, entre partout, réponds à tout. On ne te tuera pas plus que si tu étais cadavre.» Au matin j'avais le regard si perdu et la contenance si morte, que ceux que j'ai rencontrés ne m'ont peut-être pas vu. *

---

*From *Une saison en enfer*, by Arthur Rimbaud

The van stalled in Caluquembe, and, "as a favor to the journalist," I was given a place in the cab of an overloaded truck. Inside, it had been totally stripped. Only a small metal plaque gave away the vehicle's happier incarnation: MANUFACTURED IN GDR, now the property of Agostinho and Zinha, a brother and sister from Huambo.

From my travel journal, notebook 2 (which begins in Tômbua with a bad drawing of the trawler *Roncador*):

Caconda, July 9, 1997

Zinha was a woman, and she was pleased with that, there on an altar between me and her brother. At a forced stop, for Agostinho to tighten the lug nuts of the tire that threatened to come off again, she stretched once more with her irremediable lack of charm. It seemed to me that cats seduce that way, by drawing out the distractions. Then she spoke, point-blank.

"Can a woman who has relations seven days after her period get pregnant?"

"What?"

"Can a woman get pregnant in the week after her period? Mine started on the 23rd, a Sunday. It ended on the 28th. Then there were seven days, until the 7th."

The cab was too small for such a personal question, the road too vast for me to escape on foot. Long ago, that is, that same morning, I got up with a praiseworthy ambition, one alone: to get to Huambo. I felt uncomfortable. I tried to shift my attention to the chickens at my feet. Live chickens, warm chickens. Pretty chickens.

In vain.

"When was it you had relations? A week later?"

"Well, my period ended on the 28th, so, after that, one, two, three...June has twenty-eight days, doesn't it?"

"It has thirty. So, if your period ended on the 28th, it's...nine days. You had relations more than a week later."

"You think I'll get pregnant? Is a woman fertile at that time?"

Agostinho still hadn't come back. How many lug nuts and loose tires could there be? I counted the chickens: there were four. Two were white, one was black, one brown. They were restless from all the shaking, from the heat of the motor that filled the middle of the cab — where Zinha sat to make room for me because there were only two seats — and from a sulfurous vapor that came out whenever the radiator ran dry. The details we overlook!

"The most fertile time is right after menstruation. I think."

"Then I'm pregnant!"

"Maybe not. It depends on the woman. Some get pregnant more easily than others. A matter of hormones — you know. Some women don't even have their periods every month. Many are irregular... Wait: it's the other way around. The most fertile time is just before menstruation. That makes sense: the end of the fertility cycle, when the body gets prepared and isn't fertilized."

"Then I'm pregnant!"

The conversation itself was like pregnancy: nothing to be done, no way of confirming.

"And if you are, what will you do?"

"Get rid of it. My boyfriend can't make up his mind. I don't much like the way he's talking. He says he doesn't want a commitment. Not till November."

"Why not until November? Either he loves you or he doesn't. He can't choose the month. You mean he doesn't want to be with you now and in November he will? That doesn't make sense, Zinha."

"I found out he's seeing somebody else. Right there in Huambo. He has to decide between us. A man can't love two women at the same time."

"You're right, not at the same time. At least not in the same way...What kind of protection do they use in Huambo? You should protect yourself. If you're afraid of having a baby—because once is enough."

"It was just this once. I usually protect myself, but we didn't have anything. Normally we use a condom."

"Can't you get the pill, in Huambo?"

"Those green ones you take every day? You can't get them in Huambo. Do you have anything for a cold?"

The savanna, at an altitude of almost two thousand meters, jolted its way past the truck's open window. A person could walk faster. The chickens kept my left foot warm. The cab was like a sieve. Zinha slept a little, spilling hair and an arm over the back of my seat.

"You'll be long in Huambo?"

"Three days at most. Then Cuíto."

"Saturday we'll get together. We'll see each other there."

"What does one do for a good time in Huambo?"

"Ah, lots of things. There are picnics on the outskirts. And a discotheque. And gatherings. Do you like that?"

"Yes."

A truck driver passed us heading in the opposite direction—noteworthy on a road without traffic. The youth's smile was as wide as the windshield as he waved. Zinha smiled awkwardly.

"You know him? Who is he?"

"Just a truck driver..."

"What's his story? Is he your boyfriend?"

"No, but he likes me. He's tried. But he's married. No married men for me."

We got to Caconda at an hour when we couldn't go any farther. It took me some time to accept the idea of Huambo—the city, the boardinghouse, Pepe, people, some grub—having to wait till tomorrow. The village had no place for a stranger to sleep. A breeze entered through one window and left through the other. The desolation was broken by the pineapple Zinha had placed before me.

On the 20th of October the engineer Fernando Marcelino, former director of the Institute for Agricultural Research in Chianga, and his wife, Dr. Miete Marcelino, director of the Municipal Library, were murdered in Huambo. The well-known couple were ambushed by armed criminals in front of the home of a close friend, the physician Dr. David Bernardino, also white.

The Marcelinos were shot with a machine gun when their car arrived at Dr. Bernardino's residence in the upper part of the city. In the backseat were two ladies. Dilar, a nun and the doctor's sister, was also killed in the attack. The other woman, Sra Zaida Dáskalos, director of the Library of the College of Sciences and aunt of the doctor, was struck in the arm and right eye and evacuated to Luanda, where she was declared in critical condition and later sent to Lisbon.

One of the couple's children, José Marcelino, escaped the attack, which at the same moment, 7:30 P.M., was also directed at the Bernardino home. "I got here before them but didn't have any cigarettes and remembered that my mother also smoked," he told *O Planalto*. "I went back three or four blocks to buy cigarettes, and as I was paying, I heard the shots. They were coming from Dr. Bernardino's house, but I had no idea that a tragedy had occurred."

This son had the misfortune to be the first to verify his parents' horrible end. "When I arrived in front of the house, I saw my parents' car stopped there, with no one in it, the motor off and the headlights on." He thought there was "something wrong with the engine" and got out to ask his friend for help. Only then did he notice the shattered windshield and, drawing nearer, the four bullet-ridden bodies inside. "My father still had his glasses on. One bullet went through the lens, which didn't even shatter. It just made a hole."

José Marcelino immediately rang Dr. Bernardino's doorbell to ask for help. "He looked out the window in fear because he thought it was the criminals. *They're* still here, get away, it just happened!" The doctor was in the rear of his spacious residence and, when he heard the shots, telephoned Dr. Miete Marcelino to tell them to stay at home. "No one answered," José Marcelino told the newspaper.

The Provincial Command of the Huambo Police began an investigation to find those responsible for the crime, but it is rumored in the city that the couple's death was politically motivated. Before Independence, Fernando and Miete Marcelino had been MPLA militants in Huambo, the city where they lived their entire lives, and had received numerous death threats.

In recent months they were among the group of intellectuals and university personnel responsible for the publication of the opposition newspaper *Jango*. The paper was connected to the MPLA, despite its articles criticizing all the parties, including UNITA, which considered itself the main target.

"They were white and influential. Besides *Jango*, UNITA felt the lack of support from intellectuals. They needed to strike in order to show who runs things in Huambo. It was a warning, and once again it was the racist card that was played," a friend of the Marcelino family told the police, according to information obtained by *O Planalto*. He was planning to leave Angola because of the growing tension in the country.

The assassination, which drew the condemnation of several figures in Lisbon, came at a particularly difficult time for the peace process, following UNITA's rejection of the results of the presidential election. Incidents multiplied through every province, especially in Bié, Huambo, and Benguela, where the government accused Jonas Savimbi's movement of mounting a secret army and preparing to return to war.

The Marcelinos left seven adult children. Besides José, another brother, João, decided to remain in the country after the crime, although he went to Portugal for a month. "To all of them we offer our condolences" (from O *Planalto*, December 7, 1992, page 3).

A UNITA leader claimed responsibility for the Marcelinos' death, at a rally for the movement held on the fifth of the month at the São Pedro Market in Huambo. The message, an anonymous note written on the back of a Front for Democracy pamphlet, added that the leader told the militants, "We've taken care of the Marcelinos' health, now it's time to clean Bernardino."

"The death of Dr. David Bernardino, which had been preceded by the death of other very dear friends, the engineer Marcelino, his wife and sister, was perhaps an attempt by UNITA to take the government's pulse, and in fact the government did not respond in any way [...] leaving UNITA to rule. [...] The lack of authority was so great that they could enjoy the luxury of holding a rally in the Benfica area to proclaim the death of Dr. Bernardino, saying that he 'deserved death.' From those words to his execution was but a short step" (from an interview with Manuel dos Santos Pinto, a business manager evacuated from Huambo, in *Jango*, August 1993, page 6).

The Picassos and the Quiocos follow on this roll the twisted neon signs of the Africa Hotel. I photographed them from behind—the deformed letters came out right to left—atop a wall that falls vertically from the fourth floor. The hotel is on a corner and gives no indication that it was destroyed inside.

Among the neon and the Picassos came José Marcelino. I met him again one Sunday afternoon. On Sundays nothing moves in Huambo except for a group of teenagers dancing in the rain in a ruined house, in the vicinity of São Pedro, around a Sharp made possible by the trade in kwanzas. José passed by on a large carless avenue as I was kneeling over a bicycle chain, next to a tank truck gutted by a rocket. (I had met him some months before, in the incandescent light of the Baía Azul, amid shrimp and white wine, stretched out on the floor with a leg that gave me gooseflesh: the week before, a glass *palette* had taken out a chunk of his muscle).

"In Huambo you can't go anywhere. We have time. Load the bicycle in the rear there. I have a place to show you."

In 1949, David Bernardino, born into an illustrious Portuguese family of Nova Lisboa (Huambo), left Luanda in a stateroom on the *Angola* to study medicine in Portugal. Two years later, his brother José followed, and in 1954 the youngest, Luís, joined them. During his years at the university David became friends with several Portuguese intellectuals through the maestro Lopes Graça and the communist associates of José. Many people of letters and politics frequented the apartment their father had arranged for them on Avenida de Roma. One of those who came by there was a young Angolan doctor named Agostinho Neto.

The year that the PIDE arrested Bernardino the father, 1960, David began working in Dundo as a doctor for Diamang, an Angolan diamond-mining company. It was there that he met one of the great specialists in African art, Marie-Louise Bastin, and awakened to the sumptuous Tchokwe art of northeastern Angola. Those were important years in David's formation, and in 1971 he returned to Nova Lisboa with two projects: founding his own hospital and decorating in the fashion of his world the house that had been his parents' and in which he would now live by himself (his mother, Manuela Bernardino, had died). The house, built in 1951, was enormous, and he remodeled it inside and out. The doctor's preferences were unsatisfied by the provincial offerings of the city's three dress shops, which exposed in their windows the settlers' lack of sophistication. But some furniture ordered from Benguela accommodated well what distinguished this house from all the others: the veneration for Tchokwe art, the passion for Impressionist painting and Italian baroque, married to the tangle of tastes acquired in London, Amsterdam, and Algiers.

David, who had no children, indulged his pedagogical preferences on the younger generation of his family. Amid the reproductions of van Gogh and Matisse and the enormous warehouse shelves full of boxes decorated with Picassos, he would sit his nephews and their friends down for slide shows, teaching them to distinguish schools of art and playing records for them—he had hundreds—so

228

they could learn the instruments and sharpen their ear. Some of those young people lent themselves to his neighborhood project, with the distribution of pigs' feet and milk in the sanzalas where the black population lived—in the spirit that in order to win over the public, it's necessary to immerse yourself in their milieu.

He was an unconventional man. He invariably dressed badly, despite being a distinguished figure, and there was something of the flashy about him—when he went to a party, for example, he would conceal his tuxedo beneath a shirt overflowing with pleats. In his native city he was a displaced person: his degree of culture exceeded that of his surroundings, and politically he was not accepted by the conservatism of Nova Lisboa, despite some of the oldest families in the city being up to their eyebrows in opposition to the regime—the Laras, the Marcelinos, the Dáskaloses, his own.

It was not Portugal but UNITA, after the 25th of April, that would make the doctor pay for his political convictions. Uniting around him some of the intelligentsia among professors and young graduates, he founded the Democratic Movement of Huambo, which would later be absorbed by the MPLA (like similar organizations that arose in various Angolan provinces). In August 1975, UNITA won the first Huambo war and initiated the witch hunt. David Bernardino was the last man to abandon the barracks of the Portuguese troops, from which he left for the airport and Luanda. In the absence of its owner, the house paid the price for him. When the MPLA government retook the city half a year later and Bernardino was able to return home, he found the house destroyed by use and vandalism, the bathtub overflowing with dung, and the furniture plundered, not one picture left, not a single record. All these things were for sale in the markets.

The doctor rebuilt his house without any faith in the future. He gave up the pictures, in order not to be robbed again, but he didn't give up art, which appeared discreetly on the walls by the hand of Maria João Leite Velho and other friends: dancers from France confronted the elegance of women from Luanda, and sorcerers' masks cast their covetous eyes upon a family of zebras. Others of Bernardino's immobile tenants protected the windows, forged into the bars in the form of doves, crocodiles, turtles, and cubist females, in undulating iron that looked out on the orchard in the rear. The house was surrounded by a wall of poetry—Fernando Pessoa, Alexandre Dáskalos, and others—written in gigantic letters so that people passing by in the street could read it.

The frescoes of Picasso and Matisse and Tchokwe art hosted in the following years a group of people for whom the doctor epitomized the hope for independence and gave meaning to the struggle for the continuance of what mattered—the university, the hospital, the library, a certain concept of intellectual dignity. Huambo had been deserted by the white population. Some friends from before were still there, living in the solitude of those who had chosen to remain behind. The intensification of the civil war isolated them. Daily life became a hell: frequent bombings, attacks at markets, systematic sabotage—it was a rare week when none of this happened. Electricity was out for months because the posts had been felled, there was no running water for years on end, to the point where everyone forgot what faucets were for—the younger among them had never seen them working.* In such an atmosphere, people survived as resisters, each supporting the other, and those who had known one another from before became even closer.

Bernardino liked to play host. His jango, lined in purple mosaics, transformed itself into a great family. The house was full every weekend, and the guests brought the best they could find to the Sunday lunch. It would take weeks to gather the ingredients. They would eat a poulet au sang, a coq au vin, a stuffed turkey. The women went to great pains to make the dessert. There was always tea, by the quart, a vice inherited from a Goan grandmother who never got to India. Tea was served starting at 6:00. The steam from the infusions dissolved among the forty-three orchids on the glassed-in porch and, when it was cold, dripped from the hares and crocodiles of the old Portuguese

---

*One child fled in panic from water coming out of the hose when, in 1997, José Marcelino turned on the electric pump outside the small house that he restored in the upper part of the city.

230

tiles. Bernardino imputed great importance to the order of objects and the ceremony of gestures. The teacups, the Russian samovar, and the cake were placed like offerings on the black granite table in his office. On the porch, for the luncheons, was the huge marble table with wrought iron that had belonged to the bakery owned by a Greek adventurer in the 1930s (the tiles, in blue ceramic, were also retrieved from the trash). One of his favorite films was *Babette's Feast*. Until the end, that was the atmosphere that he tried to re-create continually in his residence in Huambo.

José Marcelino parked his car at the spot where his parents were assassinated on October 20, 1992. The neighborhood was ravaged by the second civil war. The dwellings were transformed into bizarre architectural caverns in which a new species of the homeless lived half-concealed in holes walled up by bricks and metal sheets riddled with bullet holes. Bernardino's house was empty. One entered it through the rear, after passing the cypresses planted by Matilde, which were no longer there. An open shed of cement and cloth was once the garage and the guest rooms. From it emerged several ragged children, who climbed the steps that formerly led to the kitchen. Only the walls still stood. The roof had collapsed, so the layout of the bedrooms, living room, and corridors was reduced to a single division—the sky of the plateau, clear at that altitude.

But there were survivors: the frieze of the Quiocos in the living room, the mask over the entrance to the hallway leading to the office, the zebra in the office, the Matisse in the dining room, the Picassos in the reading room, several African drawings scattered on the walls, and the flight of the iron doves suspended on the windows. The dream of a man haunting an emptiness of rubble and weeds.

"Don't go in there! Don't step on anything except the cement floor. The place has never been demined. Just two weeks ago a child died in a garden on the avenue that had been 'cleaned.'"

Bullets and rain have long since eroded the poetry-covered plaster on the side of the house. Perhaps the grating with the birth date of Bernardino's mother, Manuela, May 6, is still there; I didn't see it. But at the threshold of the main door continues the posthumous homage to Miete Marcelino, written by Bernardino himself.

Close, close the door,
just as she would want:
may her memory
meet with your favor.

Contrary to good sense, which his friends tried to instill with desperate phone calls from Luanda, London, Brussels, and Geneva, Bernardino refused to leave Huambo, at a time when war was clearly about to return. He was murdered on December 4, 1992, in Cacilhas, at "his" hospital, by the same men who killed the Marcelinos. His house was a kingdom with room for the entire city. The death of these three was more than a political crime. For Huambo, it was an act of eviction. The war recommenced, officially, on January 5, 1993.

These three had become the resistance in Huambo, which, contrary to what was thought, was not the MPLA resistance. Because the MPLA turned its back on Huambo and they did not. It was a resistance of providing at least an image of something other than total destruction. They wanted, in their stubbornness, for the city to function. Luanda didn't give a damn. They were there because they loved the land, so that people could have a normal life, so there could be electricity, water—that's what they were struggling for.

Such love of the land is transmitted through work, not through rallies, "down with," "kill!," or "viva!" Such love of the land is planting a tree and later being able to pick the fruit. Those three stubbornly went on taking care of their tree. And they were completely abandoned by Luanda. But UNITA appeared not to know.

It's strange.

UNITA found their presence an affront, an ideological burden. How do people survive adversity? As a group. Because they weren't from a ghetto, like Luanda, they were a family with ties not of blood but of complicity. They created an atmosphere to bear it all. They listened to classical music, heard ballet on cassettes sent to them from

London. Or opera. Until Bernardino's death it was like that. They didn't know how to use a weapon; the meetings were to keep their souls alive.

In 1992, I showed up early, at eight in the morning, went into the house. David and his older sister Carmito were there, with music playing at full volume. Classical music throughout the house. And a Huambo that was more and more its own ghost... The music in the morning. Fresh coffee. And afterward Sunday lunch, and the man's optimism. The lunch, the coq au vin, the Sunday cake...

Luanda held no appeal for him, he lived there preparing for his return, loaded down with medicine, soy, and all that. He was a man of refinement who liked things done right, with care. It was not for nothing that so many generations lived in that house.

Miete was a warm, fascinating woman and a militant. She worked with the Organization of Angolan Women for years, without becoming embittered, always gentle, doing the simple things without feeling humiliated. Dilar, the missionary, lived in Cuando Cubango and taught the peasants to read and write. She was arrested by UNITA in 1975 in Bié, accused of being Fernando's sister. She got out because the nuns intervened. She went on, traveled, had been in the Far East. She stayed in Cuando Cubango, teaching women how to crochet, how to sew on a button, and telling frightening stories. They were gentle women, with large families, children all around. The very image of mothers, not matriarchs. Whole women.

Perhaps it would not be respectful to their memory to find out who did the killing. I signed the manifesto for peace at the time of the bombing of Huambo. I think the destruction of Huambo went to the very heart. Of the city and the people.

All that politics... It's disgusting! I don't care who did the killing. What matters is they died. I miss them, loved them.

Maria Alexandre Dáskalos, granddaughter of Stamatis, daughter of Alexandre, niece of Manuela, cousin of David, has the gift of poetic clairvoyance, along with other gifts that she learned later. She knew that war would return worse than ever in 1992, knew that once again her friends would die. She told this to an ambassador in Luanda. He humiliated her with one sentence: "I'm here to handle the blacks. Whites in Angola are the children of poor immigrants."

The clairvoyance began two generations earlier. The piano is the most hated instrument in her family in the post-Independence era, because in Huambo it was transformed into an instrument of torture. After the city was occupied by UNITA, the MPLA returned in February 1976, bringing with it people of the worst category. Every day at mealtime, Maria Alexandre's maternal grandmother would hear banging on the piano in the house behind her own. She was very intelligent, the grandmother.

"The piano is being destroyed... The sound of it is making people ill, covering something cruel."

The youths of the Organization of Angolan Pioneers had their flag, and everyone in a three-block radius had to stand at attention when it was raised. Anyone who failed to do so was shot or imprisoned; the boys of the OAP were training to be future leaders. The peasants who didn't know or were distracted were taken into that abandoned house—it had belonged to a music teacher who fled months before—and tortured to the sound of the piano so it would drown out their screams. Terror makes use even of a piano.

This is Maria Alexandre's problem with classical music. It reminds her of what she would rather forget. There was always music coming back to her in the days following each killing of family and friends.

A seventeenth-century oratorio, in Sintra, greeted her in her first exile in Portugal. It was huge, with a likeness of Christ larger than she, from Madeira, with real hair. It was winter, and the dampness ran down the walls, encircling the table and the orange compote.

But it was not yet time for prayers.

On August 8, 1975, three activist MPLA youths were killed by an FNLA grenade on the top floor of the post office building in Huambo, on the old Praça General Norton de Matos, across from the governmental palace. With them was a camera-laden Japanese journalist, Ian Canecava, who was also blown up between the walls. For years, Maria Alexandre couldn't go by that corner. Maninho Saraiva, Fadário Muteka, and Gildo were her closest companions.*

Two days before, flying to Luanda, Maria Alexandre attempted, as always, to warn everyone that people were going to die. In the FAPLA barracks it was said that Huambo was a lost cause and that they had known it for six months. They did nothing to save the lives of their militants. At the FAPLA general staff she heard another phrase that would stay with her forever. A terrible phrase: "The revolution needs heroes."

It was the definitive blow for an MPLA militant. The party knew of the vulnerability of its cadres in Huambo, a small group that promoted political action among the rural population. They were easy prey in the first purge carried out in the city, after the truce was signed at the beginning of August 1975 ending five days of combat—the first Huambo war.

"The lyricism vanished with that phrase, because I was in love with Huambo. All the people of the high plains—whites, mixed-race, and blacks—hoped that the city would be spared from war because it was the country's granary and, also, because the Mbundu were the largest ethnic group in Angola and there was a sense of the wrongness of the policy toward them. UNITA is very unjust to the MPLA whites of Huambo because it doesn't recognize that they too hoped. UNITA doesn't even recognize the drama that they lived through in the MPLA, where they were mistreated. Some survived. Others didn't. There was the group in the interior, those who because of MPLA connections had to flee from one village to the next. People I've haven't seen since."

---

*Fadário was the twin brother of Faustino Muteka, vice minister of administration of the territory in the Unity and National Reconciliation government (1997), a politician with a long career in the MPLA. Gildo was the brother of General Faceira, a leading figure in the FAPLA and later in the FAA (he was one of the Angolan officials with the greatest responsibility for the fall of Mobutu Sese Seko when head of an important Angolan contingent that allowed Laurent-Désiré Kabila to enter Kinshasa). Saraiva was the nephew of the poet Viriato da Cruz (founder of the MPLA and one of the first to perish in the Stalinist hardening of the party: he died of starvation in 1973, in a village in the People's Republic of China).

People stop being seen. Maria Alexandre found a different city when she returned in 1976. The human geography she knew had disappeared. The "asphalt" had been taken over by a new population, and in the sanzala, she found the same women very thin, very old. S. José de Cluny, the girls' secondary school that she had attended, was once impenetrable; the pupils had never seen the novitiates' garden, because the day students had no access to it. But the war had come there too, leaving everything open so that Maria Alexandre could see inside. The cedars had been wiped out, and the damages to the nuns' cells, to the novitiates' quarters, were plain to see. To her it is a symbol: that which she had thought to be a secret, never in her life to be discovered, was suddenly there, naked. She can't forget it, the wall coming down. Like many other walls . . .

Maninho Saraiva's apartment had four large speakers that hosted afternoons of listening to music. Rainy afternoons in which the water fell in the motionless air, adding excitement to the tunes of Vinicius de Moraes and the best of Chico Buarque and the poems of Eugénio de Andrade and Manuel Bandeira, along with *Em defesa de Joaquim Pinto de Andrade*. Or the works of Lenin, in the "oven-refrigerator" collection: they had titles like *The Oven*, with a picture of a gas oven on the cover, or *The Refrigerator*, but inside, on paper of very poor quality, were the forbidden classics. *Battleship Potemkin* was shown at that house.

Maria Alexandre, at eighteen the youngest child and among friends who were close to thirty, had the key to the kitchen. They gave her a free hand in certain culinary adventures, but she was not allowed to have parties, because at that time the liberated lifestyle had not yet emerged. (Young people were beginning to date earlier. "We were freer because of the climate," miniskirts, bikinis, and hot pants became commonplace, "but the great Angolan excess came after Independence with the revolutionary dynamic and the freedom demanded by all.") She could also read the books, leaf through banned pamphlets, and listen to political conversations.

During Christmas holidays she would go back there. She took in the ruins. She visited people, the mothers of girlfriends in the absence of those friends, and renewed her ties with dried mushrooms, pickles, compotes—she learned to make the prunes in sauce that one pierces with a needle. And thus went an entire afternoon, on a pilgrimage, hands grasping whistling old teakettles, eyes feasting on Portuguese-language *Reader's Digests* from the 1940s. She listened to absurd tales of lions and jaguars, the tales that anyone who lived long years in the jungle possesses.

That grandmother, not the daughter of Dáskalos but of the other one, Deolinda, the one with the piano, went to Angola at the age of twelve, grew up in the Hotel Paris in Luanda, and gave birth in a hammock because she was caught in the middle of a war between two tribes in Kwanza Sul. She married a man from São Tomé who also wanted a farm, so they installed themselves in the bush, where they spent twenty years. One day she went to get water at the well, and nothing came out. A boa constrictor was covering the pipe. Things like that. Maria Alexandre's mother was deathly afraid of lions; she'd seen them passing in front of the house when she was four or five.

The son went to meet her there, in 1987, with a basket from the Huambo nuns, a young Daniel in the rain baths of Huambo, because there was no running water.

Daniel left the country at the age of three and returned when he was six. Those were the Algerian years: Arab women and Turkish baths, Persian poetry and Ethiopian dissidents from the Menghistu Haile-Mariam regime, female resisters from the FLMN, the women in whose memories reside the terror of the civil war; all those people who later died. And the Catholic church, which reconciled Maria Alexandre to her faith.

When he returned to Angola, Daniel said, "Mother, I don't want to go sightseeing." Maria Alexandre always loved traveling around the island of Luanda. She knew things had changed when they were able to go to the end of the island, when the Soviets had left that private beach after sixteen years.

Now, she doesn't want to go to the island. As her son says, "There's nothing there but ruined houses."

Zaida Dáskalos experienced an omen in Huambo before she was

killed. In Luanda, her old ostrich egg, which had withstood evacuations, occupations, and attacks, cracked with a sharp sound in her daughter's home, alerting her to what she would understand only later.

An opera, at infrequent intervals, was all that Maria Alexandre could bear to listen to. The tea kettle can be heard clearly as I wait for her in the living room where in absentia an old hotel clock ticks away.

DYING FOR NOTHING

Shouts were the silences born
of the trees solemn motionless
witnesses to the swift gestures of death
selecting men in the street.
Fear was the courage of dying for nothing.

Fernando Marcelino

On the outside of David Bernardino's house was written, in charcoal, "There remained to us vultures on the plate, and we knew that [...] people."

The missing part was ripped away along with the plaster by a machine gun burst.

The inscription comprises three verses of an unpublished poem.

The destruction of the Huambo libraries began in March 1993. The main document depository, the Municipal—which had been under the directorship of Miete Marcelino—was in the line of fire, in the upper part of the city, and "in the popular parlance of war it could be said that it was a barrier."

Roberto Caetano Paulo, provincial delegate of the Ministry of

Culture in Huambo, recalls that UNITA was on the hospital side and the government on the palace side.

"After the troops wrecked the library in the battles, the soldiers and the population began to sabotage. They began with the furnishings and ended with the literature."

The furniture before the memory.

"Part of our archives ended up in the markets. We found documents from the civil registry, both old and recent. The delegate from Culture began a verbal investigation," verifying that in a few months Huambo had lost historical documentation that made possible the reading of this entire century in the plateau, and further back. The province is now beginning a rudimentary work "at the end of the twentieth century. We have the promise of furniture from Portugal, and we've made progress toward restoration of the building that was formerly the municipal council."

The same with the Museum of the Plateau, which is in ruins and surrounded by grass not yet demined — it is not a metaphor. The old books disappeared. They reappear from time to time in the squares, at inflated prices, which means that not all the plundering of paper was to light fires. Here one finds an encyclopedia in a private home, there a scientific collection that someone wants to sell. There was a children's library in the small building of the Cultural mission, but it vanished, and the only children's story that remained was on the other side of the street, in the rubble of a house on the corner of Avenida Joaquim Kapango. Under the fallen roof and the twisted iron are Mickey Mouse and Donald Duck in the midst of flowers, everything painted in gigantic scale, where the kindergarten was.

"We're repurchasing everything we can. We've entered into negotiations with a lady who has law books worth five hundred million kwanzas. The museum was almost destroyed. There were some stuffed animals in display cases, and books on the lives of ancestors, history, and cultural figures. Index cards and photogravures, sculptures and Mbundu masks. One of the best paintings of the Kandumbo Rocks was in the hands of a third party, and he came around to sell it. Now we're looking for more in the field of literature."

"Do you know what that inscription is on Bernardino's wall?"
I read it from my notebook. Caetano Paulo didn't know. But an employee of Culture, whom I hadn't noticed during the interview with the delegate, showed up at our place the next morning. Pepe came to wake me, because "There's a man outside who has something for you."

"It's the literature," he told me. "On the wall it's incomplete."

The man showed me the remains of a book from the General Overseas Agency—Lisbon, 1951, stained and full of mold, with a cover but very few pages. *Subsídios etnográficos para a história dos povos de Angola—Ikuma ñi mianda iá Tutchokue (Provérbios e ditos dos Quiocos)*, by João Vicente Martins. On page 30, and the last in irregular handwriting, was the key to the poem on the wall:

We deceived love
in the hips of the serpent.
We kneeled in the hypnotism of the milk,
We protected the venom of the nests.

At the end.
There remained to us vultures

                                  on the plate
and they tasted to us of death.

The orchards forbidding trespass,
undulating in zinc, in clumps of earth.
The land without acres.
But there was never a lack of tea for dinner.
They filmed the funeral

                                  to kill him.

He last on State television
and we unfurling once again

                                  for good

the white mourning cloth of the bay:
the neon saber.

Signed "Lídia." "A friend of the family," one of the Marcelino sisters told me, much later, in La Paz, cutting the matter short in the cold of the Altiplano. The spelling errors on the bullet-scarred wall are a semantic lapse worth considering. And it also proves that poetry can be written with bullets, to the pride of the owners of Angola: poets who bastardized themselves in war and warriors who tried to cleanse themselves in verse.

The proverb on page 30 of the book is "rísu riá–fua, tulu mu-ári." Literal translation: "The eye is blinded, the dream goes on."

"No one escapes his destiny," said Sebastião, a policeman sent from Tete to the Immigration office in Zumbo. He is right. My only hope for a ride to Tete, when everything appeared to be going well, is the car sent for a cadaver that's in the heat. It's known that the vehicle already left from there; what's not known is when it will arrive. There are no phones in Zumbo. I'm beginning to think that when it comes to maps, I'm jinxed. I've entered Mozambique by the only district in Tete that has no land communication to the rest of the province.

The hippos, voluminous balls of fat, go on floating, weightless in the water. The canoe approaches. It's like this daily, the tangent of disaster. The female, if it is a female, has already noticed us.

The man died in a traffic accident on the Kanyemba highway, in Zimbabwe, hours after I passed through there. In this wilderness, it is difficult to come to the aid of accident victims. To make matters worse, all were drunk, as no one denies, and the jeep skidded on a bridge, smashing against the riverbank. Against all the evidence, the account of the accident concluded it was a case of witchcraft, relates Sebastião, amused.

"There's magic here. People with spells on them. Amulet-crocodiles in the lake. They're people transformed by sorcery into animals. Whoever wants to get someone uses an amulet-animal, and there's no resisting it. That person ends up being dragged into the river, and the crocodile-people grab him and take him to their hiding place, where they leave him to rot."

The accident happened Tuesday night, but the victims weren't found until 10 the next morning, and the first rescue team didn't get there until 3 P.M. The dead man from Tete was swelling in the sun since morning (and two were seriously injured). Things got no better when the team arrived with him at the only funeral home in the area and learned that all the refrigeration drawers were full. They had to look for another mortuary and finally found one with an opening in Zambia. The head of Immigration in Zumbo spares me no detail:

"Luckily they kept throwing water on him while they looked for another morgue. The swelling went down a little."

The canoe draws nearer. Now a confrontation seems inevitable. It's a female! They understand the risk. They're maneuvering fiercely. The rocks do their job, keeping the animal away. If they run out of rocks, that will be the end. They don't. Hippopotamuses are herbivores, but the largest number of fatal accidents in Africa involve them. In Zumbo, the only transportation is by river and in canoes and with oars—there are only three outboard motorboats, but they belong to the "project." The hippos react badly when they're disturbed and kill anything within reach. The females are especially dangerous when they have young to protect. The fishermen know this, but if they waited for the hippos to leave the water, they'd never go in. Since they couldn't kill them—the "Boers" of the project have passed legislation protecting them—so the alternative is to flee or to scare them away with noise, which doesn't always work. The rocks are the last resort: all the canoes carry half a dozen as ballast.

Charles and Marcelino threw two rocks when we crossed from Kanyemba to Zumbo. They slapped their hands against the canoe, made noises, ordered me to stay calm. It turned out to be only a mass of vegetation floating in the current. The other three masses we saw later were real hippos, in their customary position: watching the surface, with a clump of thick hair on their heads. The crocodile we passed also caused us no problem: it was quite close but didn't move, limiting itself to rotating its body to stay parallel to us. The three of us laughed.

A lovely crossing: one hour since Kanyemba, skimming along in the canoe in the afternoon humidity, with the brick-red sun disappearing into the Zambezi mountain range. Charles and Marcelino had rowed upstream for two hours to buy two cases of beer in Zimbabwe. It was night when we arrived in Zumbo: no place to eat. It's pointless to mention the rest (no electricity, no telephone, no water, no road).

The faint sound is the breathing of the hippos in the river. The loud sound is the bureaucratic minimalism of rubber stamps and typewriters.

The terrace of Immigration is built on a base of old stones that antedate the current masonry. Slaves were once sold on this spot.

Zimbabweans, Zambians, and Mozambicans climb the stairs of the terrace as if emerging from the water, and enter the house to get their "passports" stamped—pieces of crumpled paper invented by three different countries in these equally milky currents. There is a triple border where the Zambezi flows into Mozambique: Mozambique is here on the other side, Zimbabwe is on the other side, but further upstream; Zambia is on this side and also upstream, with another river between her and us, the Luangwa, a tributary of the Zambezi. Zumbo, Kanyemba, and Feira (the Zambian post) are a crossroad of nothingness, points cut off from their respective centers. A lot of fishing goes on, and fish circulate in quantity—they are eaten in Harare, Lusaka, and even Lubumbashi. Water is, therefore, the sole nationality.

The fishermen climb the slaves' stairs, the stairs where I was trapped for hours by the floating hippos. The post has a flag on the mast at the rear of the terrace, and I can pretend, from this high vantage point, that Immigration is a boat bearing the flag of FRELIMO, forbidden the use of the river.

Sebastião is handling the stamp, and the director comes and goes in postmortem acts of bureaucracy. No word of the car for the Tete corpse.

The flatboat comes up from Cahora Bassa around the 15th of every month, the trip taking two or three days. It can't be too soon for me: close to that date I have to make it to Quelimane. It's impossible to rent a boat from the fishermen, because they are not built to withstand the lake storms: in the late afternoon, a breeze rises in the middle of the lagoon from which the shore cannot be seen, stirring up waves worthy of the high seas. The alternative, since the car doesn't show up for the dead man, is a slow one: by canoe to Feira and from there seven hundred kilometers of impossible road following the Zambian side along the westernmost part of Mozambique, then returning to the country by way of the Catete frontier. More than enough to finish off my body: my eyes are already sandpapered from so much dust; weary, they burn, and my neck is petrified.

I slept off this exhaustion on a mat in the open air. Sebastião introduces me as his guest, and for two days he will share with me the little he has: condensed milk—at the third meal it oozed from the small hole in the can in a creamy thread, lettuce from his garden, *nshima*, dried and boiled fish. The first night I stayed on the porch of his cement dwelling. He lives in the enclosure around the house belonging to the Party, in what must have been servants' quarters: a small bedroom with boarded-up windows, a latrine cut into the floor, chickens everywhere, mats overhead, and a storage room without a lock (Sebastião kept it closed with a pair of handcuffs on a nail).

The other policeman at the post—there are only two in Zumbo and not enough work—came after dinner to talk about the new moon, share the voracity of the mosquitoes, and trade war stories. The two men fought on opposite sides: Sebastião for the government forces, his colleague for RENAMO. It wasn't yesterday, but neither was it that long ago. At a fire overlooking the silvery skein of the Zambezi, they discussed the conflict calmly. They have ideas. They did not speak of hate. They laughed.

They will face each other in the office the next morning, as on any other day, with no bitterness, because there was none the day before. Since Jamba there have been no obvious signs of violent warfare.

Destroyed houses, ruins, bullet-shattered walls, abandoned dwellings, the displaced in communities of huts, the desolated look of a Pyrrhic peace: in Zumbo, war is everywhere. But it's in the past, it's gone elsewhere—forever, they hope.

Charles and Marcelino had this written on their faces. There is a resurrection on this side of the road. The two of them, and the other two, and those I met later, are boatmen on the Indian Ocean. Their river, this river, leads to a bank of coral.

Two thousand years ago, at the time of the Han, the roads pointed at the Chinese skies the wisdom of the steles—monuments limited to a flat surface, containing a graphically perfect inscription. The direction was not random: "Lovers orient themselves so the morning light will make their gentlest features more beautiful and soften their unattractive ones. Turning toward the bloody West, the palace of red, the warlike and the heroic."*

It is still early in this terrace of slaves. But even earlier to the west, behind the mountains, where it has not yet dawned. Sebastião sweeps the house with a straw broom at 6 A.M. The day at the post always begins with the same routine.

Not counting the huts with pompous names—"Cahora Bassa," "Lusaka"—where everyone lives, Zumbo has two streets: Riverfront, which has no houses and can barely be seen through the tall grass; and Main Street, parallel to the other, only several meters long, where the few solid buildings are located. Immigration, palace, Party. The palace is a large residence. The administrator isn't in. The Commandant—we use his rank as a proper noun, because no one ever calls him anything else—insisted that the foreigner be the official guest of the residence. There is no furniture, except for two beds in the administrator's enormous bedroom. But a strange invisible presence moves among the rooms, creaking the rear door and evanescing in the scorched quarters of the patio.

---

*Victor Segalen, *Stèles*

The administrator's brother was an artilleryman. He manned bazookas in the war, not shouting as he fired. It's said he went crazy from the noise. He doesn't speak and isn't shown to anyone.

I didn't sleep there. As I was about to go to bed, the candle revealed a horde of cockroaches: they had emerged with the night, covering the pillows and backpacks, describing arcs upward from my feet, climbing the walls. An inferno. The rats were no bother, because I couldn't see them: they scampered inside the suspended ceiling. Sebastião?

"Let's go to my house. But there are roaches there too, you'll see. You just didn't notice them yesterday."

There were, but in Sebastião's room they had more space to climb: the plates from which we ate, the bread we'll be having for breakfast, and some hanging clothes. I counted only six, not six thousand.

Five! I killed one. Sebastião refused the sofa and slept on the mat, also giving me his only blanket.

"Without a mattress they'll suck your blood! You'll wake up with your skin flayed."

The project has something to do with safaris and natural conservation, of the bush and the lake. The fine for unauthorized hunting is sixteen million meticals. Hunting hippos is a prison offense.

The accident had a sole survivor, a Mozambican who was thrown clear of the vehicle. He fainted and, when he came to, managed to make his way on foot to Kanyemba to get help.

Luckily, I escaped riding in the funereal jeep. For the first time in the journey, the heat is malarial.

VILLA MISÉRIA

"Fish eat fish."

The youth appeared at the corner, fleeing, his shoes making a desperate sound easily heard at that hour. We heard the running and the shouting before we saw him.

"It wasn't me! I didn't do anything! I didn't do it!"

He lunged into the avenue, his one last chance to make it to the water, lose himself in the blackness, leaping in headfirst, hoping they wouldn't get him if the tide was in. Low tide wouldn't do; he wouldn't be able to swim or find the necessary depth to cushion the bullets. To make it to the water he had to show himself, break his run perpendicular to the buildings and dash across open ground under the yellow light of the street lamps.

He shouldn't have left home that evening. Pascoal told him not to go out—Pascoal who had helped him dig a shelter in the sand, a hole in the shape of an inverted cone wherever he wanted it, on one of the island beaches, just deep enough for the wind to pass above their heads without blowing out the fire used for cooking funje. That was where they lived, in one of the holes next to other holes that made up a village where they felt safe. The city ought to be seen from there, Pascoal told him, because the only thing the city could offer them were the viaducts and steps in the rainy season, and the garbage dumps the rest of the year. The city didn't need them.

Pascoal. A good friend. In his head the youth tried to reach him mentally on the other side of the darkness, his thoughts flying above the bullets faster than his steps over the pavement. Nothing was visible, not the palm trees, not the cars, not the crowd hunting for fish in the ponds left when the sea drains toward Roque Santeiro. A few lights and nothing else, only the platform forever aground at the end of the island, like a cathedral pointing heavenward.

If he got out of this, he'd take off the earring. He didn't want to remove it, because it was a remembrance of the war; he'd put it on in Malanje after the first attack. It was nicer than painting his nails. Pascoal painted his white. It was okay but not for the youth. Pascoal, on the other side, was with the fishermen now. The youth was only a short distance from the sidewalk now, and maybe he would get away. But maybe not. What if they caught him? Maybe the sewage pipes from the construction work would protect him, if the tide wasn't in. He had a pain in his throat and felt he was running in place, his eyes tripping over the slowness of his feet. Kota Amélio had warned him: the police in the city chase anybody who wears an earring.

He looked behind. He shouldn't have, because he lost his balance and fell. Before hitting his head, he longed for everything he had hated in his life. Sleeping in a hole in the sand, the poverty, the salty smell of the sea in his dirty clothes, the crushed fish the fisherman gave him when he helped drag in the nets, the cold in the dry season, the girls who shooed him away in Bordão on Saturday nights, the security man at the Franco-Angolan Association who once gave him a beating. Pascoal was sleeping now, after smoking some grass.

The policeman emerged from behind the same corner, his machine gun pointing upward, held by three fingers and supported by his thumb, ready to fire. Vertically, the gun had more power. He came screaming like a hyena, out of control, the youth saw it in his eyes, saw it before he fell and struck his head, curled up in a ball when the policeman, standing over him with his legs spread, pointed the machine gun between his eyes.

"You want to die? You want to die?"

The youth stopped moving after loosing a cry, his voice cracking, the whimper of a wounded bird, which faded into sobbing and disappeared in a thin thread of glistening blood that ran from one ear to the pavement.

A truck full of ninjas appeared at the corner of the Hotel Presidente, spilling light from its sirens onto the facades of the avenue, like a lasso in some spectatorless rodeo of violence.

The boys of Lobito Velho have invented a trap for catching seagulls. They sink two sticks in the sand, at water's edge, upright, then tie a string between them. They fashion a long loop, with one end attached to a stone. They place bait between the sticks. The gull catches the bait in midflight, passing between the sticks and catching its beak in the snare. The knot tightens from the bird's momentum, choking it in seconds. The boys hurl themselves upon the bird, break a wing, and begin plucking it still alive.

Other forms of meat are turtle, shark, seal fat, and dolphin.

Akuá, born into a country at war, explained to me that this wasn't violence. Fish eat fish. People eat people.

Today I'm a lady. That's what they made of me. And it was the only thing in my life that wasn't preordained. One morning when I was eight years old—one of the cold months, I don't remember which one—my grandmother slowly raised our window curtain with her fingertips. She was feeling the danger. The PIDE had surrounded the house. Soldiers with rifles and two men in plainclothes came in and arrested my father, who was in bed with pneumonia. The man couldn't get to his feet in his last moments: they grabbed him like a coat hanger, under the arms, and took him where he couldn't hear our screams. They gave no explanations. My father was a metalworker in the Lousal mines, manager of the workshops. He might have had ties to the Communist Party. He might not. We never saw him again. We never found out what happened to him, not even after the 25th of April, or where they took him, how long he was a prisoner, or the conditions in which he died. The same thing happened to an uncle of mine. They disappeared like those who die before birth.

My misfortunes began with the PIDE. My mother was a dressmaker. With my father's disappearance she deteriorated financially and lost patience with her children. She stopped being the humble mother, affectionate and loving, that she was. No more kisses, moments of happiness, bedtime stories. She turned religious, saying her rosary all the time, sacrifices and masses to bring my father back someday. I couldn't stand to see it, a woman drowning in holy water.

I left for the hills. I was a shepherdess and begged in the countryside, from Monday to Saturday. I led lambs, I can't forget it, to a haystack full of rats, rats hairless from age and fright. It was the rainy season. I cried on wet straw. I couldn't stay there. Then there were the pigs, horrible, you can't control them. Lambs, like dogs, flock together. Pigs will run away to the thicket. They're the devil.

I spent my teenage years without love, and when I finally found it, I found it wasn't meant for me. That was life for me, I got burned on wood that wouldn't catch fire. The first time I fell in love was with the Grândola family's heir. He gave me a child and then went back to the future they had planned for him. He never left his own world; it was stupid of me to dream that he would, but at that age, seventeen, you haven't learned anything yet.

At eighteen, in 1964, I was in Lisbon studying nursing at a polyclinic in Campo Grande. I frequented a sweetshop on the ground floor, and one day on the table was a newspaper with Salazar's face on the front page. I put out his eyes, in the photograph, with my cigarette. Scum! I've suffered so much because of you—and I went on burning. A man I knew by sight, at another table, got up and went to the telephone. When I tried to leave, there was a car at the door. They ordered me inside. It was the PIDE.

They took me to a prison, I don't know its name. They put me in a cell all by myself. I was there for nine months. I couldn't defend myself, because I was never interrogated. Nine months without knowing what day it was. No one came to talk to me. Until one day an inspector visited the cells and noticed me. I was very pretty, at twenty. As soon as he saw me—sitting on the floor, my hair long—he summoned me to his office. He grabbed me, took me away in a black car, and didn't stop until we were by the sea, in Guincho. He offered me my freedom: I would be released if I agreed to live with him. He was older, married in Portugal. His wife was French, fine, well bred, an educated lady, and they had three children. He treated me well. His wife never found out. He set me up in an apartment. He wouldn't leave me for anything. I went to hotels in the Algarve, in the times when not many people were there. He took me to Madrid, nice places, on weekends. He had PIDE contacts.

I was with him for two or three months. Then I tried to run away. But Lisbon is small. One day in Baixa I was in the street, and a car blew its horn. It was him. I went back to living with him. But that wasn't what I wanted. I started thinking: here I am in a PIDE's bed.

I managed to get to Mozambique with some money from a Spanish lady in Lisbon, when a gentleman showed up with a group of girls. He promised me a job in a restaurant, but it turned out to be a cabaret. He kept my identity card to buy my ticket to Mozambique. I went to the airport and called a cousin of mine, who asked me not to leave. But I was already on my way.

I stayed in Luanda for forty-eight hours. The other women continued to Lourenço Marques, but he and I didn't. He took me for a tour of the cabaret district, so I could understand what he was doing. I realized I was lost... That same night, there was a single hotel room for the two of us; he made advances, and there was an argument because I didn't want to.

I came to Beira and was received by the owners of the house where I was going to work. The job was in the Dom João V bar. I wore the costume of a queen, with fake jewels, ruffles, curls, all those crazy things, and would stand there with the "king" on display for the customers. It was the times. The establishment had another part, the cabaret, and the owners began pressuring me to work there. But it was as queen that I met people. I made the acquaintance of a Portuguese lady who gave me a helping hand, as a companion. Until her husband discovered where I worked. I finally managed to become the cook in the bar instead of being in direct contact with the men. I created a scandal, yelled that I didn't want to service the rooms, until the man with the contract showed up one day. He slapped me twice. "You're a cheap Lisbon street whore! And now you're here acting like a lady," he shouted at me. "You're going to work till you repay me for your ticket."

I had to pay for my ticket. He sent me to Tete. I left in September 1969. Or was it December? From the commotion at my arrival, and suddenly discovering the kind of work they wanted me to do, I started screaming. A crisis. I was out of commission for a month. Sometimes I wasn't in my right mind.

The PIDE inspector came here right at the beginning, because he discovered the Spanish woman in Lisbon. I was caught unawares by him one night; they told me he was waiting for me in the bedroom. He told me he wasn't here for revenge. "I came to say I didn't want you to ruin yourself, but you're ruined." He asked me to return, go back to a good place, but I didn't want to. In Lisbon, he would spend hours explaining things to me—I had a bad upbringing, he thought me very immature—and he gave me books.

I didn't marry the one I loved, I married the one I met. It was in Tete that I met my husband, twenty-three years older than I was. He loved me deeply. I never succeeded in loving him, but I thought I should respect him. He died in 1991. We had two children. He was the one who made me a lady here. I started in the hotel business with the Beira Alta, a good restaurant. Then it was the Solar das Andorinhas—I chose the name because of the way the two of them go together, the calm, the eaves, and the memories of the land . . . I thought they would bring me peace. After my husband's death I came here, and tell me if it's not the best location in the city.

There were five children in my family, three boys and two girls. The brother I was closest to, we were shepherds together and lived in the fields. Later he ran away to France and Spain. He was a twin . . . I wasn't a good mother. Children are mirrors of us, but what did I have to show them? I'm rough. I gave what my mother gave me. My first son shot himself to death in Lisbon, because of drugs. The younger one found work in Beira, but he's mixed up in drugs too. He never has enough money. He's no longer respectful of me. Last week he lit a cigarette right in front of me. There's nothing to be done. Now he asks me for the car keys.

I don't want to go back to Portugal. It brings back unpleasant memories. I wasn't happy there. Bad things happened there to me. I lost my brothers and sister in a car accident, I don't recall the date. Look it up in a newspaper of the time, an automobile accident in which the entire family died, on the Santiago do Cacém road. They died because there was a mass in Santiago for the soul of my older son, which the priest in Grândola refused to give because my son committed suicide and suicide isn't Catholic. The car went off the road when they were on their way to Santiago. It caught fire. Five deaths, the only family I still had.

I started writing at the age of eleven, inspired by the death of my grandmother. I had never seen a funeral or a grave. I was working in Beja, and one night I began to write. I have childhood poems, I have a poem from the night my brother died. There are doves, shepherds, dogs in "The Night Became Sad." Black shawls, candles, and me, so far away. In 1985 I walked through the hills around Grândola looking for the places I had been with my brother. The trees were still there where we had carved our names with a knife, and the rocks too. They were places that belonged to us. What does it matter now? He's dead.

Sometimes I close everything up and go to my country house on the Zambezi. It's on a hill with small birds, the sunset, doves getting ready to roost; in my mind I can see the Alentejo. I live in Africa, but there are moments when I'm in Alentejo. Sometimes, there in the country, I can feel the wheat rustling, the endless sea beyond the grassland. It's called the Quinta do Cajueiro. We had to have documents, so we gave it that name, because there was an enormous cashew tree. I finally got rid of it, I don't know why. But I do have a lovely mango tree. I'd like to be buried there, where I had a happy life with my husband. Whatever happens, whether it's joy or sorrow, that's where I go.

I came to know things at the country house... There was an old man there named Maxiquitane, who dropped dead in the street after my son's death. He used to say he'd never had shoes or clothes, but he wanted to be dressed like a white man when he died. I honored his wish and took care of the funeral. The Cajueiro was one farm that was never robbed, even when there were thieves on the neighboring land. I was never bothered when I went there, not even on the road at night, and I would carry money with me without any problem. Later, in 1994, I went to Beira, and they told me about a woman who could explain certain things. I looked her up and spoke to her about Maxiquitane. The woman told me that the old man wasn't letting anything bad happen to me. It was him, from beyond, watching over me.

I didn't pay any mind to it for many years, but there are mysterious things even if we don't want to believe. Dona Aninhas, in Beira — she's another one — told me one day: The tears of a mother are the ill fortune of a child. Why did you leave your homeland without saying good-bye to your mother? That gnawed at me for many years, and in 1985 I went to Portugal. My mother was there, paralyzed. She died eight days later. "I was waiting for you, who made me suffer all these years." It was coincidence, it had to be. Or was it? . . . Have they told you about the crocodiles here in Tete? There's a sorcerer who transforms the dead . . . A dead man can be clothed in the form of a crocodile, a hyena, a snake. The sorcerer uses the power of that person to heal and such things.

The house at Cajueiro had two doors. One night, two snakes came in, thin ones that weren't scared of me. They stayed in the middle of the living room, standing, with their tongues out. I covered my face with my hat and lifted my feet. My adopted son yelled. They left. One black, the other with a small yellowish stripe.

When he was alive, Maxiquitane suddenly developed a fever, and his mouth swelled up. But it came and went by itself. On the farm, they used to say it was *mizimo*, a spell, and he admitted it was from an *inhazalumo*, a snake. Because he had to take part in a *batuque*, he left to make the preparations: he found some *pombe*, a drink made from wheat and sorghum, *massanica* (wild apple tree) brandy, meat (goat or ox), hired a group to play the drums, and invited some healers and dancers. That's how it went, from Saturday night till sunset on Sunday. With the batuque, the old man's problems disappeared, and when he died and the snakes appeared, that lady in Beira asked me what did I think about the snakes? She said the old man loved me and protected me. "The snake is that man, who follows you." She told me to go home. "Why did you give up your shrine? Go home, pen up the dogs and cats, and put everything the old man liked around the orange tree: white cassava stew, boiled rice, dried fish, and tobacco."

I did so, and the next morning there were snake tracks, the marks from their bellies…I tried setting up my husband's shrine, but I couldn't focus. The woman in Beira also told me when a snake was killed, there would be great destruction, because the snake was Maxiquitane's wife. I performed those ceremonies, but when I felt frustrated, he came, in the same position around the orange tree. I began to have respect. I gave orders that no snake should ever be killed there again. But one day they killed a snake, which tried to escape by wrapping itself around the orange tree so that it would be remembered: I am Maxiquitane. But they killed it. Why? asked the snake with its eyes before it died. After that, another snake killed Joana, a monkey, and King, the dog, and the chickens. All of them killed by a snake, in the same afternoon. At night, a snake was hiding in the garden I have growing against the wall. My son opened the door, and my other son, the little one, shouted, "Inhoca!" and closed it, and the snake got caught, and I cut it up with a knife.

I began to be afraid of living there. I haven't slept there in three years. I have a meal, stay until sundown, but I don't spend the night. A short time back I gave a batuque for a lot of people, I went to his area and brought all the old people from Catipo, over a hundred people, an all-night affair. For Maxiquitane. Now I manage…Anyone who tries to rob is crazy, a rational person doesn't do anything like that. The farm is pretty this year, everything's back to normal. Either that or I'm feeling stronger.

I thought about killing myself with a glass of Mazodine. I wrote a letter to my children. And just as I was about to commit that act of insanity, the snake showed up, near the orange tree, and, raised, swayed back and forth. I threw the glass to the ground and went to bed. I never again thought of suicide.

I've sometimes had the urge to run away, abandon everything. I took a blanket, eighteen meters of white cloth, and underwear, put everything into the car, along with canned food. I was going to stay wherever the gasoline gave out, in the middle of the forest. I went by the cemetery to say good-bye to my husband's headstone. I was already on the road when I turned back, to get a floral wreath. I didn't get any farther. The car, which had never had any problems, refused to start. My workers pushed it in the middle of the night, you can ask them, without any sign of the car moving. I walked home, and the little one hugged me, crying. A feeling of peace came over me, and I had dinner that day like any other. That was a month ago. The car is still in the shop, a nice touring car, a modern Ford... I don't even think of getting it back. The mechanics can't find out what happened with the motor that night; there's nothing wrong mechanically. The Opel is a loan from a lady who's away on a trip.

Now I would like to be happy with the man I love. But the city won't let me. White man and black woman, no problem. White woman and black man, you can't have that. Tete is just like it was when I got here. There was no independence for skin color. He's a surgeon, a good man, very gentle, very intelligent. Younger than me. He's married, but the culture here is different, you can have more than one. It's just the problem of race. And he doesn't even want to stay with her, he wants us to live together. She shows up at my door raising a racket, she's been here in the middle of the night, she's come into the house and broken things. When I don't see him, I get upset. I don't sleep in my house, I can't take it, everything's there, closets full of clothes. Jorge is selling his things, I've been told.

I sleep here, and when he can, he comes to see me. The city talks about it and points fingers at me. If I didn't have to depend on them... But with a restaurant, if the customers don't like something, they avoid you. We started meeting outside the city, in a small village. That's where I go with him, I leave here at midnight if necessary, we have so little time together, days off and weekends. An old man in the village, a friend of mine, heard about the people in the city not liking it and had a small square hut built. "I don't care what they say in the city. Here no one will bother you. It's yours, for love." That's where we go. You see before you a crazy old lady, falling in love at the end of her life. But it's good. I went back to loving a man again. I'm afraid they might harm him. Tomorrow I'll show you the hut, when we go to Wiryiamu. It's there—love where once there was war.

I've aged quickly. I used to be beautiful, you know? Here in Brome I performed Our Lady of Fatima. I've done a lot of theater: *In Search of a Son*...There were good things in my life, trips, safaris. I feel at peace at Cajueiro. I want to be buried there, at the entrance gate, for everyone to step on me. In a white robe that I've already sewn, in a shroud with no coffin. In the midst of this romance, I've become a child. It was from suffering. I love everything that suffers. I've done charity, raised two boys besides my own. Eighteen and nine. I wouldn't like my life to end badly. I hope it will end well.

At one o'clock, it started. The Sixth Company carried out the assault simultaneously in Wiriyamu, Juwau, Chaola, and Jimusse. In all these places the massacre was done in the same way. Here's what they did: It was a Saturday, people were drinking pombe, among friends, lots of them in the traditional drinking spots. The commandos rounded up the people, put them in the larger huts, and set them on fire, and the people burned to death. Those who tried to run away were shot or bayoneted. They even got the children and threw them into the burning huts. Jimusse was where the largest number died, but they put the monument here. In Jimusse they herded the children and the women into one place and the men into another. They lined the men up in single file, and three armed soldiers ordered them to run so the commandos could see who scored the first hit. Some managed to get away by zigzagging as they ran. Women and children saw their parents and husbands die right in front of them. At the end, the commandos threw grenades at the groups of women and children.

That was more or less the style.

The operation was run by two great figures of the PIDE-DGS, Chico Kachawi and John Cangonlangondo. Later, Chico died stupidly, in a bathroom, a woman threw a grenade at his back. They were the leaders of the Sixth Company. This makes us think that the operation also had a component of personal revenge for Chico, because he had a weakness for women and one of the women he'd taken was from Chaola. The woman ran away and married another man. The attack began in Chaola; the helicopters coming from Tete passed there first.

Half an hour before starting the massacre, the Portuguese Fiat bombers flew overhead. But something funny happened: instead of bombing the villages, the planes dropped the bombs on the *machambas*, the cultivated land. And in the helicopters some soldiers pointed to an escape route for the population. That proves there was disagreement about what was going on.

The Tete Operational Zone did everything through PIDE. Even Inspector Sabino, who was the PIDE chief here, was subordinate to Chico and John. They were black men, but their hatred for blacks was incredible.

There were several things that hastened the massacre. One of them had to do with the population's stubbornly returning to stay in the villages controlled by the Portuguese. Also, a short time before, the Sixth suffered an ambush, a little past kilometer 19, and swore vengeance for the wounding of the commandant.

Days earlier, another thing, a ZOT airplane flew by here and was hit by FRELIMO. All this sped up the process. It was a case of premeditation.

There was a cattle herder of Portuguese origin who showed up in this area to buy animals. One day he was approached by FRELIMO troops. They stripped him of his shoes and clothing and sent him away. He arrived here in the village, very tired, and Wiriyamu himself, who was chieftain of the zone, gave him a mat, and the men rested under a tree. Later he went to Tete to tell the ZOT that there were terrorists here and that the terrorists had the support of the population.

That Portuguese herder said to Wiriyamu: I was with them, and they asked for my help; the next trip I took, I said I would bring food for FRELIMO. The Portuguese set up a meeting with the guerrilla and was at the place they'd agreed on, he waited and waited, blew his horn, and no one appeared. But he was accompanied by another white, in civvies, that some of the children recognized—he was military, they'd seen him in the city. The FRELIMO guerrillas heard the car horn, but they were a little late, and when they got there, the Portuguese had gone. They asked chief Wiriyamu about them, and the population warned them about the military man who'd been there. He had come to check out the information the herder had provided the commandos. He must have told Tete that the population was with the terrorists. I think that sped up the operation—Operation Marosca, December 16, 1972.

We all seem very small in the shade of the tamarind tree. Abid takes me back to the city. The bone mausoleum has been violated.

The glass has stopped shaking inside my forehead. I am finally calm, lying in a stupor that seems to have always existed. The fatigue that drains through my legs, arms, and neck finds a voice, still far away and weak. The voice takes on body in the totally empty dream, occupies it, expands all through the muscles. A balm spreads, aquatic, in my sleep. It is a lament I hear as I float amid the several currents of sleep. I don't open my eyes.

"These Tatas are no damned good! The government buys them because the ministers get kickbacks from India, and in the end we're the ones who have to ride around in them."

Our Tata, old and small, succumbed to the weight of the passengers, three times its capacity, plus their baggage.

The chassis broke in half, ridiculously, as in an animated cartoon.

We are stopped at an isolated spot in the night, in the hundreds of kilometers that cross Kafue National Park, one of the largest in Africa. I remain immobile with one foot in each hemisphere, neither awake nor asleep, a defensive trick I've learned from dogs. Words spill, sticky and bothersome, spoken in the nauseating blend of sweat, mosquitoes, and manioc that fills the Tata. Now comes the lamentation, nearer, more funereal, in a cortege. It becomes clearer, forming words. Can it be hymns? The people elbowing one another in the Tata fall silent and listen, whispering.

Greasy anguish hangs in the air. I have the urge to slice through this claustrophobia with a martial chop from the edge of my hand, top to bottom and side to side, with a cry of liberation. Why don't they open the windows?

In the night, no one sees anyone. The hymns walk, dragging the noise of footsteps on gravel, to disappear into the night. Whoever is singing has the sky ahead and God behind. The power of the hymns passes through the Tata, a dead can full of bated breath.

"Their brother died two days ago. They walk in mourning along the road."

The polyphony of mourning found its way into my sleep, floating, on the gravel that surely must explain the aching in my eyelids. All positions are uncomfortable, and my body responds only to the insect of sweat that runs down my neck and soaks my kidneys and groin. From time to time, or perhaps it's just an impression, the Tata shudders in fright. Small cries, laughter, and all the passengers lunge for the closed windows. They're on top of me, stepping on me in the confusion, and I know that all of it, the weight of the hymns against the dirty glass, the laughter for the dead man with no candle, the oppression of the dark, the rhythmic steps, the children crying for their loved ones, all this happens outside of me, on a straight purple road with angels at its end, smelling of the sickly perfume of the walking wake and manioc.

They told me, in the morning, when the emergency vehicle arrived — a small, old Tata — that the elephants had put on a memorable spectacle during the night, just a few meters from us. All the passengers saw it but me.

Nothing can break the endless desolation of the journey. Only a bullet. I can give away the ending: it didn't happen.

"Get down!"

It would have been impossible to see who fired the shot. We threw ourselves onto the seat when we heard the sharp explosion, but we realized at once that it was only a blown tire. We stopped to change it. We exorcised our fear by laughing at it.

Jaime climbed out to change the tire. Aguiar's helper, he rides in a honeycomb in the freight—schoolbooks—though the cabin has room to spare.

"He rides up there. It's his place, you know, Angolans have their customs, their traditions, and they don't like to be bothered. They like being by themselves. They don't mix with other people."

With his finger, Aguiar points to his forearm. Color is destiny.

The night was too cold.

"What happens when it rains?"

"He has a tarpaulin. He manages. It's his place. We have to treat them a little rough. They like it."

It's Jaime who keeps Aguiar's weapon and the cartridge belt when the truck stops somewhere or we approach a police checkpoint. Jaime hands Aguiar what he asks for, from under the tarpaulin, through the driver's window.

"Jaime! Give me the gun! Give me two sodas! Give me the bread! Give me the dried banana! Give me the meat!"

Jaime gives it. He does his duty, not speaking.

As we left Benguela, we heard machine-gun shots from the firing range.

"To me, that's a bad sign. If there's no war, there's no need to sharpen your aim."

The stretch from Benguela to Lubango is one of the most dangerous in Angola, one of the richest in tales of bloodshed: the pursuits, the combat, the ambushes, the mountains where FAPLA garrisons were lost, FALA camps, SWAPO bases. The trip is long and painful. It must be completed in two days because the road is awful — the last forty-eight miles alone, from Cacula on, take four hours. Normally no one travels after sunset. In wartime, it's a guerrilla's paradise. In the bizarre Angolan peace, it's territory for the "armed bands." Truck drivers from Benguela head for Huíla armed and in convoys, usually with escorts.

The tension in Aguiar's truck could be cut with a knife. A week ago his son, who also drives the Benguela-Lubango-Winhoek route, was fired on. They were trying to hijack his cargo, and he didn't stop. He managed to escape but arrived in Lubango with bullet holes in his truck. A week and a half ago, two policemen were found dead on the same section of road, attacked at an isolated patrol post.

Once, on the road from Lucira to Benguela, Aguiar and two more trucks were ambushed. Luckily, they were carrying arms, ammunition clips, and pistols (with tracer bullets). Even so, seven passengers in one of the trucks died in the skirmish.

"We stood up well to the gunfire. They had to run off. We left. Three days later we were told dead guys were found there with their guts exposed. One of the bandits used to be a policeman, Sankara, well known, he organized the thing."

In places with potholes, gangs take advantage of the vehicle's slowing down to leap on board and toss out whatever interests them. They then jump off and collect the goods. By the time the driver becomes aware of it, it's too late.

"Happened to me once, with commandos on the Luanda road. They're terrible."

There's a third technique: grab on to the truck, open the door while it's still in motion, and stick a gun in the driver's face. That's the riskiest approach.

Aguiar waited for two days in Benguela for a column of trucks going down from Luanda with merchandise for Brigadier Mandinho, commander of the Rapid Response Police of Cunene. It was the right column—it had an escort of ninjas—but it encountered major difficulties on the Lobito road. Aguiar asked me if I was willing to leave without anyone. Obviously I was.

That was the first safety rule we violated. After that we didn't respect any. Aguiar rattled off the itinerary of dangerous places: Talamajamba, *Coruteba, Coporolo,* Pedreira, *Contentor, Massonge* . . .

"Jaime! Give me the weapon!"

Aguiar shoved the small Makharov down his shorts when night fell. A Kalashnikov came through the window and fell on my knees.

"Is it loaded? Look, I don't know how to use it if that becomes necessary. I was never in the service."

"You'll know. If it's necessary, I guarantee you: you'll know."

A struggle, the tire. My nerves hum louder than the crickets.

A village is nearby, we can hear voices if we don't talk. We shouldn't be here, at this time, in this night, in this cold, under this threat that doesn't materialize.

"Screw it tight! Put the nuts on the bolts in the right order. Did you put them on in order? Nut number 1 goes on bolt number 1 and so forth."

This road crosses an archipelago: Benguela is a coastal city. Farther out is the ocean, islands as far as the eye can see. The country doesn't exist as it appears on the map. Once you leave the Atlantic, you enter nothingness.

We crossed these islands, and the asphalt disappeared; below, sinuous canals. War was the erosion, eating away at the land and its inhabitants. Benguela is terra firma. Lubango also. Huambo and Cuíto once were. What's in between is indescribable. No one is from the place where they are living—men and women were tossed the way rough seas toss boats onto the dunes. Islands: we pass through them while the rags they wear pass through us, the dust that covers them, the gruel and fruit pits they stir over the fires. Islands devoid of color, rising out of the bush, their feet anchored, stripped of any right, even the right of flight.

There! It might have been a jackal. We no longer see ibises, those long-beaked birds.

Every village is an island. Every person also. They drift along the edge of the continent that was once theirs: the memory of their parents, the memory of the group, the religion of their grandparents, and now the language of their children, the salt they don't have, the fire that they must go ever farther to find. Benguela, Luanda, Lobito: in Angola only the shores are terra firma, and the greatest worry is being submerged. Beneath the water there is no more news. The rest is a shipwreck—Angola has no interior, it has territorial waters. Sometimes there is a geodesic mast, a red ribbon with a sword cutting the horizon. It's a reminder of the ship's pilot whom, years ago, the subjects saw tumble slowly from the crow's nest.

The flag. The beloved homeland: half blood, half mourning.

On the rocks and thick trees, on the ruins, are graffiti. Aguiar carries cans of spray paint in his truck and at strategic crossroads adds one more graffito. AGUIAR UAMANO OVIRONGO. Aguiar knows all the lands.

At large intervals are weed-choked exits to the great abandoned farms: Calahanga, Caribo, Embanda, Cabinjiriti, Camuvi. Cattle, sisal, agriculture...

At one or two places the canal is interrupted where islands join— Catengue, Quilengues, it will be late when we arrive, after more problems; I'm speaking of two hours spent securing the Volvo's hood surrounded by drunken policemen dragging a man, also drunk, handcuffed and with chains on his feet. We pass by lands with skinned goats hanging from a nail, warm sodas smelling of fish, misshapen pots with greenish sauces and boiling bones, cigarettes sold by the unit, flies satiating themselves on bread. Treasure Island. Night falls upon these scenes like a punishment. The candles highlight the darkness they bear inside, sour smoke clings to our clothes, hovering at the level of eyes shut until it passes.

"That guy's driving without any lights!"

He missed us because he stopped a little ahead. A truck, another crazy, was coming blindly toward us, we couldn't see the monster five meters away. He parked in a path cut into the bush. Voices speaking Mbundu could be heard. They lit a fire.

"Get the triangle. We'll put it up again when another car comes. Otherwise they'll rob us. That's what they're getting ready to do."

Jaime was struggling with the wheel. We went to the bonfire of the invisible truck. They were charcoal burners, wandering around the province looking for wood. There's a code of honesty that has survived and makes business possible: no one touches bags that don't belong to them, and no one carries off bags without knowing whom to pay for them. Aguiar, a Benguelan from Alijó who's been in Angola for fifty years, taught me Mbundu during the trip.

"*Hame dukombé dikassi logopita ondjira.*" I ask for safe-conduct.

The charcoal burner wasn't to be impressed by so little. He didn't raise his eyes from the roasting meat.

"All of us are visitors here too. We don't belong to this road. We were pushed here by the war. We ought to be on our way. My whole family, I don't know about them. They're somewhere..."

On another island.

On the drive to Cacula we passed a traffic accident. The wrecked vehicle was still there, in a ravine. The corn was scattered along the road. Survivors are picking it up. They have been there since the accident, three days ago, mute and hoarse from crying. Only the eleven who died made it to Lubango.

"The dogs of the Bay of Tigers were caught like this: The settlers prepared a large cage and put an Angolan native inside, or someone who

272

showed up looking to make some money. They put the guy in a smaller cage inside the bigger cage, after making him run a little so he'd be dripping sweat. The dogs would come at night. They would smell the man's scent. But he had a rope attached to the door, and when the dog came in, he would pull it, and the dog would be trapped. The man would spend the night there with the dog drooling and barking. It wasn't risky, he was in a safe place. The settlers would sell the dogs. Fierce dogs. They attacked anything they saw."

José Nada is one of the oldest settlers from Madeira in Lobito Velho. He lives by the inner waters of the bay.

HATE INK

When you shed it,
observe
the blood:

color is not

a wound.

Teresa Chilambo, 35, husband died in the war, four people at home, makes her living gathering wood.

Alice Vissopa, 49, raises four orphans (their mothers died, and one father disappeared in the jungle, the other died in the mines), has a small parcel of land.

Joaquina Nagueve, 31, had two husbands, one disappeared fifteen years ago, the other has been in Luanda for the last two years, has seven children, lives by selling fermented drinks.

Adélia Jepele, 35, husband died of disease three months ago, has six children, lives by selling corn meal.

Jacinta Vondila, 45, husband died three years ago from disease, five children, makes her living gathering wood.

Firmina Susso, 40, husband died in the war, four children, makes her living gathering wood.

Clementina Chova, 24, husband arrested three years ago in Luanda, two children, makes her living gathering wood.

Maria de Fátima, 27, two husbands, the first killed in an ambush, the second is with another wife in Benguela, three children, makes her living gathering wood.

Margarida Jondo, 43, husband died three years ago from disease, four children, makes her living gathering wood.

Teresa Chicumbo, 24, husband enlisted four years ago and no word since, three children, lives off smuggling.

Maria de Natividade, 30, husband died in the war, five people at home, lives off smuggling.

Flora Massanga, 32, had three husbands, the last is in Luanda with another woman, five people at home, has a small parcel of land.

Joaquina Chacuvala, 39, had two husbands, one died of disease, the other in the war, seven people at home, lives off smuggling.

Regina Negueve, 24, had a husband who left for Lubango three years ago, lives with five other people at home, has a small parcel of land.

Josefa Chissuva, 59, husband died from disease, raises two orphans whose parents died in the war, makes her living gathering wood.

Madalena Salassa, 35, husband died in the mines, five people at home, makes her living gathering wood.

Maria Nagueve, 50, two husbands, one in UNITA, the second has another wife, raises two orphans whose mother died from disease and whose father left for Luanda with another woman, has a small parcel of land.

Margarida Naombo, 60, husband is blind, raises three orphans whose mother died in an attack and whose father has another wife, makes her living gathering wood.

Celestina Cuvanja, 69, husband died of disease, raises three orphans whose mother ran off with another man and whose father died.

Evalina Dumala, 63, husband died from disease, raises four

orphans whose mother died from disease and whose father left with the troops, makes her living gathering wood.

In September 1992, the health center for the Huambo periphery invited single mothers living in the area to enroll. In two weeks, 693 showed up. The center served a population of close to 70,000 people, representing nearly 12,000 families. Five of every hundred, therefore, were single mothers. "They came from the villages to the outskirts of the cities, mainly for reasons of physical safety. They came with their husbands or reunited with them once they arrived in the cities," explained *Jango* in the edition of the eleventh of that month, with a list of names. "Afterward, the husbands disappeared. Some died of disease, the majority in the war; others emigrated to other cities without their families; some took other wives—and the women were left behind, with the children. They can't read, they have no profession, they know only how to work the land, but they have no land. They came from the villages that were burned, destroyed, they lost the social ties (family and community) to which they belonged, they took up with other men, pariahs like themselves. Now the men are gone, and the women, alone with their children, have nothing, not even legal recognition of their existence."

Fourteen years of fighting taught Domingos that the worst thing about war is heroes. Carrying a bag of groceries, Domingos stopped in front of Sylvester Stallone. The actor wore a lacework of ammunition over his nude trunk, ready to puncture reality and the audience with a mortar. Domingos evaluated Rambo without nostalgia. Rambo ignored Domingos. Neither blinked. "Shows at 10, 12, 2, 6, and 10."

"I used one of those. It's an RPG7. I used it, I know all about it. It fires from the side, like in golf. You yell when you fire the bazooka so you won't go deaf or crazy. You don't drink water after stepping on a mine, if you're not dying of thirst."

Domingos Pedro, 31, Angolan, is a refugee in Mongu, capital of Western Zambia. He was in Rivungo (Cuando Cubango) when the conflict began again in 1992. He decided to flee by crossing the Cuando River. He survived the war to live in poverty along with thousands of other Angolan refugees piling up in the great camps of the Zambian northwest.

He comes from Camacipa (Bié). His family stayed behind, as is also normal among a large part of the Angolan population affected by the war—the best-loved relatives vanished somewhere, in an attack, ambush, evacuation, not saying good-bye. A kind of death without the closure of mourning that frees the survivors, now separated, for a new cycle of caring and loss.

Between birth and war, Domingos has no biography: it was merely the brief time it took for him to grow big enough to hold a machine gun in his hands, hatred on his lips, and fear in his legs. At twelve he was already incorporated into FAPLA (for the generals in Luanda, the poor and the *bailundos* [refugees] are never really children, they constitute only an anonymous reserve to be called to the front; it's the same on the other side, or worse, because in the countryside it is less noted).*

Domingos went over to UNITA seven years later. For two convincing reasons: one, he was captured; two, MPLA and UNITA had long since ceased needing an ideal on the part of their soldiers—discipline was sufficient. Just change the prisoners' uniform, or not even, and put them back on the path they came from. There were times when it was not like that, when the headiness of liberation manifested itself in various symptoms. But for that there were the Soviet-style torture chambers in the São Paulo jail in Luanda, the concentration camps in Lunda Norte and Lunda Sul, where killing was done by starvation, or the Maoist reeducation centers where prisoners were brainwashed by being forced to weed for years on end.

It's not easy to cure the past when the present is not resolved. Domingos, who left the refugee camp because he refuses "to do forced labor to make money for others," lives in the most degrading of the slums on the outskirts of Mongu. His possessions amount to a small unfurnished hut where he and another refugee, António, ward

---

*As had already happened in the peace of Bicesse, "compliance" with the Lusaka Protocol led to open demobilization and reintegration of "groups at risk," including underage soldiers. The same officers who kidnapped children and adolescents from their families, from schools, and from Angola's future were transformed into the best friends of the army of children with eyes aged by panic. From their new administrative positions in the state apparatus, they made demands "on behalf of" the social and civilian reinsertion of the minors, exhibiting lists of names and numbers. No one stopped to think that those lists were frightening admissions of crimes and as such merited trial and conviction.

off hunger on interminable days sitting on mats. Their area has neither light nor water. The town is dirty and tiny, thorny bushes delineate the streets, a labyrinth of goats amid the must of the trees and the savanna and the plague of excrement impregnating the sand. The shore of exile. The panorama is majestic there. The vast mesa of the Zambian forest is interrupted, like a veranda of trees along the coastline, to allow the passage of the endless Zambezi plains.

"If you don't speak-know their language, there's no work."

Domingos censored himself when I went into a supermarket, even before the cashier could make a reproving gesture toward his dirty, cracked feet. Any other day, Domingos would have stayed at the door.

"He's with me."

Like an animal. No: an animal isn't shooed away, because it's no bother. A refugee is lower than that, Domingos explains. Unemployment, for the Angolans of Mongu, is much more than lack of work. As the shelves roll past, he asked for permission from me to get what his stomach needs: coffee and dough, crackers and soda.

He has a son fourteen months old, but he doesn't live with the baby or with the woman because he doesn't have the money for the three or four cows that would buy his Zambian fiancée from her father. He lives by handouts or working as a guide: for little money Domingos, like other refugees, crosses the Cuando illegally, hired by traffickers interested in entering without danger and leaving with diamonds. The adventure is profitable for the buyer: a "green tucker," for example, which costs 140,000 or 150,000 Zambian kwachas in Mongu, can be bought in the UNITA zones for 40,000 to 50,000.

Seven years in Luanda, seven years in Jamba. Domingos possesses exceptional lucidity. His conclusion about the two movements that used him is, "That's not liberation. Nothing to liberate anymore. In the end, it's business. One is oil, the other is diamonds and mercury. The people don't get any of it, the people have no part in it. The people die. Santos started to veer away after the death of Neto. And Savimbi, they say he never was the government, but a boss should treat his employees well. He has the engineers, the teachers, the doctors, and how does he treat them? Nothing! They don't live, they don't move, they don't earn."

Domingos and António bathe at the home of a Zambian friend, in the neighborhood next to his, a place for Zambians who are merely poor, not less than that, and have the benefit of water in their prefab houses. (The imbalance that war creates: on the other side of the border, not even the municipal administrators have water. It's a luxury that flows only where it always did: in the rivers.)

Next to the Rambo poster there are other actors, advertising Indian films in the video cubicle packed with young people and sweat. *Come and Get More.* A blond woman bronzed with oil exhibits two strands of cartridges crossing her breasts. No movie theater can rescue Domingos from a brutalizing melancholy.

"I see war films and think it's all without any courage. You never think it can end. But in just a moment, a second, it ends, and that's all. You run away, you step on a mine, you take a bullet."

Domingos should curse his intelligence, because it's obvious he torments himself with the knowledge of what life has done to him. He has the same strange red reflection on his forehead that rises from fires of withered weeds by the river. The fires run in the direction of the wind, parallel, some ahead of others, raising an exhaust of smoke and ashes and a muffled drone. They recall the killer cars in the Australian desert after the war in *Mad Max.*

"There's nothing left over of normality, we can say it that way."

On the third day, Clarindo Kaputo sent his driver to pick me up. The visit to Vorgan was authorized, we are honored to have a journalist with us, he's going to grant us an interview. The director received me in his office. Kaputo has a vinyl long-play on top of his cabinet, *Che Guevara Speaks*, an edition of *The Lusiads*, and, close at hand, on the desk, *Gemstones* (Eyewitness Editions), a profusely illustrated manual with all the precious stones that man robs from the subsoil. The door to my hut is emerald green.

What type of station is Vorgan?

C. K.: At present we have great freedom in setting editorial lines. Fundamentally, of course, we defend the Party. Every editor here is free to write whatever he wants — of course, within a not very rigid set of guidelines — and can have his point of view transmitted. We have a grid of programs, in ten or eleven national languages, the ones most spoken in the country. We also transmit in English and French for our listeners on the borders of Angola. We have a variety of programs dedicated to health and entertainment, and other programs that try to locate certain people.

We receive letters from listeners asking if they heard a certain name correctly, the name of a relative they've lost touch with — not only the war but the 1992 events dispersed lots of people. Many have disappeared, you know.

Is it possible to keep track of the peace process through Vorgan?

C. K.: Absolutely. And more than that. The positive moments make people more open, which is when the messages are more clear. But when danger lurks, there isn't much willingness to pinpoint the location of a relative. That's interesting.

What moment are we in now?

C. K.: In a moment of great anxiety. No one knows exactly which way the boat is heading. We think there are efforts being made to derail the process. There's definitely a lot of apprehension on the part of the populations, not only those residing in areas under UNITA but those under government administration as well. No one wants more war. They're tired, but there are still elements wanting to make war, because I think they prosper under it.

Jamba Inn Number 1 has sixteen permanent guests—they await "demobilization." There is no lighting; it's better that way. They see nothing, the darkness abashedly hides a nightmare silhouetted against a sickening smell. When you enter, your eyes fasten on the vertiginous floor, and your stomach turns back. The occupants in six rooms and a hallway are piled on top of one another, almost all of them blind or amputees, and still others deaf. One might say their immobility owes to all these misfortunes: they do not see, do not hear, do not move. They speak, and those with no tongue gaze with deafening silence.

Inn Number 1 was the first reception center for the FALA handicapped, created at the start of the war when Savimbi and a handful of men established their headquarters in the southeast sector of Angola. In Angola, death is cheap. The higher price is staying alive, when life is merchandise you'd like to get rid of. In 1976, the inn was a prime example of the FALA's dedication to its heroes in the struggle: the men who had paid with pieces of their flesh. They have mines at the end of their crutches, grenades where hands are missing, and bombs within reach of their eyelashes. A business of barter, their war: a foot for each step forward, a finger for each delay, a man for each inch of land, a cry for each pain. A generation for each prophet.

Gregório has a palpably kind voice. He looks at the sky with proud bearing. In his greenish blue eyes is an endless year of clouded seasons. What he sees is a certainty, far beyond the tallest treetops of Jamba, that casts its shadow over us: the final judgment and the reuniting with peace and with those he loves in the heavenly promised land. He says this is what he wishes for my lost faith, before singing a duet, an Mbundu Seventh Day Adventist hymn that I record because it is the only gift he has to offer.

No one will admit it, but chemical warfare is practiced in Angola. "Toxic bombs. Gas. An orange brightness. In four days your legs give out, and you can't talk," relates a paralyzed man as he tries to hold a radio on his unsteady knees. Gregório is blind. "I have no images left. I live a dark life." Gregório Lucas Sapelinho Feko Satuala. At the inn since 1985, the time of the offensive on the Cazombo front.

How did you solve the energy problem? There are no generators.

C. K.: There's solar energy, automobile batteries hooked up to the transceivers. This war made Angolans, even the uneducated, into people with an elevated perspective of life. With a big imagination.

We have here mechanics who've turned gasoline-driven cars into diesel and the other way around. That applies to radio as well. The correspondents still use dynamos to charge batteries.

The antiaircraft guns are scattered in the sand, pointed upward in every direction like a monument to the war that needs no public square. Silence reigns, as in the rest of Jamba, except for the wheezing of a bellows. Then the sharp clang of a blacksmith's anvil is heard.

For two decades, Oficemgue (Central Workshops for War Matériel) repaired equipment damaged in combat or captured from the enemy. Tanks, armored vehicles, transport trucks went back into combat courtesy of the Jamba mechanics. Miracles were performed. Today, Oficemgue is an atelier at peace. The antiaircraft guns are deactivated. They are part of the weapons handed over to observers in the UNITA disarmament zone. They were too bulky to be taken by helicopter to one of the sites for destruction of war matériel.

The Oficemgue mechanics are now smiths who fashion agricultural and household utensils. A chassis is transformed into a plow. The sheet metal of a truck yields several irons, the old-fashioned kind that use hot coals, or replacement parts for a Mercedes engine block. Spoons are fashioned from stainless steel or aluminum, as are small portable heaters. The forge was manufactured right there. Sheet metal was cut to make fan blades that were then welded in a circle onto a round piece of metal that provides the air for the forge. "It's called an adaptive forge: the wheel is a hubcap from a motor vehicle, the belt is a piece of cloth, and we also made the lever. I think that with all that, the forge is complete."

Vorgan is always spoken of as a radio station yet to be domesticated. To you, is that praise or criticism?

C. K.: It would have been bad for us to be domesticated, because we wouldn't be expressing what's in the soul of our journalists. It would also have been bad because, in the moment we're experiencing, the natural forms of information — if I may use the term — are very distant from what is being done today.

Vorgan combats an entire apparatus, people who are veritable propaganda machines. For example, a roaming gang attacks a group of citizens, but soon afterward, two, three, five days, a week later, the necessity becomes apparent, because a mine was planted, to patrol, to intervene, to defend the populations, because that's the only thing that keeps us here. We have to be vigilant. We issue cautions, contradict many lies...

Before the UNITA leadership installed itself on the plateau, Jamba had generators, telephone links, foreign visitors eating cookies and goat meat on the jango of the District of Cooperation. The Old Man was in the house that today has only the governor of the Bastion, and politicians from the Free World, including the supreme Bothas of South African apartheid, came to applaud and support the struggle against communism in Africa. Journalists came and sent back dispatches, fascinated by the white gloves of the Jamba traffic policeman (what ever became of him?), writing about the harmony of a new but profoundly "authentic" peasant society that used no money. "Socialism, Negritude, Democracy, Nonalignment."

Jamba was born out of nothing, from a pact between UNITA and the sole inhabitants of the zone, the elephants. It was built to withstand artillery and aerial bombardments. It has a fragmented layout of small clusters scattered over an enormous area, consisting of thatch cottages spaced far apart and half buried in the ground. The clusters are linked by four-lane tree-lined streets with landscaped plantings in the middle and not a car in sight.

Masonry is almost nonexistent except for the Vorgan complex, which inside a one-story building and two tin-roofed container studios projects all its camouflage toward the skies from which one day are sure to come the "MIGs of terror." The station is surrounded by a minefield, "since UNITA thwarted surprise attacks that tried to sabotage the Voice," explains Clarindo Kaputo as we circulate about the installations, greeting men in ad hoc uniforms. A mine exploded last night in Jamba, with a blast that interrupted, two kilometers away, a euphoric ceremony around a bottle of wine. "It was a goat," Kaputo told me the next morning.

One of the slogans of Vorgan, a radio at war, is "A people that doesn't know how to defend itself will always be mistreated."

The electronic mail from Bailundo, which makes use of the communications that were once in Jamba, was laconic on April 1, 1998:

"Good morning and have a nice day.

"01—Thursday April 1 Vice President António Dembo, Sr. Sakala relocated to Luanda representing our Leader Dr. Savimbi in furtherance of the Lusaka Protocol. When conditions are established, Dr. Savimbi will also move to Luanda.

"02—Our radio Vorgan has now gone off the air."

I remember the exact hour I left Angola. It was at night. The frogs in the river made an infernal racket. A guerrilla fighter took me in a plastic boat through treacherous channels. Some opened into the main current and led to the other bank. The rest were watery dead ends, tree-covered pathways where crocodiles lay in wait, floating with thousands of yellow eyes.

How to explain a land with no life? No space, everything is limit and enclosure. The step to be taken is pointless, the step already taken was wrong. You could see the route of moons my heels have left in the sand. From such a place one returns empty. The soul attenuates. It does not cross the river with me.

In September the first tides of winter begin to stir. On a motorcycle, the only vehicle in the region, I flee this unhappy country— Angola is behind but still too close. I ride, clutching the owner, the veterinarian, my only hope of getting away. I found him lying on a mat, shivering with malaria. I implored him, paid him. He rose from his sickness to do me the favor of taking me as far as the Mongu road—nine hours through bush and sand.

It is a painful run through the savanna, straight through, with no headlights, fighting the sand that sticks to the tires and wheels. We overtake owls, felines, baobabs, and sleeping villages, huts and palisades erected in the middle of veritable islands of white sand—the moon separates them from the rest of the opaque landscape—where only dogs cross our path.

"They're savage because they have no owner, no one in the villages gives them anything to eat."

There are inevitable stops: the bike buries itself in sand, or the pain in the veterinarian's arm becomes too acute. Two days ago he broke a bone in his elbow when a dog overturned his motorcycle. Normally they come from behind, then run ahead of the bike.

"Wait for them! Keep your eye on their muzzle. You'll see the exact moment when they're going to jump. That's when you have to yell. They're not expecting it. They'll hesitate for a couple of seconds, then they attack again. One's coming now, it's about to jump, careful! Now!"

Terror opens its jaws, ready to bite, to inject with rabies.

This is Carlos Seixas's account.

The fires were lit one after the other in the cold, dark night. Hundreds of mutilated men gathered around the fire with their wives and children, in groups, availing themselves of shadows, obliging the day to burn longer. They spoke of the future, their backs to the war, drew up plans, gazed—those who could still see—at prophecies hidden in the glowing embers. It was the night of demobilization in Bonga, the barracks area for those maimed in the war.

Somewhere, a drum awoke, background to the conversation. It rose in a progression of imperceptible gestures, film frames of sound, each identical to the one before, but in sequence they formed an ascending movement: a rhythm emerged above the crackling voices. The speakers looked toward the sound, the drum, the drummer. That was the first sign of obedience.

It could be any one of them. A slave's only power is to be chosen. The drum seized a man, yanked him from the somnolence of alcohol, with a leap that brought him close to the fire, a leap that paralyzed the frenzy of the flames on his smooth brow, maddened his laughter, ignited his half-closed face with a diabolical spark. A man had been subjugated.

The drum accelerated, whipping the man with its rhythm but never touching him, making him run in circles and jolts, striking out around him, a whip filling the air with its sound. The crack of the drum galloped on the broken back of the dancing man, a euphoric animal laughing in the circular arena.

He was a normal man but with one leg. At his gesture, a child approached, removed his wooden leg, and left. The man continued dancing on his left leg, circled the flames, spinning with them, at the behest of all, incited by a thousand clapping hands, dizzy atop one winged foot, furious in the fermentation of his own sweat. A roar of voices penetrated his ears, throbbing through the veins of his neck and inflaming his fingers in spasms, as he blindly embraced and unequivocally surrendered to the master, the only master, the God of Thirst and Forgetting.

The drum called forth another man, thrust from the darkness by an avalanche of shouts and clapping hands. He was normal too but with one leg. A child approached, removed his wooden leg, and carried it away.

The two men were dancing now, crazed by the dance; the strangeness of the celebration; the symmetry of their misfortune, one with a right leg, one with a left. They embraced each other and spun around the fire, in rhythm, their temples dripping sweat, their eyes closed from the fatigue in their chests, bodies, bones, their gestures merging with the ceaseless imperative of the drum.

The power of the drum possessed the crowd sitting on the ground, huddling in the cold, hypnotized by the spectacle. The drummer's fever spread to the other bodies, to all, in an oceanic convulsion.

The couple danced and danced. Dust rose from their two legs until an infernal orange cloud, made neonlike by the fire, embraced them. In their ecstasy, amid the dust, the fire, the rhythm, the shouts, the madness, the dance of the amputees, they fused into one man, a whole man with a left leg and a right leg, a single dancer with two legs of flesh and ten toes for balance, a complete creature, a child of God and therefore perfect.

An ephemeral son of Bonga.

The drum, climax achieved, cast the celebration over a precipice, stopping abruptly. The drummer, free at last, fainted from exhaustion.

Two children approached through the cloud of dust to attach two wooden legs.

Three and a half months later, Henri came to meet me at the airport in Maputo, after my flight from Quelimane. He had arranged another contract, another country—again, a country where he had been for years. The street kids had grown. Now they were as tall as he, and they recognized him by the nickname they'd given him earlier: Little Mulatto.

We made up for lost time like simpletons. A play on the avenue, a curry at the fair, beset by a diminutive vendor of films: *The Law of Fuck*, *American Pornography*, *75 Positions*, *Blacks and Whites*. Billiards: laughing like yokels at the tables that hide mountains under the worn felt. A jam session at the Tchova with the only Rasta in history who doesn't smoke ganja. The minigolf, the capital's megadiscotheque, for the perfume of the ladies and the gin. A Saturday afternoon as if on a date, eating beef sandwiches with mustard at the Arcádia, with the sun landing on the old round marble tables.

Henri, however, returned to Oudong. Old Norodom died at the end of 1996—half a year earlier. What was left was the house of his driver and bodyguard.

There was still Sokim, running toward him with outstretched arms, weeping. Henri continues to wear the gold and the Buddha. He tells me of bouts of melancholy. He has a parrot tattooed on his back. The animal has yet to say a word to me.

"That night in Oudong, nothing happened."

In the distance, where the road is indistinguishable from the grass and the grass bears up the sky to become the horizon, appears an unmistakable silhouette. At first it is nothing more than two wavering lines disconnected from the ground, a vertical line crossed by a diagonal line: a machine gun on a bandolier. A vertical line crossed by a horizontal line: a machine gun held in the hand. In the van in the next instant, only the engine breathes, taking us to the encounter, to the range, the trigger, at the mercy of the guerrilla. UNITA or government?

Five days in Lubango without being able to leave the house, waiting for the phone to ring with a ride to the other side of the line. A waste.

Raúl, the local logistician for Nuova Frontera, diagnosed the cause for the impasse: because of lack of basic conditions of safety, no trucks are leaving Huíla for Huambo; the more experienced drivers are waiting for the situation to improve and are stuck, keys in pockets, at the luncheonette next to the stop for the Namibe bus; there have been almost daily attacks on the road, attributed to roaming gangs. Huambo is a long way off, the four-hundred-kilometer diagonal stretch across the center of the map of Angola is colossal: two days, after the two wars, it's a miracle if you do in a day what used to take five hours. UNAVEM suspended land transport between the two cities, including convoys of vehicles with armored escorts. Provisions from the Portuguese Logistical Company in Huambo to the mission's regional headquarters in Huíla are now sent by air; all I could do was set out on my own, at the first opportunity; at this point, stopping meant going backward.

Cristiano and Gianni, of Nuova Frontera, took me to Cacula, where the Italian organization had an integrated agricultural and training project. Cacula is a fork in the road: to the left, Benguela; to the right, Huambo.

A People's Republic banner flies from the flagpole of a destroyed gas station. All the intact buildings are recent, and they are huts. I've been authorized to be thrown into a jumble of people and weapons in a flying pickup. In all, besides the bags, twenty-six passengers and six machine guns squeezed in, with their sights on the road. The police, in blue uniforms, provided an escort. The soldiers, in dark glasses, prepared for the expected.

Younger than the agents, the Angolan Armed Forces youths are placed at strategic points on the road, theoretically to guarantee protection to travelers. They are the ones who, without pay, food, or communication, fire on food trucks and grab what they can, from watches to women. They then flee, only to appear hours later before their victims, to offer help. On the way down from Benguela to Lubango, I had already learned that the critical points on the map were in proximity to "posts" and "patrols."

A silhouette took on the shape of a man. Soldier or guerrilla?

Friend. He just needed tobacco, because his mouth was dry. The vehicle continues, with the smiling greetings of the onboard escort. The passengers, starting over from zero, reerect the euphoria of departing, the distancing of danger, the serenity of the empty road.

I will not make it to Huambo today.

BEAT

red
strawberries
on the vine
pre
sent
of the
season

black
cats
hungry
for them

You want to know about the war in Bié?

We killed one another to the last man. Without quarter—we didn't leave the house even for the funeral. That's what a civil war is. Madness around the dinner table. Ours made us go too far. We exterminated entire lines, from the youngest to the most defunct, from those who hadn't even been conceived to those whose souls were no longer being prayed for. We died at home and in the cemetery, in bed, at the gravestone, in the field. In Cuíto they also killed the dead, the war reached even them, it didn't waste them, it claimed them, they died twice. The living, many more times. In Bié we are survivors or the resuscitated, and you can't say which I am. No one has the courage. We would have to pluck out our eyes, so nothing remained in the sockets, to confront the truth. But there would also be an inverted image in the hollow of the spoon. That's how you eat passionfruit.

Recall with me: The bombs would come from the air, and the air is anywhere you try to breathe. They knocked down doors, shattered glass, devoured stone like termites—look at those lacework castles. The bombs split open graves and profaned homes, relatives and ancestors warmed themselves under the same blanket. The tenants lost the certainty of what world they inhabited. This or the next, here or beyond, yours or mine?

Try this mountain water, crystalline from a spring, and spit out the taste of phosphorus onto these feet that have been burning me for a day. Know why the plants have all become dwarfs? They drink from the rivers. This soil is made of gunpowder. It feeds off footsteps, and your walk is a powder trail. The plantings are full to the point of exploding—the grenades buried themselves when they fell belly down, others are cultivated to kill later. It rained a lot this year, rains that were with us from the cholera season to the scabies season. The spring still flows. If you scratch the plantings, they ooze pus, if you go there, you'll see it and you won't go back. In the yards we erected crosses with the wood we found there. We know the places—how could we forget them?—but the children were born later.

A geography is to be discovered in two spans of fever: the apartment where I pulled up floorboards to burn; the bedroom where I dug graves; the windows that I covered with bricks; the terrace to which I took firepower; the mortar in which I ground roots; the night I played the batuque drum; the body we possess before dying.

We loved each other, it's true. We loved earnestly, in the manner of end-time sects, attacked by the fire descending upon them. In the imminence of the end, in a harbor of faith of the elect, of the damned, each coupling a failed prophecy.

Kiss me. Your lips are the old rust-colored brandy of Villa Miséria, the most protected building in Bié. There was a bell tower between our delirium and the enemy artillery. The others, without a tower, were at their mercy: mothers and children doubled over, sitting, floating in feces, sleeping for weeks on steps not big enough for lice.

Villa Miséria.

I kiss you in this night that we have become. We are on the veranda of the villa, which remains boarded up. Notice that the bombs fall in the distance. They're coming closer, though. The brandy and our desire dance in this encirclement. Before long, one of us will be dead or in a peace process, and afterward no one can guarantee you will know that I loved you, if by chance you love me. Someone put music in the Villa Miséria Discotheque, DJ Ângelo, the manager, archangel of the cassette, named chief of the Cultural Division of Civil Defense! But it wasn't the position that made him special: Ângelo is a paraplegic and the only dance instructor in our province.

I speak to you of reasons to kill and to deserve to leave. Was it worthwhile today to find me and say that you're still alive? We went on, it's a habit, our inertia degenerates into combat. On February 10, 1993, one of the truces was broken. It was because of Terrible, a captain. He was crazy, or half crazy. He decided to cut down a tree, the last one still standing in the square where the police barracks was located. A demarcation line passed through there. A string was the line. Running between houses, through the streets, you here, them there. Don't step across, or you won't know what separates you from those who'll open your skull like a nux vomica. Terrible cut the string. The trunk fell, and the branches came down on the enemy side. The enemy forbade us to take away the wood. They argued about the trunk. It was a Friday. The next day, the captain decided there was no solution: the thing to do was steal it. Twelve days of hard fighting followed, frantic combat.

People died over that wood.

People also died because of a Sharp found in a house from which we rousted the enemy. It had a magnificent sound. Through a megaphone they demanded the return of the Sharp. We said never. We fought for a bunch of days just because of that. But we never did give it back. It was a good one, that Sharp... You ask me for reasons, and I speak to you about a time without values or food or sense.

Foliage instead of bananas. Branches instead of potatoes. Boiled manioc leaves instead of manioc root. Garbage. A cow whose owner makes cuts and then dresses them so he can have meat without killing the animal. Cat for breakfast. The revolting, redeeming taste of the first rat. Abundant salvia rejecting insects without salt. A woman so desperate she chews on rotten dog, indifferent to the pestilence. A running man carrying bits of a man in a sack.

The horror. Come near and partake of my breath: I am that homeland. That child too. See him kicking a human skull as his football. Not because he is evil. The skull was available, nearby, and dry. You and I know the norms of humanity: skulls are buried, balls are round. No one gave him the chance to learn that.

An ancient hunger strangling your stomach, and you at the window, wanting to leave, and your father in the middle of the street, asking for help that you cannot give him, wounded by a bullet that lay in wait for him, ambushed like you. The dogs falling upon him the moment he goes out to ease your hunger, and the distressing bark, the cries from the shedding of the same blood that engendered you, begging you to save him, and you appealing, no, no, but envying the dogs in the end, envying them when you turn your eyes to the beasts that today, through that hydra that nuzzles the redness, will devour and vomit your last reason for living.

War isn't your father-sonofabitch-whore-mother-brother-friend eaten as you watch by savage rage. It's your envy of the dogs, a hungry and animal envy. It will pass — all you have to do is eat — but for the rest of your life you will bear the nightmare and the shame that you pretend to hide from the view of all. Because in Cuíto the walls tumbled, and the roofs revealed the scars of the survivors, the resuscitated, in the pornography of the days. In our city, consisting now of one street, only a single room remained, property of all: absolute pain and the fear that it will return.

The judgment has been announced, it will take place soon. We have rounded that ending that swallows up creatures, we of Bié, and look what became of the church, which is still closed. Learn from it. The saints are nothing but wood when God condemns you to the ice of hell. Remember the sacred thing that I'm confiding to you: immortality, a certain time, in Cuíto.

After the orgy there is no hatred and no cure for it. The shrapnel cuts out your tongue, and you grope for words to scream. Who was your enemy? It was the FAA soldier who handed you a cup of salt through the hole in the front line, so you could give him the ammunition and perhaps the weapon with which you were soon lashed. It was the UNITA guerrilla who demoralized you by announcing, night after night, that tonight was the final attack. In the end, you no longer know who you are and what compass orients you. Your books are wet, your glasses are fogged. Hate supposes a degree of soul, which you have lost the right to speak for.

The line of shapes turned its back to the rising sun, to the eucalyptus, and to the soccer game. It stood there with slumped shoulders, facing the spot where the morning wind fled in whirlwinds of dust. A youth walked with dull steps, howling at the heavens. It was late when I asked for a place to sleep, and I still had to wait five minutes outside while the official, his back visible through the window, parroted endless Inshallahs by radio. On the table by the threshold was an imitation-leather flyswatter that looked both efficient and comforting, a box of matches, a metal ashtray, and a pad of English, with words and phrases in irregular handwriting, in blue and red.

Chico is learning the essentials of life: "Walking, playing, selling, waiting, buying." It's very early. The interrupted night lives on in painful eyelids. Early as it is, there is no assurance of transport to Huambo. Everyone is cold, and everyone warms himself with fear. The howling is terrible, and the youth repeats it. The small UNAVEM team in Caconda has been reduced to an Egyptian who's reading *The Secret Talks between the Arabs and Israel*, twelve hundred pages, first volume, by Mohamed Hassanin Hakal. This book is read from right to left and leafed through from the last page to the cover.

Chico, the "local staff," sleeps in the chaise longue on the porch to the music of the crickets. He has deposited his fatigue in his left hand, open like a skiff, in the same position as the moon.

The spoken newspapers of the plateau headline a massacre. Two days ago, in Cusse, fourteen people were decapitated, one learns. The enemy arrived in a village to steal cattle, rounded up the people, and cut off their heads and hands. Who it was, on which side? There was another attack in the Vila Nova zone. There are attacks almost every day. José, the driver of a truck crammed with people and animals, says, "It does no good to be afraid. All you can do is put your soul in God's hands."

"What about those who don't believe in God?"

"Don't tell anybody you don't, or you'll travel alone."

José is a Catholic and wanted to be a priest. The war ruined his vocational plans at the age of eighteen. He was with the troops from 1984 to 1991.

"That was when I left. Not left, deserted. Or I'd still be there. Tell me, what have I got out of life? Nothing. No enjoyment. Zero. In Angola we say, 'Make use of life while you've got it, because it won't last long.'"

The youth reappears with a piece of iron resembling a crowbar. He's in plain sight, but no one sees him, cloaked in the invisibility of the insane. I lay my backpack on the ground and sit on it. I cover my head with the long jacket bought at the used-clothes store at the Chioco Market in Lubango, leaving my kidneys exposed but wrapping my ears in fetal comfort. I can pretend that, in the center of the world, I am outside it, protected from it. I have only a small opening to follow the youth's movements, and no air comes in through it. The poor soul leaps about as if possessed, feigns a childish series of martial blows. He makes a sound that must be his idea of horror. José had the truck roof covered with chickens. Inside: flour, passengers, goats. An ark of life, delirious and apprehensive, serpentining through the mined grass. When the goats fell feet upward, it was necessary to stop and right them. When the chickens, a bunch of thirty, slid onto the windshield, hanging by bonds around their feet, a helper of José's would open the right-hand door and, still in motion, crawl onto the fender, stick a leg across the hood, and launch the fowls back onto the roof.

The youth rams the iron bar into the ground, smashing an imaginary head. At this hour none of the stores in the market—the soccer field is in the market area—have opened. For him the head isn't imaginary. His violence is concrete, and his crime, unpunishable, is irremediable.

Chico's cabala is written on a rectangular card with the upper corners cut off, the kind used inside new shirts to stiffen them. The teacher is a Portuguese military man on leave from the team site. The crazy youth reappears on the field. Crawling, he approaches three goats tied to a post. He caresses one of them, slowly and at length. He hugs it in a way that brings forth the heat of the animal's coat. There is a guest annex, but Chico can't find the keys to any of the rooms.

I sleep in the team's small house, in the part that until recently belonged to a Malayan peace observer. The room has orange walls, two shelves, a table lined with disgusting greasy newspapers, and a pilled mattress. S. R. DAHIYA—DEPUTY COMMANDANT. The bed has four posts that, in the absence of mosquito netting, raise a mendicant's canopy. There are two insecticides on the shelf, two empty packets of Dunhills on the table, an empty package of "dairy for coffee and tea" on the floor, and an enameled mug with caramelized sugar at the bottom. There is a calendar with a naked blond woman lying on her stomach and seen from behind, photographed so that the light shows, without detail, her gilded pubis beneath the uniform line of her buttocks. Other photos and clippings cover the inside of the door. Asians in the press and a calling card from someone unimportant. And the singer Ada Kentamaan. It must have been heat that the youth was looking for from the goat.

CUÍTO RAP

Ai-uê, Bié–ê!
Bachalo lo sihué
Ai-uê, Bié–ê!
What was seen in Cuíto
With my pals
I remember, uê.
What was seen in Cuíto,
with my pals
let me li-ive!
What was seen in Cuíto
With my friends
I remember.
The nine months, uó, uó,
of resistance
we cooked potato
and papaya, oranges
with crawling bugs,
and then another day came:
news, hunger, and death,
we invented things to eat
without tasting li-ife.
After a time
the rains stopped
the hunger and the drought, uá–ô
where can we eat?
The beat is far off,
I remember
Qualonda suanono.
Sometimes we didn't even talk
and always hunger in our face.
Let me li-ive!

—António Augusto,
fifteen years old

Joint studies undertaken by the Christian Children's Fund and UNICEF between 1995 and 1997 revealed that 97 percent of the children in Bié had been exposed to warfare. During the conflict from 1992 to 1994, 27 percent of the children in the province lost their fathers, 89 percent were exposed to bombings, and 66 percent witnessed the explosion of land mines. Sixty-six percent of the children had seen people dying or being killed, which left them a legacy of psychosocial trauma. The same research, whose results were released in October 1998, revealed that 10 percent of the young boys took part in combat, 33 percent were wounded, and 38 percent were victims of mistreatment.

"The children of Bié also suffered hunger, thirst, various epidemics, nakedness, separation of families, setting off of mines, transport of war materials, sexual assaults, long marches, lack of medical care and medicines, and the absence of instruction or bodily and environmental hygiene."

As a result, many of the children "suffer pains in the head or stomach and are fearful that something bad will happen in their lives."

"When I got out of the truck, Aguiar handed me a Nescafé with powdered milk. I hugged the cup with both hands to steal its heat. Jaime was pulling up stakes: the hospital cot on which the boss had slept, atop the trunk's hood, the blankets that covered him, the breakfast stuff. The fire was put out with sand. A boy who had also slept there took out a cigarette. He squatted and lit it from the small pile of embers. He closed his eyes in pleasure, inhaled, exhaled. The smoke was consumed by the small sounds of first light, mingling with the morning fog that had not yet dissipated, leaving the cattle, the palms, the roofs, the foothills in the distance. Aguiar started the engine.

"Leaving—the only perfect peace."

Of Namibe I retain this photograph: a seignorial house in ruins on the main avenue with a collapsing roof and empty windows and an equally old wall that is an extension of the facade and on which can be read, in what remains of the plaster and the paint effaced by the rains, a calligraphy of worn, perfect letters: AGOSTINHO NETO.

In the center of the photograph, of the wall, of the avenue, between today and AGOSTINHO, stands a public lamppost, with no glass or bulb. Only the post.

The lights went out tonight, and the entire city was in the dark for several minutes. The lamppost proved its superiority: it betrayed no one, because it was already extinguished.

Behind the colonial facade is a void filled with garbage. That's on the second negative, taken from a different angle: the place where the wall was split from top to bottom, dividing the image in two and giving it the effect of a collage. On the exterior, other facades in the same style as Algarve or Minas Gerais; inside is the garbage. There's an avenue in the middle. At that precise moment there is no traffic. A solitary peasant has stopped between the walkway of bygone decadence and the walkway of present-day rot. He is indecisive but alert, his back turned to AGOSTINHO.

A policeman came and harassed me for having photographed the wall. He demanded the roll of film.

Agostinho Neto, near death, was taken to Russia, where he died in 1979. At the demented suggestion of the Soviet ambassador in Luanda, his body was kept in Moscow to be embalmed. Unknowingly, Angolans mourned before an empty casket. It's said that his successor, who daily thanks the sun when it sets over the unfinished mausoleum, didn't find the necessary money to keep the Father safe from rats.

I could have explained to the policeman that it wasn't the wall I had on the roll; I had photographed only the lie. He wasn't worried about the past. Young, he had been born without it.

I remember arriving in the city and the bus stopping at a small rectangular plaza of one-story houses. The bus smelled of tangerines all the way from Humpata. Namibe smelled of cake. There was a bakery on the corner of the square.

"Good morning! Do you bake cakes?"

"Yes. But not today."

Speaking of hotels, a great shock for me happened in 1977 when I was dating my husband. I stayed at my grandmother's house in Huambo, and he went to a hotel. I wanted the best for him, and the best was the Ruacanão, where my mother got married in 1953 (the menu must be in one of these drawers). When I went up to the room, I couldn't believe it: the carpets were torn, the rooms empty. When he opened the closet door, bullets and a cartridge belt fell out. He left and went to an inn run by an uncle of mine, with no clean sheets because there was no water in the pipes. Before Independence, in Huambo there were two young girls who read the *Comércio do Funchal*: me and a friend who lost a finger in the war in Cabinda and who had far-left brothers studying in Portugal. The brothers sent us *Das Kapital*. Obviously we didn't manage to read it. In secondary school I was called before the PIDE twice—I defended certain ideas fiercely. I would read clippings from the *Comércio* in the Religion and Morals class. My classmates would say to me, "You don't know what communism is, they're going to do away with the neon lights. Do you know what it means to have all the lights out in the city?"

Strange how these things happen...

————

The Bay became an island when the water receded. Once everyone went there over a spit of asphalt. Everything changed when the houses lost their owners. The water conquered the road and separated this handful of sand from the continent.

No one has returned to the island. Those who once lived there forgot the way. The others saw no point in trying to tame a curse.

The domesticated dogs stayed behind. Being on an island annihilated any reflex not needed in the struggle for existence. Litters were born into increasing brutishness. Migratory birds with foreign nests, schools of fish reflected in the moonlight, scorpions poised to inject pain, spiny cacti: all were beyond reach. The only mammals on the island, the dogs, finally lost the memory of suckling.

With the years, the war came to the coast, but they could not take advantage of the corpses. They barked, ran in circles, and fought, their teeth bared with rage. Losing vision, they are slaves to smell. Burned by the salt and by the heat alternating with cold, they sniff the blood. They avoid the church, a whitewashed volcano in the midst of the smooth sand, a clear eye in the center of the hurricane of dunes, the only building the winds have not obliterated, the paleness of Paradise. They have learned to bite the water, to hunt fish. They are now completely separated from the desert and what lies beyond. Breezes do not carry here the sounds of the jungle. None of them knows what a river is, or smoke, or the caress of a hand on their coat. The bay is a beach spined with fear. It's said the dogs eat people, and people don't try to learn the truth. That's the nature of tigers.

Visible in the distance, the lights of Tômbua fade with the birth of day. The desert appears in all its expanse as a sheet of sand pinched between two superimposed oceans. The *Garoupa* finds no currents adequate to its hull. The fish don't travel to allow themselves to be caught, explains Master João, relieved at our failure. We were never, after all, far from land.

The pines on the beach, even at a few knots, grow rapidly on the horizon. We round the lighthouse that still stands—although extinct—at the edge of the inner waters. The sparkling sand; the drooling dogs; the roar of the seas that will never be more than two. The bay is on the maps but doesn't exist.

On the dock, someone caught, in full flight, the fleeting shape of the rope.

"Mother, teach me good sense," sang the woman in a language of the north. "*Nseruse, mamā, nseruse nserusango!*"

The river slumbers in a valley of warm breezes, and another city lies in its hot breath. In the riverbed, boats pass straining under the ashes of war. Galleons with the powder of bones, the lime of the dead born in the plateau, fascinate and terrify the broad Zambezi plain.

"You can't resist me! I'm RENAMO. I speak the grammar of Relvas. I'm no one's family, I'm the crazy woman of the province."

Dessai laughed at her without malice. The woman ran her fingers down the richest man on earth, between his eyelids and his broad bearded cheeks, love and infinite languor in her gesture.

From fear to the seashore. Walking ahead, lamenting the cities without sun, to the unharmed ocean, like a salt payer tattooing in white the nameless sand.

"Why are you drying my eyes?"

"Because I like you. Now I'm going to the Chingar to drink. Want to come with me?"

"Yes."

"How much time do you have?"

"None."

ACKNOWLEDGMENTS

José Eduardo Agualusa and Ruy Duarte de Carvalho
Adelino Gomes and Francisco Sena Santos, because they asked
me to "call when I could," blackmailing me not to give up
Maria Alexandre Dáskalos (it's true that the angels weep)

In chronological order of their help and generosity: David Winhurst
(for the only credential that protected me), António Costa Moura,
François Gunod, Henri Valot, Eduardo Lobão, Carlos Seixas, Luís
Filipe, Mário Tavolaj and his team in the central office of the OIM
(the endless patience of James, Luz, and Sabrina), José Martins and
Miguel Vidal Pinheiro in Luanda. Mahamane Cissé (for having
proved that "mint tea is a human right"), José Serras Pires, António
Marques, João Marcelino, and José Vaz de Carvalho in Lobito.
Manuel Fernando Jerónimo, Alice Suzette, and César in Benguela.
João and Laurinda Tavares, Tó Mané and Ivo Ferreira in Namibe.
Vasco Martinho (and the fisherman of his ANGESP) in Tômbua.
Carlos Arede, Cristiano Agostini, Gianni Morelli, Franca Gattoi and
the Nuova Frontera team (also Rui and Domingas) in Lubango.
Giuseppe Juffre and José Marcelino in Huambo. Captain Dorival
Moraes, Captain Gerardo Espinosa (Uruguay), and Captain Monteiro

(Brazil) in Cuíto (they were on my side against stupidity). Sara and Lara in Chitembo. Major Rui Neves (FAA) in Menongue. Captain Spies (Brazil) and Major Anok (India) in Caiundo. Ana Maria Miranda in Bagani. Captain Carrey Olivera (Uruguay), Gladys Higa, Analía Ramos, and Papagaio Mussili in Jamba. The Lubasi family in Sinjembela (cornmeal, water, and gentle words: a salvation). Ambassador Francisco Falcão Machado (and his unparalleled staff) in Lusaka. João Rosão, João Alves de Matos, Monteiro, Victor, and the friends of Merzzario in Lubumbashi. Sebastião José Mariano in Zumbo. Abid Karimo and Mahomed Ahomed Dessai (some whiskeys are unforgettable) in Tete. José Paulo Hertz and José Vaz de Albuquerque (the comb I didn't have the money to buy really *was* rosewood; it's still pretty) somewhere along the Zambezi.

A special debt above all others I owe to the Portuguese contingent of UNAVEM III, especially to the Logistical Company in Huambo and the Transmissions Units in Lubango and Menongue (they were a second home). Three names, again among many others: First Sergeant Pratas, Captain Lourenço Merca, and Captain Soares da Costa.

Beatriz Marcelino, Arlindo Barbeitos, Ana Paula Tavares, Maria Idalina Portugal, Helena Amaral, Manuela Gomes, and José Milhazes.

Last, but like the first, a UNITA guerrilla, Colonel Nunda. He was ordered to escort me in Cuando Cubango. He carried out his duty with dignity. I suspect, even today, that he saved my life. It was also obvious that he risked his own.

GLOSSARY

Aka!: Quimbundu outcry of anger, shock, or gloominess.

Al Berto: Alberto Raposo Pidwell Tavares (1948–1997), one of the most original poets of his generation in Portugal. He studied architecture, visual arts, and painting before turning to writing in the 1970s.

Angolan liberation movements: In 1961 the MPLA, under Agostinho Neto, rebelled against Angola's colonial power, Portugal. Two major liberation movements joined the MPLA: the FNLA under Holden Roberto in 1962 and the UNITA under Jonas Savimbi in 1966. They soon began to compete. The MPLA, with its main stronghold in Luanda, represents the interests of the metropolitan elites and is influenced by and oriented toward Portugal. The FNLA, founded in Congolese exile in 1962, has its headquarters in Angola's northwest and continues the tradition of the former Congolese kingdom. UNITA, at home in the Angolan highlands, is supported by the largest ethnolinguistic group of Angola, the Mbundu or Ovimbundo. The three movements signed a treaty with Portugal forming an interim government on November 11, 1975. Six months later, a fierce power struggle broke out, and, except for brief intermissions in 1991 and 1994, it continued until early 2002. A cease-fire and peace settlement were agreed on following Savimbi's death.

Baía dos Tigres (Bay of Tigers): Located in the south of Angola at the edge of the desert near the Namibian border, its name refers to a large population of tiger sharks. In 1865 Portuguese fishermen attempted to settle nearby but failed due to lack of fresh water. Later a small fishermen's colony, with simple fish-processing facilities, was developed in the bay area. Food and water were brought in first by ship. A water pipeline was built but was broken by the surf in the mid-1970s. This resulted in the bay's complete isolation and the absence of permanent settlement for over two decades.

Bailundos: ethnolinguistic group in the south of Angola that belongs to the Mbundo or Ovimbundo. The Bailundos still maintain their traditional migratory existence, mostly as migrant workers. To refer to somebody as Bailundo is to label him backward and ignorant, but it is not uncommon, especially among urban people in Luanda and Benguela.

Bakongos: ethnolinguistic group living in Cabinda and the area between the Atlantic Ocean and the Cuango River. The Bakongos (or Quicongos) are primarily farmers; their main crop is manioc. In the sixteenth century, the Portuguese introduced a monarchic society among them.

Barotse: a Bantu-speaking people in western Zambia, known also as Lozi. They primarily cultivate cereal on the upper Zambezi's fertile floodplain. Hunting and animal husbandry are also important to their livelihood. The name refers to the land occupied by this tribe.

batuque: a drum and ritual dancing to the drum.

Ben-Ben: another name for Arlindo Salupeto Pena, UNITA's former military chief. He joined the rebels' organization at the age of thirteen. From 1997 until his death in 1999, Pena served as FAA's deputy military chief under the GURN government.

Benguela: capital of Benguela province. Founded in 1617, it is also an important harbor on the Atlantic coast.

Benguela Railroad: Constructed from 1912 to 1923, it initially covered 1,348 kilometers, connecting Angola's Atlantic coast with the country's eastern border, and with southern Africa from the city of Elizabethville/Lumbashi in the former Belgian Congo/Zaire. Today most of the system is in disrepair due to civil war.

Black Cockerel: UNITA emblem (see Vorgan).

Cajú, Cajaneiro: Portuguese for "cashew tree."

Capelo, Hermenegildo, and **Ivens, Roberto:** Portuguese scientists and discoverers who, from 1877 to 1880, traveled through Angola. In a second trip, in 1884 and 1885, they went from the west to the east coast of Africa, from southern Angola to northern Mozambique.

Capulana: part of the traditional African wardrobe for women, to be wrapped around the hips.

Catete: town in northwestern Mozambique, at the Zambian border.

Cavaleiros: suburb of Lubango, in southwest Angola.

CFB: see Benguela Railroad.

Chioco: market in Lubango.

Chipango: royal compound, Mwata Kazembe's exclusive and sacred grounds.

Chota: Mwata's palace.

comba: memorial service for someone deceased, to be held eight or thirty days after the funeral. The word derives from the Quimbundu and means "to sweep away the remains."

dos Santos, José Eduardo: Agostinho Neto's successor in 1979 as president of the MPLA. He had escaped to Zaire in 1961 in the wake of the Portuguese crackdown on the MPLA and eventually made his way to the Soviet Union, where he studied at the Oil and Gas Institute of Baku in Azerbaijan. He became the first foreign minister after Angola's independence in 1978, and in 1992 narrowly won the first democratic elections in the history of Angola and became president.

FAA: Forças Armadas Angolanas (Angolan Armed Forces). Its formation as an organization for both former UNITA fighters and members of the Angolan military forces was agreed on in the Lusaka Protocol, a result of peace talks between the Angolan government and UNITA (see Lusaka Protocol).

FALA: Forças Armadas de Libertação de Angola (Armed Forces of the Liberation of Angola), the name of UNITA's military division.

FAPLA: Forças Armadas Populares de Libertação de Angola (People's Armed Forces for the Liberation of Angola), the name of the Angolan army until FAA was formed.

Fazenda: an agricultural estate.

FNLA: Frente Nacional de Libertação de Angola (National Front for the Liberation of Angola), founded in 1962 by a group of refugees in the Congo under Holden Roberto. During the civil war that followed Angola's independence in 1974, rival factions fought for control over Angola. The FNLA as well as UNITA were supported by the United States, its Western allies, and South Africa; the MPLA, which eventually won, was backed by Cuba and the Soviet Union.

FRELIMO: Frente de Libertação de Moçambique (Front for the Liberation of Mozambique), founded in 1962 as a result of a merger between three formerly independent liberation movements. Since Mozambique's independence in 1975, FRELIMO, a single political party, has been dominating the country's political life.

funje: porridge made of corn.

Ganguela: ethnolinguistic group in central Angola believed to be the oldest Bantu-speaking people in the country.

Honwana, Luís Bernardo: Mozambican writer, journalist, and documentary filmmaker, who is also an accomplished photographer and one of the heads of the Organization of Mozambican Journalists.

Huambo: Founded in 1912 as Nova Lisboa, capital of Huambo province, in central Angola, it became the country's second largest city, after Luanda, and the country's cultural center. It also was an important commercial center, but during the civil war, especially in 1992 and 1994, most of its infrastructure was destroyed.

IOM: International Organization for Migration, a nonpolitical, humanitarian organization that coordinates and supports the resettlement of refugees in Angola, where 2.5 million citizens have become refugees as a result of the civil war.

Jamba: (Umbundu for "elephant"). UNITA military base in southeast Angola until Savimbi moved to the central high plains in 1991.

jango: Umbundu word for a round or square roof made from straw that rests on pillars, which can be found in public places in almost every Angolan town or village, providing a place for the locals to meet informally.

Kabila, Laurent-Désiré (1939–2001): Born in what was then the Belgian

Congo. When the Congo gained independence in 1960, he was a youth leader in a political party allied to Patrice Lumumba, the new country's first prime minister. In 1967 Kabila founded the People's Revolutionary Party (PRP), which set up a Marxist ministate in South Kivu; it came to an end in the 1980s. Kabila spent most of the next decade in the Tanzanian capital, Dar es Salaam, selling gold mined in eastern Zaire. He came to prominence again in October 1996, when he led a revolt by ethnic Tutsis in South Kivu. With support from Museveni's government in Uganda and the Rwandan military, he united the Tutsis with veteran anti-Mobutu guerrilla groups to mount a full-fledged rebellion. In 1997 he led a seven-month rebellion in Zaire (now the Democratic Republic of the Congo) that toppled longtime dictator Mobutu Sese Seko. Kabila was killed during a shoot-out in his palace in 2001.

Katanga: see Shaba.

Khan, Nusrat Fateh Ali (1948–1997): world-famous Pakistani vocalist and singer of traditional Sufi music.

Kigali: capital of Rwanda.

kissange: native musical instrument.

kota: Angolan form of addressing the elderly, an expression of great respect.

kwacha: Zambian currency.

kwanza: Angolan currency.

liamba: Quimbundu for marijuana.

little brother (maninhos): form of address among UNITA members that has become a synonym for them. It is used by UNITA members to distance themselves from the socialist address, "comrades."

Lourenço Marques: Former name of Mozambique's capital, Maputo, it is a seaport on the Indian Ocean with close to one million inhabitants.

Luanda: Capital of Angola, founded in 1576, it is the country's chief port and largest city.

Lunda: Bantu-speaking ethnolinguistic group belonging to the Ganguela group, also known as Tchokwe or Quiocos. Originally settled in northeastern Angola, where the country's large deposits of diamonds are located, gradually expanded into present-day Congo and Zambia. It is believed that they are descendants of an ancient hunting culture of the savanna. The Lunda have maintained impressive schools of sculpture and have a strong sense of cultural heritage. They are also known for their excellent building and business skills.

Lusaka: capital of Zambia.

Lusaka Protocol: peace treaty signed on October 31, 1994, by the Republic of Angola and UNITA under the auspices of the UN, after a year of negotiation. As a result, the UN agreed to send further peacekeeping operations to Angola. This protocol supplements and strengthens the previous Bicesse Accords, signed in Portugal in 1991, particularly in the area of human rights. The Bicesse Accords had collapsed after UNITA disputed the results of the September 1992 election.

machamba: term used in Mozambique for cultivated land.

Machel, Samora: Born in 1933, he became a FRELIMO leader in 1966. In 1975, he became Mozambique's head of state and served until he died in an airplane crash whose cause has never been fully investigated.

maka: Angolan word for aggravation, argument, chaos, or problem.

Mau-Maus: rebel movement against the British colonial regime in Kenya, known for its atrocities against white settlers.

Mengistu Haile Mariam: military ruler of Ethiopia from 1974 to 1991. As an army officer, he contributed greatly to the overthrow of Emperor Haile Selassie in 1974. Emerging, through violence, as military chief by 1977, he sought Soviet aid, established a socialist people's republic, and fought off Somali incursions and Eritrean rebels. He was elected president in 1987. Regional rebellions increased, while Soviet aid receded amid economic deterioration. Mengistu abandoned socialism, but, unable to mobilize military resistance, he was forced to flee to Zimbabwe in 1991.

metical: Mozambican currency.

Mobutu Sese Seko (Joseph Desiré Mobutu, 1930–1997): One of Africa's most tenacious dictators, he was born in what was then the Belgian Congo. During the last years of colonial rule, he worked as a journalist and joined Patrice Lumumba's Congolese National Movement. When

Congo became independent in June 1960, Lumumba, the country's first premier, chose Mobutu to be his private secretary and, soon afterward, named him chief of staff of the army. In September 1960, Mobutu led his troops against Lumumba, who was murdered the following year. In 1965, Mobutu seized power permanently, declaring himself president, and began to wear his signature leopard-skin hat. He is credited with developing a sense of unity in Zaire, which was made up of diverse ethnic groups with no common language. He promoted the use of three languages to complement the official language, French. Western nations backed his corrupt regime until the cold war's end, because it was seen as an anticommunist bulwark in the region. In the 1990s, Mobutu's health declined, and he largely withdrew from government. In 1997 Kabila overthrew the Mobutu regime.

MPLA: Movimento Popular de Libertação de Angola (People's Movement of the Liberation of Angola). Founded by Agostinho Neto in 1956, it became Angola's state party in 1975 and remained the country's most powerful political organization after the multiple-party system was established in 1991. In 1992, under President dos Santos, the MPLA officially turned away from Marxism-Leninism and adopted democratic socialism.

Mucubal: small ethnolinguistic group that inhabits the southwestern edge of Angola between Cubango and Cuando. The Mucubal are nomads, known for their tall build.

Mucuissa: ethnolinguistic group from the southern Huíla province.

Mueneputo: name for the Portuguese king.

Mwata: "husband of all"; it is also the name of a dynasty of Lunda potentates.

Neto, António Agostinho (1922–1979): physician, philosopher, and poet who served as independent Angola's first president, from 1975 to 1979. A founder of the MPLA, he became its chief after power struggles won by the pro-Soviet faction in 1957. In 1961, under his leadership, MPLA began the fight for independence from Portugal. In 1975, Neto proclaimed the People's Republic of Angola. He died of cancer in Moscow in 1979.

NGO: nongovernmental organization.

ninjas: Originally, highly skilled warriors organized in secret societies in feudal Japan. Kung Fu movies and comics introduced their martial arts to Angola, where members of the infamous special police unit are now called ninjas.

Old Man: UNITA members' name for their chief, Jonas Savimbi, following an African tradition that prevents subordinates from calling tribal chiefs or elders by their given names.

Ovimbundo: Bantu-speaking ethnolinguistic group in the central western part of Angola. Also known as Mbundu, its six million members are Angola's largest ethnic group, about 37 percent of the population. They are excellent farmers and are famous for their animal sculptures.

PAM: Programa Alimentar Mundial (the UN's World Food Programme), largest worldwide food-aid program. About two million of Angola's twelve million people depend on it.

PIDE: Polícia Internacional de Defesa do Estado (International Police for Defense of the State), Portuguese secret police. It existed until April 1974, when a military coup ended a forty-eight-year dictatorship in Portugal.

pombeiros: wandering tradesmen in eighteenth- and nineteenth-century Angola, who traded weapons, alcohol, and fabric for locally made products or slaves from the backcountry.

pula: colloquialism for Caucasians, used specifically in Angola.

pumbo: a marketplace located in Angola's hinterland.

Quelimane: town on the Indian Ocean, 940 kilometers northeast of Mozambique's capital, Maputo.

Quibaxe: town in Angola's Bengo province that has been especially hard hit by the civil war. Although of little strategic importance, the town became a battleground, changing hands between the government and UNITA many times.

Quimbundo: ethnolinguistic group that dominates a large territory between the Atlantic Ocean and the Cuango River. Historically they were known as great warriors and statesmen. By the late fifteenth century, they had formed the Ndongo kingdom, ruled by the Ngola, from which the Portuguese derived the name Angola. The Quimbundos developed an advanced agriculture-based society and excelled in cultivating coffee. In the islands around Luanda, the Quimbundo communities made their livelihood from fishing.

quinta: small estate.

Quioco: see Lunda.

Relvas: author of a well-known grammar textbook that is used throughout the entire Portuguese-language area.

RENAMO: Resistência Nacional Moçambicana (National Mozambican Resistance), established in 1976 by the Rhodesian security services, primarily to combat anti-Rhodesian guerrillas based in Mozambique. South Africa subsequently developed RENAMO into an insurgent group opposing the Front for the Liberation of Mozambique (FRELIMO). RENAMO made a strong showing in the country's first democratic elections in October 1994, winning majorities in the country's five most populous provinces and becoming Mozambique's largest opposition party.

Roberto, Holden: He founded the FNLA in 1962. When the MPLA took over FNLA's headquarters in 1976, he had to leave the country. Today he serves as opposition leader in Angola's parliament.

Sah'lomon: a second-rate singer from Zaire.

Salazar, António de Oliveira (1889–1970): Portuguese dictator. After the military coup of 1926, Salazar was briefly minister of finance, and in 1928 was recalled to office by General António de Fragoso Carmona. He became premier in 1932. In 1933 he introduced a new constitution that established an authoritarian state. Political opposition was effectively suppressed. In his final years he devoted considerable resources to suppressing revolts in Portugal's African colonies.

sanzalas: primitive houses or shacks of the poor black population.

Savimbi, Jonas Malheiro (1934–2002): a founding member of UNITA in 1966. In 1974 he was included in the interim independent government with Neto and Roberto, but he returned to armed opposition when Neto's Marxist government was established. Aided by the United States and South Africa, he led a guerrilla war over much of Angola between 1975 and 1991, until a cease-fire was achieved. He ran for president but refused to accept his defeat in the 1992 elections. UNITA then resumed armed conflict with government forces, initially with much success. After reverses in 1994, UNITA signed a new peace accord (see Lusaka Proto-col). It offered Savimbi one of two Angolan vice presidencies, which he declined. With renewed warfare in 1998, the government said it would no longer recognize the 1994 agreement or deal with Savimbi, instead supporting and recognizing a splinter group, UNITA. Savimbi was killed in an FAA offensive in February 2002.

Shaba (formerly Katanga): province in the south of the Democratic Republic of the Congo bordering Angola and Zambia, rich in mineral deposits.

Slavery Museum: a small church located on a ledge above Luanda's beach, where in former times slaves were blessed before being sent off to America or Europe.

soba: Quimbundu for "tribal chief"; also synonym for "chief."

SWAPO: South West African People's Organization, a Namibian liberation movement founded in 1960 in what was then called South West Africa, aimed at ending the exploitation of natural resources and racial discrimination (apartheid) by the government of South Africa. After 1975 SWAPO fought a guerrilla war for Namibia's independence from Angolan territory, and in 1976 the UN General Assembly recognized SWAPO as the only authentic representative of the Namibian people. Namibia finally gained independence in 1990, and Sam Nujamo of the SWAPO party became the country's first president.

Tchokwe: see Lunda.

UCAH: Unidade Coordenadora da Assistência Humanitária, center for humanitarian help.

Umbundu: Bantu language spoken by four million people (38 percent of the Angolan population) who originally settled in southwest Angola. Angola's ethnic fabric was irreversibly changed by the civil war. Today the majority of Umbundu speakers live along the coast and in Luanda.

UNAVEM: United Nations Angola Verification Mission, the peacekeeping mission in Angola, carried out by seven thousand UN Blue Helmet soldiers, ordered by the UN Security Council to oversee the redeployment of Cuban troops and implementation of the peace agreement between UNITA and the Angolan government.

UNITA: União para a Independência Total de Angola (Union for the Total Independence of Angola). After splitting with other nationalist parties over ideology and strategy, Jonas Savimbi created UNITA in March 1966. With its base in Jamba, in southeast Angola, UNITA gained most of its domestic support from the Ovimbundo ethnic group. With military aid from South Africa, the United States, and several Western European countries, UNITA built one of the largest armies in Africa. In areas under its control, UNITA reinvigorated chieftainships, established a barter economy, mined diamonds for international export, and maintained strict army discipline. During the war to overthrow Portuguese colonialism, UNITA often fought the other major liberation movements, the MPLA and the FNLA. In 1974, when Angolan independence seemed inevitable, UNITA allied briefly with these groups. But the alliance soon fell apart. In 1975 South Africa supported UNITA in trying to take over Luanda, without success. The following year, UNITA abandoned the cities and launched an insurgency war against the Marxist-Leninist MPLA government. In the late 1980s, UNITA entered into negotiations to end the war, which resulted in elections in 1992. When it became obvious that Savimbi would lose, UNITA accused the government of electoral irregularities and attacks on demobilized UNITA soldiers and again took up arms. In 2000 Savimbi declined an amnesty for UNITA fighters offered by President dos Santos in return for giving up weapons.

UPA: União dos Povos da África (African Peoples' Union), a liberation movement founded in the Belgian Congo in 1958. It merged with the FNLA in 1962.

Vorgan: Voz Resistência do Galo Negro (Voice of the Resistance of the Black Cockerel), UNITA's radio station.

ZOT: Zona Operacional de Tete (Tete Operational Area), the military territorial division in the northwest of Mozambique during the colonial war.